THE MYSTERY AND MEANING

OF THE DEAD SEA SCROLLS

THE MYSTERY AND MEANING
OF THE DEAD SEA SCROLLS

THE
MYSTERY AND
MEANING OF
THE DEAD SEA
SCROLLS

HERSHEL SHANKS

RANDOM HOUSE

NEW YORK

Library of Congress Cataloging-in-Publication Data

Shanks, Hershel.
The mystery and meaning of the Dead Sea scrolls /
Hershel Shanks. — 1st ed.
p.   cm.
Includes bibliographical references and index.
ISBN 0-679-45757-7
1. Dead Sea scrolls. I. Title.
BM487.S453   1998
296.1′55—dc21   97-29391

Book design by Carole Lowenstein

CONTENTS

ILLUSTRATIONS,
MAPS, AND PLANS

ILLUSTRATIONS

MAPS AND PLANS

INTRODUCTION

Half a century has now passed since a bedouin shepherd discovered a long-hidden cache of scrolls in a cave in cliffs above the northwestern shore of the Dead Sea. The details of that initial discovery will probably never be known with certainty. Who found the scrolls, how, under precisely what conditions—such questions are by this time shrouded in mystery. Even the date is uncertain; the 1930s, 1942, and 1945 have all been suggested as alternatives to the generally accepted date of 1947, probably February of that year. What is not in doubt, however, is the age of the scrolls themselves. They date to the time of Jesus and shortly before.

Between the early 1950s and 1956, archaeologists and bedouin vied with one another to find more scrolls, and eventually a library of over eight hundred different manuscripts was recovered. The bedouin were the clear victors in this quest. In one case, the bedouin explored the richest cave, now known as Cave 4, right under the noses of archaeologists who were excavating the nearby ruins of a site called Qumran, hoping to learn more about the scrolls from this ancient settlement as it emerged from the sand.

Of the eight hundred manuscripts, fewer than a dozen were in any sense intact. The rest were mere fragments—about twenty-five thousand of them—many no bigger than a fingernail. Acquiring these fragments from the bedouin turned out to be more complicated than acquiring the intact scrolls from the initial cache. Yet it was critical that all these fragments end up in the same place to assure that each manuscript could be maximally reconstructed. An arrangement was worked out between the authorities and a Bethlehem antiquities dealer nicknamed Kando, who had become the middleman for the bedouin, to purchase their finds. In this way, all the fragments were eventually acquired by what was then the Palestine Archaeological Museum in Jordanian-controlled east Jerusalem.

Beginning in 1953, an international team of young scholars was assembled in Jerusalem under Jordanian auspices to sort out these thousands of fragments. Most of the seven-man team, which included no Jews, were Catholic priests. In retrospect their accomplishments were remarkable. While the task of identifying fragments will never be completed (even today new pieces are being fit into the puzzles), by 1960 this team of scholars had not only identified the pieces of the eight hundred documents and arranged them as well as they could, they had also deciphered and transcribed them so that they could be easily read.

Meanwhile, by 1958 Israeli and American scholars had published the seven intact scrolls from the initial cache.

Most of the intact scrolls were easily readable by anyone who knew Hebrew or, in one case, Aramaic. The fragmentary scrolls, however, presented a more difficult problem. These too were mostly Hebrew, though some 25 percent were in Aramaic, a closely related Semitic language that was the vernacular in Palestine at the time of Jesus. But, on average, about 90 percent of each of these documents was missing and there were few obvious fragment joins. Letters were frequently dim and uncertain. That the scroll team was able to produce transcripts of these fragments, with some reconstructions of missing parts, in so short a time is an enormous scholarly accomplishment.

By 1960 the contents of the collection were reasonably clear. More than two hundred Dead Sea documents were books of the Hebrew Bible. These varied in size from a tiny scrap to a complete book of the prophet Isaiah. Other manuscripts were nonbiblical books, known from later medieval copies, such as Jubilees and Enoch. In the case of such texts, the Dead Sea Scroll fragments could be reconstructed relatively easily since the later copy formed a template into which the fragments could be fit.

But hundreds of Dead Sea documents were completely unknown. It is these that proved most fascinating, both to scholars and to the public. Most of the documents were written on either goatskin or sheepskin. A few were on papyrus. One especially intriguing intact scroll engraved on copper sheeting identified over sixty sites of buried treasure. The various texts were bewildering—previously unknown psalms, Bible commentaries, calendrical texts, mystical texts, apocalyptic texts, liturgical texts, purity laws, Rabbinic-like expansions of biblical stories, and on and on. How to make sense of it all?

From the outset it seemed clear that some of the scrolls reflected the views of a distinct Jewish sect, which scholars soon identified as the Essenes, an obscure Jewish movement described in some detail by the first-century Jewish historian Josephus. In recent years, however, the Essene hypothesis has been increasingly questioned, as we shall see.

Another aspect of the scrolls proved more sensational: In many respects the published scrolls seemed to mimic Christian doctrine—though most of them dated to a time before the Christian era. Was Jesus to be found in the scrolls? Was Christian doctrine, long thought to be unique, foreshadowed by the scrolls?

It was such questions as these that aroused—and continue to arouse—wide public interest in the scrolls. The French scholar André Dupont-Sommer, who was not a member of the scroll publication team, sought to draw a direct line between the Dead Sea Scrolls from Qumran and Christianity, arguing that Jesus was prefigured by a character in the scrolls known as the Teacher of Righteousness. In a now-famous passage, Dupont-Sommer wrote:

> The Galilean Master . . . appears in many respects as an astonishing reincarnation of [the Teacher of Righteousness in the scrolls]. Like the latter, He preached penitence, poverty, humility, love of one's neighbor, chastity. Like him, He prescribed the observance of the Law of Moses, the whole Law, but the Law finished and perfected, thanks to His own revelations. Like him, He was the Elect and Messiah of God, the Messiah redeemer of the world. Like him, He was the object of the hostility of the priests. . . . Like him He was condemned and put to death. Like him He pronounced judgment on Jerusalem, which was taken and destroyed by the Romans for having put Him to death. Like him, at the end of time, He will be the supreme judge. Like him, He founded a Church whose adherents fervently awaited his glorious return.[1]

Dupont-Sommer greatly influenced the prominent American literary critic Edmund Wilson, who wrote a best-selling book on the scrolls, reprinted from a series of articles that appeared in *The New Yorker* from 1951 to 1954.[2] Wilson, following Dupont-Sommer, claimed that the Qumran sect and early Christianity were "successive phases of a [single] movement."[3] Wilson drew out the implications of Dupont-Sommer's position:

> The monastery [at Qumran], this structure of stone that endures, between the waters and precipitous cliffs, with its oven and its inkwells, its mill and its cesspool, its constellations of sacred fonts and the unadorned graves of its dead, is perhaps, more than Bethlehem or Nazareth, the cradle of Christianity.[4]

This position was given credibility by factors entirely unrelated to the content of the scrolls themselves. The publication team was largely Catholic, indeed largely Catholic priests, and, foolishly, they refused to release the texts of the unpublished fragmentary scrolls. This decision, understandably, led to accusations that the unpublished scrolls were being withheld because they undermined

Christian faith. Ultimately the refusal to release the scrolls resulted, in the words of Geza Vermes, a distinguished commentator on the scrolls, in "the academic scandal *par excellence* of the twentieth century."[5]

In 1991, after considerable struggle, as we shall see, the hitherto secret texts finally became available to all scholars. Since then scroll scholarship has burgeoned. It is now possible to attempt an assessment, which provides the occasion for this book: What *do* the scrolls tell us about the period from which both Christianity and Rabbinic Judaism emerged?

It is clear that the scrolls have not fulfilled the extravagant expectations that their discovery first aroused. Dupont-Sommer was wrong. Jesus is not in the scrolls. Nor is the uniqueness of Christianity in doubt. But the scrolls do tell us a great deal that we had not previously known about the situation of Judaism at the dawn of Christianity.

The scrolls also tell us much about Judaism at the time the Temple still stood in Jerusalem and about the roots of Rabbinic Judaism, the direct ancestor of all major Jewish denominations today, which emerged after the Romans destroyed the Temple.

Finally, the scrolls tell us about the Bible before the authoritative canon was established in the second century A.D., at a time when different versions of the biblical books circulated within the Jewish world.

The scrolls thus provide a unique insight into a religious culture at a time of unparalleled religious as well as social ferment. The earliest of the scrolls dates to about 250 B.C.; the latest to 68 A.D., when the conquering Romans destroyed Qumran on their way to Jerusalem, which they burned a bare two years later, effectively ending the First Jewish Revolt against Rome.

In 332 B.C. Alexander the Great defeated Persia and conquered Judea. Thus began a process of Hellenization that would profoundly affect all aspects of Jewish culture. Greek cities were established in Palestine (Jerusalem itself became a *polis* in 175 B.C.); Greek temples were built and dedicated to non-Jewish deities; Greek was soon spoken throughout the Jewish world, along with the vernacular Aramaic and the increasingly less frequent Hebrew.

Upon the death of Alexander in 323 B.C., his empire split into two major parts: the Seleucids in Syria to the north and the Ptolemies in Egypt to the south. During the third century B.C. the Seleucids and the Ptolemies fought no fewer than five major wars, with Judea as a battleground and a prize.

During this period in Judea, social tensions heightened—between the Hellenizers, who introduced Greek ideas and customs, and those traditionally inclined Jews who opposed Greek influence, between the sophisticated cities and the conservative villages, between urban aristocrats and rural farmers, and between rich and poor. Many Jews found their faith and the continuity of their world threatened by these Greek intrusions. The book of Ecclesiastes, with its theological skepticism and occasional praise of reckless hedonism, is an example of the profound effect this new culture had on traditional religious commitment.

In about 175 B.C. Jason—who had Hellenized his Hebrew name, Joshua—bribed the Seleucid monarch Antiochus IV to depose his brother and in his place appoint Jason to the office of high priest in Jerusalem. In gratitude, Jason briefly changed the name of Jerusalem to Antiochia and erected a gymnasium in the capital, where Greek sports were played and Greek philosophy was taught. Josephus reports that Jason "at once shifted his countrymen over to the Greek way of life."[6]

Later Antiochus issued a decree banning circumcision, religious study, and observance of festivals and the Sabbath, and forced Jews to worship his gods and to eat forbidden foods.

Such radical Hellenization inevitably brought on the Maccabean revolt, giving birth to the Hasmonean dynasty of Jewish kings and high priests (142–37 B.C.). What began as an anti-

Hellenistic revolt, however, soon turned into a pro-Hellenistic dynasty. Political intrigue was rife among the Hasmoneans and the highest political authority (the king) was soon combined with the highest religious authority (the high priest). Religious schisms widened and antagonistic religious parties vied with one another. On the festival of Sukkot (Tabernacles), which is celebrated with palm branches and a lemon-like fruit called *etrog,* the populace threw their *etrogim* at the high priest. In a civil war during the early years of the first century B.C., dissident Jews joined the Syrian king Demetrius III in an attack on Jerusalem, while the Jewish king Alexander Yannai (Jannaeus) hired Syrian mercenaries to defend the city. Yannai crucified eight hundred of his subjects for supporting his enemies.

For the elite, whose elaborate tombs and elegant mansions have been discovered in Jerusalem, this was nevertheless a prosperous time. In the prime residential section of Jerusalem, Nahman Avigad of Hebrew University has recovered not only their opulent residences, including beautifully paved ritual baths, but also their fancy dinnerware and costly furniture.

In the mid-second century B.C., however, a small group of Jews, perhaps offended by the rampant materialism they saw all about them, perhaps distressed by the degradation of the priestly class, which had merged with the Jerusalem aristocracy, moved into the Judean desert to live in isolation. They settled at a place now called Qumran. Who these people were will be a major subject of this book. If in fact they were the keepers of the scrolls that were later found in this area, their leader held the title Teacher of Righteousness. It is clear that they rejected the Jerusalem Temple—or at least its priesthood.

At about the same time, other Jewish religious groups or sects were emerging. Of these, the Pharisees are the best known. To them are attributed the sources of the Oral Law—the Talmud of the later sages—that formed the basis of Rabbinic Judaism, the post-Exilic Judaism that spread throughout the diaspora after the destruction of the Temple by the Romans and the later expulsion of the Jews from Jerusalem.

The second major grouping, the Sadducees (Tsadukim), claimed to be descended from Zadok (Tsadok), the original Solomonic high priest. On this descent rested much of their claim to power; although they objected to the usurpation of the high priesthood by non-Zadokites, they nevertheless often aligned themselves with Hellenistic Hasmoneans.

A third, much smaller, group was the Essenes. They too objected to the non-Zadokite usurpation of the priesthood, but they were far more rigid in their adherence to and strict interpretation of religious law and less willing to adjust to the political realities of Hasmonean rule than were the Sadducees. Even the Essenes, however, could not entirely escape Hellenistic influences—for example, in the dualism (characterized by contrasting forces, such as good and evil, that control the world) that often permeates their religious writings.

While these were the major groupings, there were many others about whom we know far less and doubtless still others who have left no trace in the historical record.

In the mid-sixties B.C., two royal Hasmonean sons engaged in a fratricidal war for the throne. One of these sons sought Roman help, and in 63 B.C. the Roman general Pompey conquered Jerusalem, effectively ending Jewish sovereignty, although Hasmonean rulers continued at least nominally to sit on the throne of a truncated kingdom for another quarter century.

Then, in 40 B.C., Parthians from the east invaded Judea, wresting it from the Romans and appointing the last Hasmonean ruler (Mattathias Antigonus). At the time of the Parthian invasion, Herod, a Jew of Idumean and Nabatean lineage, subsequently known as Herod the Great, was serving as a Roman procurator. He promptly went to Rome to convince the Roman senate that only he could restore Roman rule. In 37 B.C. Herod led an army against the Parthians and after a bitter fight reconquered Jerusalem.

For thirty-three years he ruled Judea, as a Roman vassal. That he was hated by his Jewish subjects is well known. The Jewish historian Josephus tells of Herod's plan to have the leading men of Judea murdered at the time of his own death because he feared that otherwise his funeral might be an occasion for general rejoicing. Without question, Herod exercised his power through terror and brutality, but a further reason for his unpopularity was his violation of traditional Jewish law. He built numerous pagan temples and even staged gladiatorial contests in Jerusalem. However, he also rebuilt the Jewish Temple in Jerusalem on so grand a scale that it far eclipsed the original building constructed a millennium earlier by King Solomon.

After Herod's death, in 4 B.C., social unrest became more open. Although Jewish client-kings of the Herodian dynasty pretended to govern a truncated Judea, brigands often ruled the countryside, and the Romans assumed more and more direct power. Riots were not uncommon, leading eventually to the outbreak of the First Jewish Revolt against Rome, which began in 66 A.D. and effectively ended in 70 A.D., when the Romans burned Jerusalem and destroyed the Temple.

Judaism during this period has been described as "remarkably variegated."[7] Some scholars have gone so far as to talk about Judaisms, rather than one Judaism. In those insecure times the traditional Judaism, centered in Temple sacrifice, was widely considered by Jews themselves inadequate to the stormy present. So, along with institutions like the synagogue, which would replace the Temple and become the focus of Jewish life thereafter, we also see the development of expectations of the end of time, of heavenly visions, of life after death, of resurrection of the dead, of apocalypses (revelations) where good and evil were to face each other in a final cosmic battle, and of messianic deliverers.

This, in brief, was the world implicitly addressed by the Dead Sea Scrolls.

THE MYSTERY AND MEANING
OF THE DEAD SEA SCROLLS

*The Wadi Qumran from the air, showing the Qumran settlement in
the center and adjacent to it some of the caves where the Dead Sea Scrolls
were found. In the distance the shore of the Dead Sea can be seen.*

CHAPTER 1

EXPLORING THE LEGEND

The story of the discovery of the first hoard of Dead Sea Scrolls may be briefly told, especially as it has been told so often.

Probably in late 1946 or early 1947, a shepherd boy of the Ta'amireh tribe named Muhammad Ahmad el-Hamed, nicknamed edh-Dhib (Muhammad the Wolf), was searching for a lost sheep. He tossed a stone into a cave, hoping to scare the sheep out, but instead of the bleating of a sheep he heard the sound of cracking pottery. When he and a friend explored the cave they discovered two large jars. Inside, wrapped in linen, they found some ancient scrolls.

Was it a goat or a sheep that he was looking for? Was it one shepherd or two? Did they enter then or only the next day? And who was edh-Dhib? Scholars have interviewed inconclusively several bedouin who claim to be edh-Dhib, and even the date when the scrolls were first found is uncertain.

In 1993, Weston Fields, the executive director of the recently created[1] Dead Sea Scroll Foundation, met yet another man who claimed to be edh-Dhib. Like many Ta'amireh bedouin, he had long since settled down in a cinder-block house in Bethlehem. But

The two bedouin, allegedly Jum'a Muhammad and Muhammad Ahmad el-Hamed (edh-Dhib), who supposedly found the first cache of scrolls in 1947.

Jars in which the scrolls were found.

he still searched for antiquities in the West Bank, selling them to dealers in the Old City. That is how Fields met him, alerted by an antiquities dealer. Fields interviewed the man who claimed to be edh-Dhib several times and even went to the caves near Qumran to test his knowledge of their location and original contents. On one occasion that year, I went with Fields to the shop of the antiquities dealer to talk to edh-Dhib, as I will call him, although I am by no means sure of his identity. In his unpublished account of the meetings, Fields described him accurately: "He had the beautiful, easy smile of the bedouin, the brown wrinkled skin, the wizened weathered look and the characteristic missing teeth. Dressed in traditional garb—a long dress-like garment, suit jacket and a red-and-white checkered *kafieh*—he looked the part, the timeless bedouin of the Judean desert."

Fields judged his age to be about seventy-five. He spoke neither English nor Hebrew; the antiquities dealer served as interpreter. Edh-Dhib obviously knew the caves well and was able to relate many of the supposed circumstances of scroll discoveries. In the words of the Fields memo, "We have confirmed that [edh-Dhib] had intimate, direct knowledge of the Qumran caves. The precision and magnitude of his knowledge bespeaks first-hand experience. He neither reads nor writes, but even if he did, none of the material [he related] is available in Arabic [so he cannot have learned details from reading about them]."[2]

But there were also problems with his story. For example, in the antiquities shop he told Fields there were about forty-five jars in the cave when he entered it. When he led Fields to the cave where he said he had found the scrolls, it was not the one that scholars have long identified as the first cave to be discovered (Qumran Cave 1) and when he was taken to the cave that scholars regard as Qumran Cave 1, he denied that this was the cave he had first found. For one thing, it was not large enough to hold forty-five jars, he said.

Edh-Dhib also adamantly insisted that the scrolls were first discovered shortly before 1938. Though he did not give the actual

A 1993 photograph of a man claiming to be edh-Dhib.

date, he insisted that he found the scrolls before he married his first wife. She was barren, and after twenty years, he took another wife. Two years later, wife number two bore him a son, who was thirty-three years old in 1993. So he was sure he had made the scroll discovery at least fifty-five years earlier (twenty years with wife one, two years with wife two, and thirty-three years since his son was born equals fifty-five years). For years, he kept the scrolls in his tent.[3] He didn't know the writing was Hebrew and he didn't know they had any value. One scroll, he said, broke into pieces and he threw it away.

When he was shown a book with the standard photograph of edh-Dhib taken nearly fifty years earlier, he laughed. "That is Musa," his cousin, he said. When Fields pointed out that the caption said the photo was of edh-Dhib, the bedouin laughed. "*I am* Muhammad edh-Dhib," he stated emphatically. "*That* is Musa."

Fields was only one of several American scholars who have attempted to identify and interview edh-Dhib. The earliest such attempt occurred in 1949.[4] Others took place in the 1960s.[5] They are nothing if not confusing. Were these early interviews with the same "edh-Dhib" Fields interviewed? When one early investigator told an "edh-Dhib" that someone else had been identified as "edh-Dhib," the bedouin replied, "Arabs sometimes have more than one name."[6]

In a 1956 interview, one "edh-Dhib" claimed he found the scrolls in 1945.[7] Other interviews with the same or a different edh-Dhib place the discovery in 1942.[8]

What we can say with confidence is that bedouin from the Ta'amireh tribe tending their flocks on the northwestern shore of the Dead Sea found some scrolls in a cave, probably in late 1946 or early 1947. We know that they found scrolls because we have them—or at least some of them—and the linen in which they were wrapped and the jars in which the linen-wrapped scrolls were placed. And we know when the scrolls first appeared on the antiquities market.

The entrance to Cave 1 is visible in the middle of the photograph.

In April (or thereabouts) 1947 the bedouin brought the scrolls to Bethlehem, the principal market town of the Ta'amireh. One can only wonder what their thoughts were then, and what arguments there were as to the scrolls' worth and who would be entitled to whatever they could be sold for. We do not know under what conditions the scrolls had been kept between the time they were found and the time they came to market, or even precisely how many scrolls were involved. In some accounts, for example, there were eight scrolls, instead of the seven that eventually came into scholarly hands.[9]

What happened when the scrolls reached Bethlehem is as obscure as the circumstances of the initial discovery. In Bethlehem the bedouin contacted one antiquities dealer, or perhaps two: Faidi Salahi or Faidi al-'Alami,[10] who may have been the same man under different names,[11] and possibly Khalil Iskander Shahin, better known as Kando. Kando may have returned to the cave with the bedouin and conducted illegal excavations himself,[12] perhaps recovering a scroll or scrolls that the bedouin had missed. In any event, the total number of intact scrolls numbered seven, either because the bedouin originally recovered that many or because Kando's excavation added to the original number.

These seven scrolls were divided into two lots, three in one lot and four in the other. Just why is not clear. They may have been found at separate times. Or they may have been divided by the bedouin as separate shares. In any event, three of the scrolls were obtained by Salahi and four by Kando. According to one version of the story, Kando paid the bedouin only 5 dinars ($14) for their scrolls, and promised them a third (or some say two-thirds) of what they fetched on the market.

There is a tendency among Western writers to denigrate the untutored actors in this drama, such as the bedouin and Kando. The bedouin, it is said, had no idea what they had, and this is certainly true. But very likely they did know that whatever they had was valuable on the antiquities market. As Harvard professor Frank Cross has noted, "The Ta'amireh were not without experience in archaeological matters."[13] They had long worked for professional archaeologists and, as Cross notes, took pride in the antiquities they found.

The same is true of Kando, who is regularly described as a cobbler. Shortly after the four scrolls came into his hands, Kando consulted a friend and fellow member of the Syrian Orthodox Church, George Isaiah, and together they took the scrolls to the Syrian Orthodox archbishop (metropolitan) of Jerusalem, Mar Athanasius Yeshue Samuel. One recent account claims that had they not taken the scrolls to Mar Samuel, "Kando would likely have used the greatest manuscript discovery of modern times to repair shoes in his cobblery, and no one else would ever have seen them."[14] This is nonsense, not only because the scrolls were far too brittle and fragile to be used in this way, but because Kando was sophisticated enough to know that they would have value to scholars. Kando always bridled at being called a mere cobbler. In recent conversations with his sons (Kando died in 1994 without recording the story of the scrolls from his viewpoint, though I urged him repeatedly to do so), I was told that Kando's father—their grandfather—had been a successful, even wealthy, businessman. In 1947, when the scrolls were brought to him, Kando himself owned several businesses, including a small shoe factory (hence the characterization of him as a cobbler), but he loved antiquities and already owned an antiquities shop. (On the other hand, could I be confident that the sons were telling me the truth?)

Salahi, who had the smaller lot, three scrolls, contacted an Armenian friend named Levon Ohan, the son of Nasri Ohan, a well-known Armenian antiquities dealer in the Old City. Ohan, in turn, contacted a friend who was professor of archaeology at Hebrew University, Eleazer Lupa Sukenik, who was always on the lookout for antiquities that came on the market. Sukenik was the father of Yigael Yadin, who was to become Israel's most illustrious archaeologist and a Dead Sea Scroll scholar in his own right. At the time, however, before the establishment of the State of Israel,

Khalil Iskander Shahin (Kando),
an antiquities dealer who served
as middleman between the
bedouin and the scholars.

Metropolitan Mar Athanasius Yeshue Samuel,
who purchased four of the original seven scrolls
and sold them in the United States.

Yadin was chief of operations of the Haganah, the underground army.

Sukenik has recorded his version of events in some detail.[15] This was 1947, the final days of the British Mandate in Palestine. Violence was rife. The British security forces had divided Jerusalem into military zones separating Jewish and Arab sections of the city; barbed wire marked the boundaries. To move from zone to zone required a military pass. Neither Sukenik nor his friend Ohan had a pass, so they agreed to meet at the gateway to Military Zone B.

On the other side of the barricade from Sukenik, Ohan removed a scrap of parchment from his briefcase and showed it to Sukenik through the barbed wire. Sukenik noticed that the form of the Hebrew letters resembled that of letters he had studied on ossuaries—limestone bone boxes—that were common in Jerusalem at the turn of the era, that is to say, some two thousand years ago (see page 173).

Sukenik immediately decided to purchase the scrolls from which the fragment had come, although he didn't say as much to Ohan at the time. Instead, he expressed interest and asked his friend to show him more samples. Sukenik obtained a pass to enter Zone B, and after looking at more fragments, he resolved to go to Bethlehem to negotiate a purchase price.

It was a dangerous journey at the time, and his wife objected to his going. In Sukenik's own words, "She said I was crazy even to think of" going to Bethlehem. Tension was especially high because on the other side of the globe the United Nations was about to vote on the partition of Palestine into a Jewish state and an Arab state. If the vote was affirmative by the required two-thirds, as was widely anticipated and as in fact occurred, the Arabs might declare war to prevent the formation of a Jewish state, and full-fledged fighting could break out, replacing the sporadic violence that preceded the vote.

Sukenik consulted his son, who was on a brief visit to Jerusalem to check on the defense of the city in advance of the anticipated Arab attack. Yadin describes his reaction: "What was I to tell him?

*Professor Eleazer L. Sukenik of Hebrew University, who was
the first scholar to see a fragment of the scrolls.*

As a student of archaeology myself, I felt that an opportunity of acquiring such priceless documents could not be missed. On the other hand, as Chief of Operations of Haganah, I knew perfectly well the dangers my father would be risking in traveling to Arab Bethlehem. And as a son I was torn between both feelings. I tried to hedge, but, before leaving, son and soldier won and I told him not to go."

Sukenik listened neither to his wife nor to his son. On November 29, 1947, he and Ohan boarded an Arab bus for Bethlehem.[16] Sukenik was the only Jew on the bus. The tension was palpable. But the bus trip passed uneventfully.

After the requisite Arab coffee and polite exchanges, Salahi brought out two jars in which the scrolls had been found. Then he produced the scrolls themselves. Sukenik describes the moment: "My hands shook as I started to unwrap one of them. I read a few sentences. It was written in beautiful Biblical Hebrew. The language was like that of the Psalms."

Sukenik told Salahi that he would probably want to buy the scrolls and agreed that he would let him know in two days. In the meantime, Sukenik would take two of the three scrolls with him to Jerusalem to examine them more carefully. Salahi wrapped the scrolls in paper and handed them to Sukenik. Sukenik bid Salahi farewell and then boarded the bus for the short ride back to the city. He was carrying in his hands the two scrolls that would become known as the Scroll of Thanksgiving Psalms, Hodayot, in Hebrew, and the War Scroll, Milchamah, in Hebrew, or, more completely, the Scroll of the War of the Sons of Light Against the Sons of Darkness (see page 165). His hands understandably trembled. A week later he acquired the third scroll, a copy of the book of Isaiah, later to become known as Isaiah[b].

Within hours of Sukenik's return from Bethlehem the United Nations passed the partition resolution by the necessary two-thirds vote. Sukenik was back in his study absorbed in the scrolls when his youngest son, Mati, who would be killed in the war that was soon to break out, rushed in to tell his father of the vote.

"I could not remain indoors," Sukenik wrote. "I went out to share the joy with Jewish Jerusalem. . . . The streets were thronged with cars from which cheering youngsters were shouting the announcement to any who might have missed it on the radio. . . . I felt myself bursting with my own news. I had to tell someone about the great discovery. I searched for friends, and was delighted to spot two nearby among the crowd. . . . My news bubbled forth. I do not know whether they believed me or even whether they heard what I was saying but in the turbulent emotional joy of that night, and sensing that I was transmitting something exciting, they responded with unrestrained delight."

The next day the Arabs attacked. Seven neighboring Arab states formally declared war, a war Israelis call their War of Independence. Almost six months later, on May 15, 1948, the State of Israel would be proclaimed in Tel Aviv.

It was only natural that both Sukenik and his son saw the acquisition of the three scrolls as portentous. In Yadin's own words: "I cannot avoid the feeling that there is something symbolic in the discovery of the scrolls and their acquisition at the moment of the creation of the State of Israel. It is as if these manuscripts had been waiting in caves for two thousand years, ever since the destruction of Israel's independence [by the Romans in 70 A.D.], until the people of Israel had returned to their home and regained their freedom. This symbolism is heightened by the fact that the first three [two?] scrolls were bought by my father for Israel on 29th November, 1947, the very day on which the United Nations voted for the re-creation of the Jewish state in Israel after two thousand years."[17]

In January 1948 Sukenik received a call from an acquaintance named Anton Kiraz, who belonged to the Syrian Orthodox Christian community, the same community to which Kando belonged, telling him that more scrolls were available.

These of course were Kando's four scrolls, but by that time he had sold them to the archbishop Mar Samuel. In April 1947, Kando had taken fragments from his lot to Mar Samuel, who immediately recognized that they were written in Hebrew. Mar

Samuel asked Kando to bring him the scrolls from which the fragments had come, and Kando apparently sent the bedouin themselves with the scrolls to St. Mark's monastery, where Mar Samuel lived. The bedouin, looking tattered and dirty, were turned away and returned to Bethlehem with the scrolls. When Mar Samuel learned from idle lunch-table conversation that some dirty bedouin had been turned away, he realized what had happened. He immediately called Kando to apologize.

Two weeks later, Kando himself brought the scrolls to the monastery. A deal was quickly struck: Mar Samuel reportedly bought the scrolls for £24, about $100. If Kando paid the bedouin their share, he retained two-thirds (or one third) for himself.[18]

Not sure what he had bought—the scrolls could be forgeries or, more likely, relatively recent manuscripts—Mar Samuel sought counsel from scholars in Jerusalem. Those he consulted included a friend at the Department of Antiquities, scholars at the Dominican monastery of St. Stephen with its famous École Biblique et Archéologique Française, and librarians at the library of Hebrew University. At Anton Kiraz's suggestion, Mar Samuel also decided to show the scrolls to the professor of archaeology at Hebrew University, E. L. Sukenik. Kiraz was to make the necessary introductions.

Kiraz and Sukenik agreed to meet at the YMCA in Zone B, and Sukenik obtained a new pass. There Kiraz brought the other four scrolls and showed them to Sukenik, who quickly recognized that they belonged to the same hoard as those he had already acquired, and he expressed interest in buying them. Again it was agreed that Sukenik would take the scrolls with him for further examination and would return them in a few days.

In the war-torn environment there was no time for the usual pas de deux by which Middle Eastern agreements are reached at leisure. Sukenik decided that the best way to close a deal quickly was to lay £2,000 sterling on the table, but he was unable to raise the money. He had applied for a mortgage loan of £1,500 with which to buy the first three scrolls, but the loan was never completed because at the last moment other funds became available. To pay for Mar Samuel's scrolls, Sukenik again sought a loan, but this time the military and political situation had deteriorated to such an extent that he was refused. He had no choice but to hand the scrolls back to Kiraz. The two agreed that they would meet again and bring their principals: Sukenik would bring the president of Hebrew University and Kiraz would bring Mar Samuel. They, rather than Sukenik and Kiraz, would negotiate the price.

Sukenik never saw the scrolls again. Kiraz advised him that a decision had been made not to sell the scrolls at that time. Mar Samuel wanted to wait until the political situation settled down so he could determine a fair price on the international market.

At this point, Butros Sowmy, a fellow monk and close friend of Mar Samuel's, decided to try to learn more about the scrolls from the American School of Oriental Research in Jerusalem, today named the W. F. Albright Institute of Archaeological Research in honor of the great Johns Hopkins scholar. The director of the school at that time, Professor Millar Burrows of Yale University, was away when Sowmy placed his call, so the call was taken by a young fellow at the school named John Trever. Since it was not safe for Americans to go into the Old City, where St. Mark's was located, Trever asked if Sowmy could bring the scrolls to the American School. Sowmy agreed and the next day appeared with the scrolls in hand.

Trever was stunned. The writing closely resembled that of the famous Nash Papyrus, the oldest fragment of the Hebrew Bible then known, generally dated to about 150 B.C. or shortly thereafter.[19]

One of the scrolls Trever held in his hands was a complete copy of the book of the prophet Isaiah (Isaiah[a]). Another was to become known as the Manual of Discipline. The third was a commentary on the book of Habbakuk (Pesher Habbakuk, in Hebrew), one of the so-called minor prophets. The fourth scroll was so twisted and fragile that it could not be unrolled. Originally it was called Scroll L because the name Lamech could be seen in the text; several years later, when the badly mangled scroll was finally unrolled, it was seen to contain some fanciful expansions on the book of Genesis; hence, it is now called the Genesis Apocryphon.

By happy chance, Trever was an inveterate and near-professional photographer. He proposed that a complete photographic record be made of the scrolls. After consultation with Mar Samuel and some urging by Trever, Sowmy agreed. To obtain sufficient film, Trever scoured the war-torn city and finally found some outdated portrait film. Although photographs were later taken by others, Trever's pictures remain the finest evidence of the content of these scrolls (except for the Genesis Apocryphon, which could not then be unrolled).

Both Trever and Sukenik had dated the scrolls with considerable accuracy, although initially the date was a major question. The paleography of Hebrew scripts was then in its infancy (see page 83). Some scholars, most notably Solomon Zeitlin of Dropsie College in Philadelphia, insisted the scrolls dated only to the medieval period.[20] Another nagging question involved their authenticity. Could they be fakes?

Both questions were resolved when Trever sent photographs of the texts to the leading biblical archaeologist and Semitic epigrapher of his day, William Foxwell Albright, at Johns Hopkins University in Baltimore. Albright's famous reply arrived at the American School on May 15, 1948, the very day Israel declared its independence: "My heartiest congratulations on the greatest manuscript discovery of modern times! There is no doubt in my mind that the script is more archaic than that of the Nash Papyrus. . . . I should prefer a date around 100 B.C.! . . . What an absolutely incredible find! And there can happily not be the slightest doubt in the world about the genuineness of the manuscript."

Because of the increasing violence in Jerusalem, two weeks later the American School temporarily closed and its American personnel returned home. In the meantime, Mar Samuel decided to deposit the scrolls in Beirut to assure their safety. Shortly after taking them there, Father Butros Sowmy was killed by shrapnel as he stood in the courtyard of St. Mark's monastery.

In January 1949, Mar Samuel, at the invitation of Professor Burrows, who had returned to Yale, arrived in the United States with the scrolls. The metropolitan needed money for his church and was looking for a buyer.

To generate interest in the scrolls, he arranged, with the assistance of Burrows and Trever, to exhibit them publicly. In October 1949, Mar Samuel's scrolls were exhibited amid much fanfare at the Library of Congress. From there they traveled to several other museums and art galleries—the Walters Art Gallery in Baltimore, the Oriental Institute of the University of Chicago, the Worcester Art Museum in Worcester, Massachusetts, and Duke University in Durham, North Carolina. Interest was high, but, strangely, no institution was ready to make an offer to buy the scrolls.

Years passed. In the meantime, Mar Samuel settled permanently in New Jersey. In desperation, on June 1, 1954, he placed his now-famous classified ad offering the scrolls for sale in *The Wall Street Journal* (see page 21).

By chance, Yigael Yadin was in the United States on a lecture tour at the time and someone called his attention to the ad. He immediately determined to buy the scrolls for Israel and arranged for an intermediary to reply to the ad and negotiate for their purchase.

After lengthy negotiations, a price of $250,000 was agreed upon for the four scrolls—an extraordinary bargain even at the time. Of course Yadin and Israel were kept nominally out of the deal for fear that Mar Samuel would not consent to such a purchaser. Lawyers for the two sides drew up a bill of sale, which was signed by Mar Samuel on behalf of the seller and a New York businessman, Sydney Estridge, on behalf of the buyer.

The parties who had been dealing on behalf of Yadin were professional negotiators. But there was one thing they could not do—

examine the scrolls on delivery for identity and authenticity. For this, a scholar in the field was necessary, and he could not be Yadin, since he would be recognized by Mar Samuel.

Yadin called his friend Harry Orlinsky of The Johns Hopkins University. As Orlinsky describes it, he was almost out the door, leaving on a vacation, when the call came: "My wife was already seated in the car and I was locking the door when the telephone rang." With a military man's instinct for secrecy, Yadin asked Orlinsky, without telling him why, to postpone his vacation and immediately come to New York on a matter of importance to Israel. In Orlinsky's account of the event: "I asked for a minute or two to talk it over with my wife. Together we decided that if Israel needed me, we had no choice."[21]

When he arrived in New York, Orlinsky was instructed on his role: "I was to assume the name 'Mr. Green,' an expert on behalf of the client. I was to take a taxi to the Lexington Avenue entrance of the Waldorf-Astoria Hotel, where the Chemical Bank and Trust Co. had a branch. I was to make sure that I was not followed. A Mr. Sydney M. Estridge would be waiting there for me; we had been told how to identify one another. He would go with me downstairs to the vault of the bank. There we would find a representative of the Metropolitan [Mar Samuel], with the scrolls ready for examination. I was to say as little as possible, and admit to no identification beyond being Mr. Green.

"The vault was stuffy and hot, and inadequately lit. From a large black trunk on the floor emerged four scrolls. The most important and impressive of them was the Isaiah Scroll, all sixty-six chapters of it."

After identifying and authenticating the four scrolls, Orlinsky went to a pay phone, called an unlisted number, and uttered the code word: *l'chayim*, to life. His mission had been successful.

The four scrolls were flown to Israel one at a time. There they were joined by the three scrolls obtained seven years earlier by Yadin's father, E. L. Sukenik. Alas, Sukenik, who had died the

"The Four Dead Sea Scrolls"

Biblical Manuscripts dating back to at least 200 BC, are for sale. This would be an ideal gift to an educational or religious institution by an individual or group.

Box F 206, The Wall Street Journal.

This advertisement, placed by Mar Samuel in
The Wall Street Journal, *led to Yadin's purchase of the four remaining scrolls of the original cache.*

*Yigael Yadin (on the right, with James Biberkraut)
left the military in 1952 and soon became
Israel's most illustrious archaeologist.*

previous year, did not live to see this happen. In 1948, when he failed to raise the money to acquire these four scrolls, he wrote in his diary: "Thus the Jewish people have lost a precious heritage."

On February 13, 1955, Israel's prime minister, Moshe Sharett, called a special press conference to announce that all seven scrolls were now in Israel. The announcement made front-page news around the world, and presumably Mar Samuel learned for the first time that he had sold the scrolls to the government of Israel.

Or did he know this already? How did Yadin manage to purchase four Dead Sea Scrolls for a paltry quarter of a million dollars? In 1933 the Codex Sinaiticus, a fourth-century Bible in Greek, was purchased by the British Museum for £100,000 (then about $335,000). At about the time Yadin purchased these four scrolls for Israel, Yale University paid $50,000 for a first edition of *Alice's Adventures in Wonderland,* only a little less than the price of one of the four scrolls.

Why were no American institutions interested in buying Mar Samuel's scrolls? Why was Yadin's representative the only serious response to Mar Samuel's *Wall Street Journal* advertisement?

Yadin himself ascribed this situation to "the false values of the market for rare books in [the United States]."[22] But there is another, more plausible explanation.

The Dead Sea Scroll caves are in the West Bank. At the time the scrolls were discovered, Jordan controlled the West Bank and had claimed it as part of Jordan, although only Great Britain and Pakistan had recognized Jordanian sovereignty. As self-proclaimed sovereign, Jordan claimed title to the scrolls. From Jordan's viewpoint, Mar Samuel had smuggled the scrolls out of east Jerusalem (and the Old City), which was also in Jordanian hands at the time. Since Jordan's claim to the scrolls had appeared in the press, Mar Samuel surely knew of it. In short, he could not give good title. Any purchaser would have to worry about a suit by the Hashemite Kingdom of Jordan, seeking return of the scrolls—any purchaser, that is, except Israel. Israel and Jordan were technically at war. For Jordan to sue Israel would imply recognition of the Jewish state, a step that Jordan would be unwilling to take.

In short, Israel may have been the only possible purchaser for these scrolls. Did Mar Samuel know this? Most likely, he did, especially when he was unable to arouse interest in the United States among prospective purchasers. And this may be why he was willing to sell the scrolls for a mere $250,000. Surely, he must have suspected that the strangers to whom he was selling the scrolls represented the State of Israel. Since Mar Samuel could not openly sell the scrolls to Israel, the disguise protected Mar Samuel as well as Yadin. The consequences to Mar Samuel, his people, and his Church of a sale to Israel could have been severe. Yadin helped him to avoid all this, and Mar Samuel could not be blamed for accepting the subterfuge.

One final irony: Mar Samuel was selling the scrolls on behalf of his Church. The proceeds were to help his people. But the papers were badly drawn. The United States Internal Revenue Service contended the proceeds were personal income to Mar Samuel, subject to American income tax. Mar Samuel resisted the claim and the government sued. Mar Samuel lost the case. Most of the proceeds from the sale were paid in taxes to the U.S. government.

CHAPTER 2

❦

ARCHAEOLOGISTS
VS. BEDOUIN

Not long after the first seven scrolls came to scholarly attention in 1948, efforts began to locate the cave where they were found. The find spot could reveal much about the scrolls, including their date (based on the pottery sherds likely to be found there, which could be securely dated). Equally important, there might be more scrolls or scroll fragments to be recovered.

The initial efforts were disappointing: Neither Kando, who had himself done some excavating of the cave, nor the bedouin could be prevailed upon to identify the cave.

Finally, the British director of the Antiquities Department under the Mandate, who had been retained by the Jordanians, an archaeologist named G. Lankester Harding, arranged for the Arab Legion, an elite Jordanian military unit, to scour the general area near the Dead Sea where the documents had supposedly been found.

After a two- or three-day search, on January 28, 1949, a captain named Akkash el-Zebn noticed freshly turned dirt in front of a small cave opening.[1] A closer inspection revealed that a considerable amount of dirt had been removed from the cave. When Harding and his colleague Père Roland de Vaux of the French École

Biblique et Archéologique Française, examined the cave, they confirmed that this was indeed the cave where the scrolls had been found. Their excavations recovered fragments of two of the seven largely intact manuscripts that the bedouin had earlier removed from the cave, as well as about seventy fragments from other documents. Extensive pottery sherds found in the cave confirmed the antiquity of the scrolls.

One would think that a search of the area for additional manuscripts in other caves would now begin in earnest. But this idea did not suggest itself to the academic mind. As Harvard professor Frank M. Cross described it, "It was generally assumed that by a stroke of fortune an isolated cache had been found. Apparently it occurred to few scholars that Cave 1 was other than a chance hiding place, or storage place, chosen by some odd but happy quirk of an ancient mind."[2]

The bedouin, however, were not so careless. In Professor Cross's elegant words: "The Ta'amireh clansmen, having made a successful debut in the archaeological field, were inclined to make a vocation of it. They ranged the sterile wastes of the Judaean desert, peering into caves, scratching in their floors, oblivious to passing months, patient and undiscouraged by persistent failure."[3]

The scholars meanwhile decided to excavate the nearby ruins of an ancient settlement, hoping to find more scrolls or learn something about the people who had placed the scrolls in the cave. The site known as Khirbet Qumran, "the ruins of Qumran," is less than a mile south of the cave. It is also known as Khirbet Yahud, "the ruins of the Jew."[4] Archaeological remains were clearly visible on the surface. At one time in the nineteenth century, the site had been identified as biblical Gomorrah. Later, potsherds from the Roman period (the period of the scrolls) were found there. In late 1951, Harding and de Vaux began to excavate. Their excavations continued under de Vaux's direction until 1956.

The earliest level, according to de Vaux,[5] dated to about the eighth century B.C., the period of the Israelite monarchy. De Vaux

G. Lankester Harding (right) and Father Josef Milik (center) confer with Roland de Vaux (left) at the excavations at Khirbet Qumran.

identified this level as the City of Salt, mentioned in the allotment to the tribe of Judah in Joshua 15:61. Later research makes it more likely that it is Secacah, mentioned in the same verse; the text tells us that it was located "in the wilderness."

The remains from this period are scant. The site was apparently abandoned for half a millennium or more, only to be reoccupied in the second century B.C.

In 31 B.C. a massive earthquake struck the area, heavily damaging the settlement at Qumran.[6] We are in the Great Rift Valley, which extends from the valley east of the mountains of Lebanon, down the Jordan Valley through the Dead Sea, then down the valley known as the Arava, through the Red Sea and on into Africa. The Dead Sea marks the lowest spot on earth, nearly 1,300 feet below sea level. In this rift colliding tectonic plates continue to produce earthquakes relatively frequently.

Although de Vaux concluded that the earthquake of 31 B.C. led to the site's abandonment until about 4 B.C., the better view now is that the gap in occupation lasted a few years at most. Then in 68 A.D. the Roman army on its way to Jerusalem destroyed the site. After a brief occupation by a Roman military garrison,[7] the site was left to the timeless wilderness and the desert sun.

Is there is a relationship between the site and the scrolls? Did the people who once lived here hide the scrolls in the nearby caves? Did they compose or copy them here? Did the scrolls belong to the library of the people who lived here? Or did the site have nothing to do with scrolls? After all, Cave 1, where the seven intact scrolls were found, is nearly a mile north of Qumran.

While the archaeologists excavating the site were attempting to answer these questions, the bedouin were looking for more scrolls in other caves in the area. In February 1952 they found a few fragments of manuscripts in a cave not far from the cave where the original seven intact manuscripts had been found. This then became known as Cave 2. The fragments were not large or extensive, but they did alert the scholarly community to the possibility of finding more manuscripts in still other caves.

The archaeological schools in Jerusalem soon organized an expedition to explore systematically the caves in the high rocky limestone cliffs south as well as north of Qumran. In Frank Cross's words, "The excitement of the search turned aging scientists into a new breed of archaeological mountain goats."[8]

In March 1952 the academics examined over two hundred caves. In one, they struck pay dirt. Cave 3, as it became known, contained fragments of Ezekiel and Psalms, as well as such apocryphal works as Jubilees, and even little pieces of unknown works, one of which refers to "an angel of peace."

Encouraged by these finds, the diggers explored the cave especially thoroughly. In the back of the cave on a ledge separated from the rest of the finds, they discovered two small rolls of copper sheeting about twelve inches high—easily the most mysterious of all the Dead Sea Scrolls discovered before or since (see Chapter 11). Actually, the two copper rolls form one document, which lists sixty-four locations where immense amounts of treasure are buried.

By the end of March 1952, the academics were exhausted. Some had contracted malaria as a result of their efforts. They were nevertheless comforted to know that they had explored most of the caves in the limestone cliffs.

Meanwhile de Vaux and Harding and their crew continued the excavation of Qumran, located on the marl terrace, a lower, softer sandstone formation between the limestone cliffs and the shore of the Dead Sea.

The bedouin, however, continued the search for more manuscripts in caves in the marl terrace itself—virtually under the noses of the archaeologists. The scholars had cunningly observed that the earlier manuscript finds had occurred in the limestone caves overlooking the marl terrace, so they logically confined their search to those caves. The bedouin, unburdened by logic, also searched the caves in the marl terrace—on which Qumran itself was built.

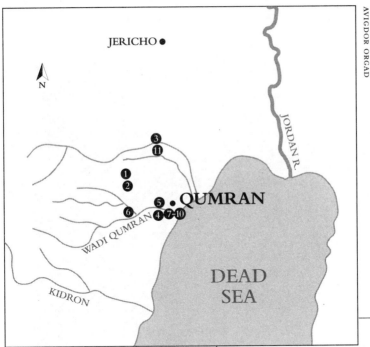

AVIGDOR ORGAD

JERICHO ●

N

③
⑪
①
②
⑤ ● QUMRAN
⑥ ④⑦-⑩
WADI QUMRAN

KIDRON

DEAD
SEA

JORDAN R.

*From eleven caves clustered around
Qumran, archaeologists and bedouin
recovered the Dead Sea Scrolls. The
caves are numbered in the order in
which they were discovered.*

*Qumran perches on a marl terrace on
the northern edge of the Wadi Qumran
at the base of high limestone cliffs. The
site overlooks the Dead Sea thirteen
miles east of Jerusalem.*

ALEXANDRIUM ●

JERICHO ●

JERUSALEM ●

JORDAN R.

QUMRAN ●
● EIN FESHKA

● HYRCANIA

HERODIUM ●

JUDEAN DESERT

DEAD
SEA

EIN GEDI ●

MASADA ●

N

AVIGDOR ORGAD

Cave 4, where fragments of over five hundred scrolls were found; today the cave can be entered from the top or from either end, as seen in the center of the photograph.

The interior of Cave 4.

The entrance to Cave 4 is only a few hundred feet—less than the length of two football fields—from where the archaeologists were digging at Qumran. Apparently while the archaeologists dug by day, the bedouin dug by night. And here they found the motherlode.

It should not be supposed that all it was necessary to do to locate the fragments of scrolls was to walk into a cave and poke around. The scroll fragments are usually covered with windblown sand and acrid bat guano. Over time, the floors of the caves, especially in the soft marl, gradually rise. So does the roof as erosion and earthquakes disturb the ceilings, which fall bit by bit, further burying any precious documents below. The dark mixture finally becomes food for worms and rodents. The scrolls themselves were often a meter or more below the surface.

The Ta'amireh tribesmen were in many ways experts. Some had previously worked for professional archaeologists. Others were working for de Vaux at Qumran. They knew to look in dry caves. They patiently excavated day after day in the hope of making a find. Even today, in caves where there have been no finds, latter-day professional archaeological surveyors often come upon evidence of these bedouin cave excavations.

Cave 4, which the bedouin found in 1952, contained over five hundred different manuscripts, all in tatters. There was not a single intact scroll among them. In most cases, only very small parts of original documents were recovered. The rest had been eaten by worms or had disintegrated from the heat and the corrosive effect of the bat dung in which they had lain buried for two thousand years.

By the time the archaeologists discovered the bedouin operation at their feet, the bedouin had removed 80 percent, perhaps 90 percent, of the contents of the cave.[9] The archaeologists were left with a mop-up operation, although a scientifically important one that allowed them to confirm the find spot of the Cave 4 fragments that they later had to purchase from Kando.

Once they discovered the bedouin digging in Cave 4, the archaeologists found Cave 5 adjacent to it. But the bedouin managed to find Cave 6, a hundred feet or so up the Wadi Qumran.

The spring of 1955 brought a new cycle of finds—Caves 7 through 10, also in the marl terrace, but closer to the Dead Sea. These caves had eroded and collapsed in ancient times, but there was enough evidence of their presence left to alert some of the excavators as they dug at Qumran.

Caves 5 through 10 are generally considered minor, because of the scant material found in them. In Cave 10, only an ostracon (a potsherd with writing on it) was recovered. However, Cave 7 is special because the nineteen fragments found in it are all in Greek. The claim that some of the tiny fragments are of New Testament writings will be considered in Chapter 5.

There was to be one more surprise. Again it was the bedouin who triumphed. More than a mile north of Qumran, in the limestone cliffs, not far from where the academics had made their one big discovery (the Copper Scroll in Cave 3), the bedouin excavated what was to become the last cave in the series, Cave 11. Apparently discovered in 1956, it proved to be nearly as rich as the initial discovery. How many scrolls the bedouin actually found remains something of a mystery, however. We know that they found at least three intact scrolls—a scroll of Leviticus written in the ancient Hebrew script used before the Babylonian exile; a scroll of the Book of Psalms, containing additional psalms not found in the Hebrew psalter; and the famous Temple Scroll—as well as numerous fragments of other manuscripts. I say "at least" three intact scrolls were found in Cave 11 because there may be more. We know only about those that have surfaced on the antiquities market or come to light elsewhere—like the Temple Scroll, which, as we shall see, was discovered under the tiles of Kando's home and confiscated (see Chapter 12). Further contents of Cave 11 may well reside in the vault of some antiquities dealer or collector. One senior scholar is, as I write, traveling the world in search of still-hidden Dead Sea Scrolls—not in the ground, but in private hands.

CHAPTER 3

THE TEAM
AT WORK

I n the early 1960s a special museum in Jerusalem called the
Shrine of the Book was built for the seven original scrolls from
Cave 1 acquired by Israel. It is an extraordinary building architecturally, lying half buried, like the scrolls themselves, with a roof
aboveground, fashioned after the lid of one of the jars from Cave 1.

The texts of these seven scrolls were published by American and
Israeli scholars in the 1950s and made available to scholars. These
editions were followed in the late 1950s and early 1960s by publication of the relatively few manuscripts found by archaeologists in
the so-called minor caves. To this period also belongs the publication of the major Psalms scroll from Cave 11.

The publication of the hoard from Cave 4, however, consisting
of over five hundred different manuscripts and about twenty-five
thousand fragments, naturally presented problems of a different
magnitude. The first problem was to acquire them from the
bedouin; if the fragments were sold hither and yon to a variety of
purchasers (antiquities dealers and collectors), it would be impossible to aggregate the fragments according to the manuscript to
which they belonged or to reconstruct a given manuscript from all
available fragments.

The Shrine of the Book in Jerusalem, where the intact scrolls are exhibited.

*The original seven scrolls are displayed in a temperature-
and light-controlled environment in the Shrine of the Book.*

Kando proved to be the key to the acquisition of the Cave 4 fragments. As early as 1950 Harding and de Vaux approached Kando to buy more scrolls. This may now seem like an eminently sensible thing to have done. But things are not always so simple in the archaeological world. The bedouin who had excavated Cave 1, as well as Kando himself (remember that he too went back to dig), were acting illegally. They are looters; professional archaeologists detest them. It is illegal for an antiquities dealer to purchase looted objects and a crime to sell them.

Kando may well have thought that Harding had come to arrest him, rather than to buy looted antiquities. Professionally, to make the offer to Kando required admirable courage on Harding's part. In the end, de Vaux convinced Kando to sell him the scroll fragments that he and the bedouin had removed from Cave 1. The price: nearly $3,000 (1,000 dinars). The scholars had now become Kando's major customer. Thus Kando was in effect immunized from the antiquities laws.

In the meantime Kando had cemented his relationship with the bedouin by taking in as a partner the sheik of the Ta'amireh tribe. This gave him a monopoly or a near-monopoly over the finds.[1]

In late 1952, Kando brought the first batch of Cave 4 fragments to the Palestine Archaeological Museum (PAM, later known as the Rockefeller Museum). De Vaux, who was president of the museum as well as a professor at the École Biblique, in cooperation with Harding, soon worked out an arrangement with Kando to purchase all the Cave 4 scroll fragments for a price of one Jordanian dinar per square centimeter of inscribed surface. (The dinar, pegged to the pound sterling, was worth $2.80 at the time).[2] This arrangement saved the Cave 4 fragments for the scholarly community.

Harding, who was not only the head of the Department of Antiquities but curator of the Palestine Archaeological Museum in Jerusalem, made another crucial decision. He assigned the scrolls to the PAM, instead of to the Jordanian state museum in Amman (which also acquired some scrolls, including the famous Copper Scroll).[3] But for Harding's decision, the scrolls might well be in Amman to this day.

The Jordanian government set aside 15,000 dinars ($42,000) for the purchase of the Cave 4 materials. PAM funds were also provided. But these and other available funds were soon exhausted—while the fragments kept coming in from the bedouin through Kando. At this point, Harding was authorized by the Jordanian government to invite foreign institutions to provide additional funds, with the understanding that when the pieces were put together and published, a proportionate share of the manuscripts would be distributed to each contributing institution. On this basis, institutions from the United States, England, Germany, Canada, and the Vatican provided additional funds. The last of the purchases was made in 1958.

While the small fragments continued to be sold for one dinar per centimeter, Kando negotiated a higher price for the larger and more elegant pieces, and he seems to have kept many of the best pieces until last. Indeed, the longest of the scrolls, the famous Temple Scroll, was not acquired from Kando until after the Six-Day War in 1967 (see Chapter 12). The last fragment brought in, in 1958, was the controversial "Son of God" fragment, with its parallels to the Gospel of Luke (see Chapter 5).

By 1961, however, Jordan decided it did not like the arrangement that allowed foreign institutions to acquire some of the fragments; it nationalized the scrolls, thereby expunging any private interest in them, whether of foreign institutions or of the Palestine Archaeological Museum, a private museum at the time. Although Jordan offered to repay the institutions that had contributed to the purchase price, it has yet to do so. Finally, in 1966, shortly before the 1967 Six-Day War, in which Israel captured east Jerusalem and the Old City, including the Palestine Archaeological Museum, Jordan nationalized the museum. In that way, as Jordanian governmental property, both the museum and its contents fell into Israeli hands.

The Rockefeller Museum (formerly the Palestine Archaeological Museum) is the home of tens of thousands of scroll fragments from Cave 4.

The legal entanglements regarding ownership of the Dead Sea Scrolls is a lawyer's dream—or nightmare. Recently, the Palestinian Authority under Yassir Arafat has laid claim to the scrolls because Qumran and the caves where they were found are in the West Bank, a few miles north of the pre-1967 border with Israel. Israel, of course, maintains that the scrolls are part of Jewish patrimony of which it is custodian.

As thousands of fragments began arriving at the Palestine Archaeological Museum in the 1950s, they were laid out under glass on tables in a long room soon to be known as the scrollery. From the outset, it was obvious that a team of scholars had to be assembled to deal with the mountain of material. To Père de Vaux, as president of the museum, fell the task of gathering such a team. Word went out to foreign institutions in Jerusalem, and through them to senior scholars in France, England, the United States, Germany, and elsewhere, that appropriate young scholars were needed in Jerusalem to work on the scroll fragments. In this way, a team of eight scholars was appointed, headed by de Vaux himself.

Of these scholars, the first to arrive, in the summer of 1953, was an American, Frank Cross.[4] That fall, one of the French appointees, Father J. T. Milik, a Pole living in Paris who had already worked on the Cave 1 fragments, returned to Jerusalem. From England came two young Oxford scholars—John Allegro, an atheist who would subsequently embarrass the team by suggesting that the messianic leader of the Dead Sea Scroll sect had been crucified a hundred years before the Christian messiah (see Chapter 11), and John Strugnell, who would later convert to Catholicism, become chief editor, and in a grossly anti-Semitic interview embarrass the project further. In 1954, two other Catholic priests arrived: Abbé Jean Starcky from France and Father Patrick Skehan of Catholic University of America in Washington, D.C. Claus-Hunno Hunzinger, a Lutheran from Germany, rounded out the team, but soon resigned. He was replaced by a French priest, Father Maurice Baillet.

Although the scrolls were Jewish religious documents, the team included no Jews. According to one recent account: "Harding and de Vaux wanted a team that would truly represent the nations and creeds that were active in biblical scholarship, with one major exception: They could not include any Jews or Israelis. It has been argued that de Vaux himself was anti-Semitic; it is certain that, like [Millar] Burrows, [John] Trever [both then of the American School of Oriental Research in Jerusalem], and many other scholars, he was vehemently opposed to the establishment of the state of Israel. But since he was acting on behalf of the Jordanian government, de Vaux could not have included Jews or Israelis on his team even if he had wanted to."[5]

The team was able to spend extended periods of time in Jerusalem through the generosity of John D. Rockefeller, Jr., the founding benefactor of the Palestine Archaeological Museum, who had also provided it with a million-dollar endowment.

The scrollery in the museum was a particularly pleasant place to work. Photographs show a fresh breeze billowing the curtains. The scholars handled the fragments with their bare hands. Some of the scholars, like Milik, examined the fragments closely with cigarettes hanging out of their mouths. When they found joins, they would normally attach the pieces to each other with Scotch tape. Forty years later, women who immigrated to Israel from the former Soviet Union would spend years carefully removing this tape with special solvents.

With the exception of Allegro, whom Strugnell called "the stone in the soup,"[6] the team members got on well together. The languages of the scrollery were English and French. Milik spoke both with a Polish accent. Cross describes him as wearing a cassock in those days, "with a dribble of tobacco ash down the front."[7] He subsequently left the priesthood, married, and now lives modestly in Paris. Although "intensely shy . . . dour, even

The "scrollery" in the Rockefeller Museum, where the Cave 4 scroll fragments were assembled into the remains of over five hundred manuscripts.

Members of the original scroll publication team meet in the courtyard of the Rockefeller Museum: Roland de Vaux (with his trademark beard) is seated directly under the archway; J. T. Milik is on his right; Jean Starcky is on de Vaux's left; and John Allegro is standing behind Starcky.

melancholy . . . , he had a quick, infectious sense of humor. When he suddenly saw the humor in a situation or comment, he would break out giggling."[8]

Milik was generally regarded as the most talented of the scholars. According to Strugnell, "Milik has more intelligence for these materials in one of his hands than any of that group," referring to the scholars who took over after Strugnell's resignation in 1990. Milik learned the handwriting of hundreds of different scribes and quickly placed fragments into what has been called "incipient manuscripts," as sometimes dozens of fragments from a single text were gathered together. He even seemed to be able to memorize the shapes of the edges, quickly identifying joins. He is also an exceptional paleographer and decipherer, able to identify hazy letters and passages and understand the sense of a document from the barest fragments.

De Vaux served as chief editor, although he functioned largely in an administrative capacity (in addition to directing the excavation at Qumran). Cross remembers de Vaux as "completely charming—brilliant, lively, warm. He wore his Dominican robes with great flair. He was a raconteur of extraordinary gifts. . . . He had wit and a gift for the dramatic."[9] It was said that before becoming a priest he had been an actor with the Comédie Française. He denied this to Cross, but as Cross observed, "He was delighted with the story." Trude Dothan, one of Israel's leading archaeologists, describes de Vaux as "one of the most charming men I ever met. . . . He had a fantastic sense of humour."[10]

The members of the team almost always shared meals, often went on holidays together, made trips to visit ancient sites, and generally enjoyed the camaraderie. Strugnell described the experience as "fun . . . very pleasant . . . We enjoyed it."[11]

"I remember," Frank Cross told me in 1993, "one lovely day, drinking Italian wine—Lacrima Christi—in a garden in Jericho with Starcky and Milik. They were good companions. I remember many nights when Skehan and I and another companion or two

*Père Roland de Vaux, president of the Rockefeller Museum, professor
at the École Biblique, excavator of Qumran, and chief editor
of the scroll publication team.*

*Frank Moore Cross, Jr., seen here at the entrance to Cave 1,
came to Jerusalem in 1953 to join the Dead Sea Scroll research team.*

would go late over to the Az-Zahra Hotel. . . . There was a lovely garden over there filled with pepper trees. We would each have a bottle of Dutch beer and talk into the night."[12]

But the scholars also had the "sense of making history. . . . We appreciated the sense of discovery," Strugnell told me in a 1994 interview.[13]

Cross has described the Cave 4 fragments as they came into scholarly hands: "Many fragments are so brittle or friable that they can scarcely be touched with a camel's-hair brush. Most are warped, crinkled or shrunken, crusted with soil chemicals, blackened by moisture and age. . . . Often a fragment will exhibit an area of acute decay and shrinkage. . . . The bad spot may draw the entire fragment into a crinkled or scalloped ball, so that the fragment is almost impossible to flatten. The script in such an area of decay may be shrunk to half or less the size of that in good areas. Often such decomposition in sheets of leather has caused splitting and fragmentation."[14]

Cross recalls one dark, illegible fragment encrusted with yellow crystals that appeared to be dried urine. With castor oil and a camel's-hair brush he carefully cleaned the fragment, slowly removing the encrustation. Gradually, the Hebrew letters began to appear. It turned out to be a fragment from the biblical book of Samuel, but it was not the version of Samuel to be found in the standard text of the Hebrew Bible, the Masoretic Text (MT). It conformed instead to the Greek translation, known as the Septuagint, which meant that the Hebrew text used in the Greek translation was different from the standard Hebrew *textus receptus* (see Chapter 9). Cross describes the moment: "I suddenly realized I had found something that to me and to other textual critics of the Hebrew Bible was earthshaking."

He was holding in his hand a fragment of the version of the Hebrew text used by the Septuagint translators. The fragment "proved that the translator of the Old Greek [the Septuagint] had been faithful to the Hebrew text he was translating. Thus the differences between the traditional Hebrew text and the Old Greek translation, for the most part, rested on different textual traditions of the Hebrew Bible. The manuscript of Samuel promised to break the logjam in text-critical studies of the Hebrew Bible. I held a key discovery."[15]

What Cross meant is that scholars of biblical texts could now have much more confidence in the Greek text, known as the Septuagint, because its variations from the received Hebrew text could well be based not on errors of translation but on a different Hebrew base text, a fragment of which Cross had just identified.

After initial cleaning, the fragments were photographed, often repeatedly in various stages of reconstruction, by a remarkable Arab photographer named Najib Albina, who worked for the Palestine Archaeological Museum. Using infrared film, Albina was often able to bring out features that could not be seen with the naked eye. Even in the case of legible scrolls, Albina's photographs were far easier to read than the fragments themselves, to which scholars would now turn only to clarify a questionable reading or an illegible passage. Many of the scroll fragments have since deteriorated and faded and letters have fallen off as the edges have crumbled. In these cases, Albina's photographs represent the best evidence of the text.

After they were photographed, the fragments were placed between sheets of glass, a serious mistake because the confinement produced dampness and warmth that contributed to their deterioration.

Some fragments have disappeared, whether stolen or simply misplaced remains a mystery. An especially beautiful fragment from a scroll of Samuel dating to the third century B.C. disappeared from a display case during the 1967 Six-Day War,[16] one unfortunate example among many.

During the 1956 Sinai campaign, Jordanian authorities feared that the museum and its scrolls might fall into Israeli hands. As a precaution, the scroll fragments were packed up in boxes, shipped to Amman, and stored in the basement of the Ottoman Bank, where dampness had a devastating effect on some of the more fragile scrolls. When they were returned to Jerusalem after the war, many had mildewed and almost all had to be re-cleaned.

As we have seen, Cave 4 fragments continued to come into the scrollery until 1958. In the end, team members were able to relate the thousands of fragments from Cave 4 to about five hundred different manuscripts. They arranged the fragments as well as they could, depending for guidance on joins, on the sense of the text, even on worm holes eaten through the text in successive layers. Then they transcribed them, in order to be able to read them without going either to the photographs or to the fragments themselves.

So well did they succeed that by 1957 they decided to make a concordance of the nonbiblical texts. The concordance was prepared by three young scholars—two Americans and a Canadian—each of whom spent a year in Jerusalem on the project. During the first year, the work was done by Father Joseph Fitzmyer of Catholic University of America, the second year by Father Raymond Brown of Union Theological Seminary in New York, the third year by Willard Oxtoby, now of the University of Toronto in Canada. (A Spanish scholar, Javier Texeidor, concorded nonbiblical fragments from other caves.)

In informal sessions, the various manuscripts were assigned to specific scholars on the team for publication, partly on the basis of their respective specialties: Abbé Starcky, for example, was an Aramaicist, so the Aramaic documents were largely given to him. To Cross and Father Skehan went the biblical scrolls. According to Strugnell, "Some [members of the team] were less energetic than others. I suppose Milik and I were the most energetic."[17] As a result, the greatest share—including most of the previously unknown texts—was assigned to Milik, whom *Time* magazine called "the fastest man with a fragment." But Strugnell and Starcky also got handfuls of these texts. Starcky, however, turned out to be "lazy," according to Strugnell.[18]

Overall, it was a gentlemanly affair. There was some horse trading, but not much. Everyone tried to be fair and the arrangements

The infrared photograph of a decayed scroll fragment (above) reveals details not visible to the naked eye on a normal photograph (below).

were all very informal. In time, however, these assignments became, as it were, chiseled in stone, as if not simply possession but ownership itself had been granted along with the assignments to the various scholars. Those to whom the texts had been assigned could now decide whether to allow other scholars to see them or not, but in no event would another scholar be permitted to publish an assigned text, or any part of it, even if the man with the initial assignment had failed to do so. As it turned out, holders of these assignments felt entitled to will their "right," as it soon became, to a younger devotee, who would thereby succeed to all the perquisites of his benefactor.

In 1960 John D. Rockefeller died, and with him much of the funding that supported the team disappeared. But something else happened, too. It wasn't just that the money dried up. The scholars also seemed to dry up. The work slowed down, not abruptly but gradually, as if the thrill of discovery had worn thin.

In retrospect, the decade of the 1950s had been a remarkable one. All the Cave 1 scrolls had been published by Israeli and American scholars (none of whom was on de Vaux's team). The team scholars had made outstanding progress on the mass of Cave 4 fragments, which had been assembled, photographed, arranged, read, transcribed, and concorded. Team scholars even published a volume containing the seventy-two fragmentary scrolls that archaeologists had recovered from Cave 1.

But then things bogged down. For the next twenty-five years Strugnell, for example, published almost none of his assigned texts. Milik published more than any of his colleagues, but twenty-five years later he was still left with a huge bundle of unpublished texts. Strugnell himself regretted that he had not "had the foresight to see already by 1960 that we were absurdly top-heavy; too few scholars were working on the project."[19]

In 1985, well over half the texts from Cave 4 remained unpublished and inaccessible to scholars who were not on the team. Even the concordance remained unpublished and available only to team scholars.

A major reason for the failure to publish was a decision, apparently made independently by each scholar, to publish not simply the text with some technical notes (called a diplomatic edition), but also an extensive commentary. Not until 1976, twenty years after the original assignment, did Milik finally publish a 439-page commentary-cum-text, entitled *The Books of Enoch: Aramaic Fragments of Qumran Cave 4*.[20] Awaiting this publication for a quarter century, scholars had hesitated, in the absence of Milik's text, to use Enoch as a basis for understanding contemporaneous Judaism.[21]

During the 1967 Six-Day War the Jordanians failed to transfer the scrolls to a "safer" location east of the Jordan in anticipation of an Israeli advance—as they had done unnecessarily in 1956—perhaps because in 1967 so little scholarly activity was occurring with regard to the scrolls. In any event, in 1967 the scrolls were simply taken to the basement of the Palestine Archaeological Museum. On the third day of the war, after Israel captured the Old City and east Jerusalem, Israeli archaeologists entered the museum to take charge of the scrolls.

One might have expected that with Israel now in control and Jewish scholars eager to work on the scrolls, new energy and direction would be infused into the scroll publication effort. But that was not the case. After the war, Avraham Biran, director of the Israel Department of Antiquities, together with Yigael Yadin, Israel's leading archaeologist, worked out Israel's relationship to the Jordanian-sponsored scroll publication team.

Israel wanted to be regarded as a beneficent conqueror. Biran recalls a visit from an emissary of the queen of Holland, asking permission for Dutch scholars to continue working on some inscriptions. "I told him, 'What do you think we are? Are we here just to grab things?' And that was the attitude we had towards the Dead Sea Scrolls."[22]

When de Vaux came to see him, Biran told him that Israel would honor the team's publication rights—that is, the exclusive rights to publish the scrolls without allowing other scholars to see them in the meantime. "Why?" I asked Biran. "You see, it would be like taking away from somebody something he's been working on. . . . We did not want to appear as barbarians who prevent other scholars from doing their work," he replied.

This Israeli politesse was doomed to fail. Strugnell related to me the attitude that prevailed for years after the 1967 war at the École Biblique, where most of the editorial team lived and ate: "It was interesting when I stayed at the French school how frequently people found parallels to the German occupation in Paris. You know, they had gone through that, and they were sensitive to what it's like to be occupied. It's a hard business."[23]

For years after the Six-Day War, anti-Zionist scholars in east Jerusalem refused to set foot in west, Jewish, Jerusalem. Milik, for example, has never set foot in Israel to this day and has never returned to Jerusalem since the Six-Day War.

As for the arrangements he made with de Vaux immediately after the Six-Day War, Biran told me: "It's only, as I say, years later, and partly because you [the author] started the whole battle for the publication . . . Look, you're right. I didn't anticipate . . . We would not touch them. It's a gentleman's agreement among scholars, you might say. That's how we do it. We honor what people [start to work on]. . . . Because we had the power, we didn't want to take it."

Biran recalled saying to de Vaux, "There is a limit of time for this to go on." But the limit was never specified. "Where I think we made a mistake, we probably should have insisted, 'All right, you have the right to publish, one year, two years, three years, whatever, five years; after that, your right expires.' . . . I think the mistake we made was in not insisting on a deadline."

According to Yadin, Israel did set two conditions on the scroll publication team's continuing to work. The first involved the title page of the official scroll volumes, which read "Discoveries in the Judaean Desert of Jordan." The Israelis wanted some acknowledgment that the publications were now continuing under Israeli auspices. The Israelis didn't quite get what they wanted, but in subsequent publications the words "of Jordan" were eliminated.

More important, according to Yadin, there was in fact a time limit of sorts: "One [of the conditions] was that they were to proceed quickly with the publication of the thousands of fragments they had had at their disposal for so many years. By then, 1967, they had published very little of the material, and this had been a great loss to the scientific world. . . . Now that we were in control, we wanted that rectified."[24]

But under Israeli auspices, despite Yadin's insistence, things continued pretty much as they had since the early 1960s. Very little happened.

CHAPTER 4

FREEING
THE SCROLLS

As early as 1976, Columbia University professor Theodor Herzl Gaster "deplore[d]" the fact that only what he called "the charmed circle" had access to the unpublished scrolls. "By the hazards of mortality, he wrote, "[this policy would] prevent a whole generation of older scholars from making their contribution."[1]

In 1977, Geza Vermes of Oxford warned that "unless drastic measures are taken at once, the greatest and most valuable of all Hebrew and Aramaic manuscript discoveries is likely to become the academic scandal *par excellence* of the twentieth century."[2]

In the mid-1980s, I addressed the issue in the pages of *Biblical Archaeology Review* (*BAR*), of which I was editor.

The problem lay in a scholarly tradition, nowhere reduced to writing but simply observed, that a scholar who is assigned publication of an inscription controls access to it until it is published. This rule is compounded by the fact that the assigned scholar has no time limit by which he must publish the inscription. In the case of the Dead Sea Scrolls, this unwritten tradition had been carried to extremes. Several of the original team of scholars had died and passed their assignments on as a kind of bequest to trusted colleagues, who then enjoyed the same unlimited exclusivity. Worse still, several scholars had assignments so vast that they could not complete them if they lived to be a hundred and twenty.

These treasures conferred enormous academic power and prestige upon the scholars who controlled them and could divulge exciting new discoveries at scholarly conclaves and in learned journals. Graduate students flocked to professors who could assign to them the academic equivalent of the crown jewels as subjects for their doctoral dissertations, thus assuring the fealty of another generation of scroll scholars created by the original team.

In 1987, de Vaux's successor as chief editor, Père Pierre Benoit, also of the École Biblique, had become incapacitated by terminal cancer, so a new chief editor, John Strugnell, was appointed from among the remaining members of the publication team, a choice subsequently ratified by the Israel Antiquities Department. A brilliant student at Oxford, Strugnell never earned a doctorate and became one of the few members of the Harvard faculty to attain a full professorship—in his case, of Christian origins—without the terminal degree. Strugnell was the first to bring Jewish and Israeli scholars onto the team. But the basic rule remained: Only scholars with publication assignments could see the unpublished scrolls. It was a rule the Israeli scholars were happy with.

Long regarded as an anti-Semite, as well as anti-Israel, Strugnell gave an interview in 1990 to an Israeli journalist, which I later published in English in *BAR,* that confirmed the worst rumors about his views. Strugnell described himself as an "anti-Judaist." Judaism, he said, was "racist," "a folk religion," "not a higher religion." He didn't mince words: "There. I plead guilty. . . . The correct answer of Jews to Christianity is to become Christian. . . . The basic judgment on the Jewish religion is, for me, a negative one."[3]

When asked what annoyed him about Judaism, he replied, "The fact that it has survived. . . . For me the answer [to the Jewish problem] is mass conversion. . . . It's a horrible religion."

John Strugnell, who came to Jerusalem in 1954 as a young, enthusiastic graduate student from Oxford University.

Alcoholism and manic-depressive illness slowly incapacitated Strugnell and in 1990 he resigned as chief editor of the scrolls. He has since recovered and returned to scroll research.

He was equally blunt about his attitude toward Israel: "I dislike Israel." Israel "is founded on a lie." "The occupation of Jerusalem cannot be sustained."

Although he had not favored the establishment of the State of Israel, Strugnell admitted that now "you've got four million people here, even though the Zionists based themselves on a lie. . . . You're not going to move populations of four million. Not even the Nazis managed that."

Clearly Strugnell had to go. Moreover, the Israelis had other reasons to be dissatisfied with him. He was an inefficient administrator who suffered from manic-depressive illness and was often drunk. At the end of 1990, Strugnell resigned, returned to the United States, and checked into a psychiatric hospital in Cambridge. The Israelis then installed as chief editor Hebrew University professor Emanuel Tov, who had already been appointed associate editor over Strugnell's objection.

But none of this changed the basic rule. The Israeli establishment was as adamant as the publication team: Only those with scroll publication assignments could see the unpublished scrolls.

During his brief tenure as chief editor, however, Strugnell had taken several steps to speed up publication. He had expanded the team, convinced team scholars (especially J. T. Milik) with particularly excessive assignments to allow reassignment of some of their texts to other scholars, and, under pressure from the Israelis, issued a "Suggested Timetable" calling for completion of work by the end of 1996.

One other thing proved crucial: Strugnell decided to publish a limited edition of the concordance of nonbiblical scrolls that had been prepared in the late 1950s and had since languished in the basement of the Rockefeller Museum, a single copy largely unused, consisting of three-by-five note cards, each of which contained the concorded word together with the preceding and following words and the location of the concorded word each time it was used. The cards were then arranged in alphabetical order of the concorded words. The concordance could be extremely useful because it would enable scholars easily to locate other instances of the concorded word that would help unlock its meaning in the text being studied.

In 1988, Strugnell had thirty copies of the concordance published in Göttingen, Germany. The title page stated that it had been privately printed "on behalf of Professor John Strugnell, Harvard University." A special Strugnellian touch proclaimed in large capital letters in Latin, "Editorum in Usum"—only "for the use of the editors."

In one respect the concordance was damning; in another it was dangerous. It was damning because it showed that by 1960 (when the concordance was completed) all of the texts had already been transcribed; it was these transcriptions from which the concordance had been made. In other words, transcripts of all of the Dead Sea Scrolls could have been released in 1960.

The concordance was dangerous, at least from the editors' viewpoint, because the secret texts could be reconstructed from the concordance—a lengthy and dull job, but nonetheless possible. It was possible because each word in the concordance could be used to create a chain to the preceding and following words. In this way the whole text could be reconstructed. Consider, for example, a biblical concordance of the King James Version: under "beginning" the concordance might say, "In the beginning, God" with a citation to Genesis 1:1. This directs us to the entry for "God," where we would learn that the word "God" appears in Genesis 1:1 followed by the word "created." In this way the entire text of the King James Version of the Bible could be re-created from a biblical concordance.

The team members were both cognizant and fearful of this possibility but were comforted by the magnitude of the task. What the team hadn't counted on was the computer. Even with a computer the task was enormous, but it was manageable.

That is what happened. Having obtained one of the few copies of the concordance, a nearly blind professor of Talmud at Hebrew Union College in Cincinnati, Ben-Zion Wacholder, together with his graduate student Martin Abegg, a computer-wise, born-again evangelical Christian, reconstructed the unpublished texts, sometimes offering improved readings. The first volume of these texts was published by the Biblical Archaeology Society (the non-profit organization that publishes *BAR*) on September 4, 1991. The publication was heralded on the front page of *The New York Times,* and *The Washington Post,* as well as other newspapers around the world. The computer used to reconstruct the texts was dubbed "Rabbi Computer." "Amazingly," *The New York Times* said, "two scholars at Hebrew Union College in Cincinnati have now broken the scroll cartel."

Not long before the computer reconstructions of Wacholder and Abegg were published, William Moffett, the newly appointed director of the Huntington Library in San Marino, California, made a surprising discovery. In a special humidity-and-temperature-controlled safe in the library were photographs of all the Dead Sea Scrolls, including those still unpublished. For security purposes, in case something should happen to the originals in Jerusalem, photographic copies had been deposited in a number of locations—Oxford University, Hebrew Union College, and the Ancient Biblical Manuscript Center in Claremont, California. The Huntington Library did not engage in the kind of research the Dead Sea Scrolls involved, however, and it was never intended that a security copy of Dead Sea Scroll photographs should be deposited there. The library had in fact obtained the photographs clandestinely years earlier as a result of an academic squabble.

In 1978 an imperious California philanthropist named Elizabeth Bechtel provided the funding to establish the Ancient Biblical Manuscript Center (ABMC); its mission was to collect high-quality photographs of important biblical manuscripts for scholarly use. The ABMC was headed by a distinguished Dead Sea Scroll scholar, James Sanders. It was Sanders and Bechtel who arranged for a duplicate set of scroll photos to be deposited in the ABMC. Like the other depositories, however, the ABMC signed a written agreement not to allow anyone to see the photographs without the express permission of the editor assigned to publish the particular scroll.

Because Mrs. Bechtel was also associated philanthropically with the nearby Huntington Library, its photographer, Robert Schlosser, was sent to Jerusalem to make the copies for the ABMC.

Meanwhile, Mrs. Bechtel and Dr. Sanders had become involved in a bitter struggle for control of the ABMC. Mrs. Bechtel met the plane when Schlosser returned from Jerusalem with the Dead Sea Scroll photos. A set eventually was given to the ABMC. But another copy was retained by Mrs. Bechtel personally. These she deposited in the special safe in the Huntington Library.

Mrs. Bechtel died in 1987, Sanders continued to run the ABMC, and most people forgot about the set of photos in the Huntington Library—until the new director, as it were, "discovered" them. He also learned that the Huntington, unlike the other depositories, never signed an agreement limiting access to the photographs. Moffett astutely recognized the goodwill that would accrue to the library were he to make the Huntington copies of the unpublished scrolls available to any scholar who wanted to see them. He believed in intellectual freedom. "Free the scrolls and you free the scholars," he said.

On September 21, 1991, Moffett announced that the library would make available to scholars microfilm copies of its photographs. The following day, Moffett's picture holding one of the scroll photographs appeared above the fold of the Sunday edition of *The New York Times.*

The Huntington in fact scooped the Biblical Archaeology Society's publication of secret photographs of the scrolls that we had been working on. At the same time BAS was preparing the computer-reconstructed texts for publication, we were also preparing a two-volume folio set of photographs of the unpublished scrolls. I still don't know the source of those photographs. They somehow came into the hands of a maverick scroll scholar named Robert

Eisenman of California State University, Long Beach. In order to give the publication of the photographs a bit more academic prestige than he alone could muster, Eisenman associated in the project a prominent New Testament scholar, James Robinson of Claremont Graduate School. Unlike Eisenman, who holds highly idiosyncratic ideas about the scrolls (Eisenman claims the apostle Paul is referred to in the scrolls as "the Liar," the archenemy of the Teacher of Righteousness, a view that has convinced few, if any, other scroll scholars), Robinson is highly respected for his solid scholarship.

Initially Eisenman arranged to have the photographs published under his and Robinson's names by one of the world's most prestigious scholarly publishers, E. J. Brill of Leiden. But at the last minute Brill backed out, fearful of the reaction of the Israel Antiquities Authority.

When that happened Eisenman and Robinson turned to the Biblical Archaeology Society, which brought out its two-volume folio edition of photographs of the unpublished scrolls on November 20, 1991, two months after the Huntington. Anyone with $200 could now purchase this edition and have all the pictures within arm's reach. The struggle to free the scrolls was over.

People often ask how I felt when the Huntington scooped us. At the time, I was delighted—and greatly relieved that the powerful, prestigious Huntington Library was running interference for the Biblical Archaeology Society. The truth is I was feeling isolated and afraid. I was, in effect, taking on the government of Israel, to say nothing of the cadre of prominent scholars, especially in Israel, who despised me for aggressively pressing for release of the scrolls. The Israel Antiquities Authority had already ordered its archaeologists not to write for my magazine. Moreover, I knew there was a serious danger of my being sued.

Suing Hershel Shanks and the Biblical Archaeology Society was one thing. Suing the Huntington Library was quite another. The Huntington was a powerful institution and it had the money I did not have to fight the legal battle. If Israel did not sue Huntington, it would probably not sue me. Now that the struggle for the scrolls is over, it all seems quite benign. But at the time, things looked very different, especially in light of the absolute determination of the scroll establishment not to be finessed by an outsider.

I felt even more relieved when I saw the initial reaction that greeted the Huntington announcement. The director of the Israel Antiquities Authority, Amir Drori, and the chief editor, Emanuel Tov, immediately faxed Moffett a peremptory letter charging the library with a breach of its "legal and moral obligation," threatening a lawsuit, and demanding an "immediate reply." If that is what they sent to the Huntington, what would they have sent to me, I wondered. The Huntington stood its ground and the Israelis, under a storm of worldwide criticism, backed down.

My fears were not unfounded. When I interviewed Drori in the summer of 1996, long after the imbroglio was over, I asked him if he had thought about suing me when we published our edition of photographs of the unpublished scrolls. "We think your publication [of the photographs] is illegal," he said. "We discussed the matter. We thought, we think, even now, that we are one hundred percent right, [but] I decided not to go to court about it." He also considered suing the Huntington Library: "I think what the Huntington did was an awful thing—to break the law. It was a one-sided decision of Huntington. They didn't ask us. The pictures were stolen material. . . . We were one hundred percent right. No doubt about it. But I decided not to go to court."

I did get sued, however. In my foreword to the folio edition of photographs I included the Hebrew text of the document known as MMT, as reconstructed by Elisha Qimron of Ben-Gurion University and Strugnell. It had already been published—but without authorization—in a Polish journal,[4] from which I copied the 133-line text. But by that time, the editor of the Polish journal, under pressure from the Israelis, had withdrawn the supplement containing the unauthorized publication.[5] Despite that, I included a copy in my foreword.

Qimron sued me and the Biblical Archaeology Society for copyright infringement. To represent him in the suit, Qimron retained one of Israel's most prominent lawyers, Yitzchak Molcho, a friend of Prime Minister Benjamin Netanyahu as well as his personal attorney, and now head of Israel's negotiating team with Yassir Arafat's Palestinian Authority. Molcho is an excellent lawyer and he all but wiped up the floor with us. We won very few, if any, points in the course of the litigation.

Molcho opened the case by going to the judge without notifying us and getting an *ex parte* court order prohibiting us from distributing our facsimile edition anywhere in the world. Immediately after getting the order, he faxed me a copy. On another occasion, while I was in Israel, Molcho, again without notifying me or our lawyer, got an *ex parte* order preventing me from leaving Israel. We had to prepare papers and go to court in order to get another order allowing me to go home.

Qimron won the case and the court awarded him a judgment against us for 100,000 shekels, reportedly the largest amount ever awarded in a copyright case in Israel's history.

At this writing, the case is pending on appeal to the Israel Supreme Court. If the lower court's decision is affirmed, Qimron will own a copyright both in the *arrangement* of the various fragments and in the letters and words missing from the badly preserved fragments that he reconstructed based on the surviving letters and words. His copyright will last as long as he lives, plus a fixed number of years thereafter. Naturally, copyright lawyers and scholars are following the case with considerable interest. It is the first time a scholar has claimed a copyright in a reconstructed ancient text.

CHAPTER 5

UNDERMINING CHRISTIAN FAITH — OF A CERTAIN KIND

The scrolls both enrich our understanding of early Christianity and, at the same time, undermine a certain kind of simple Christian faith—the naïve notion that Jesus' Jewishness was accidental or incidental and the belief that his message was wholly new, unique, and unrelated to anything that had gone before, astonishing everyone who heard it.

Until the eighteenth century, the Age of Reason, most Christians accepted the Gospels as literally true, as reliable biographies of Jesus. Contradictions among them could be "harmonized," so that each Gospel supplemented the other.

Thereafter, the Bible became subject, like any other text, to scholarly analysis and criticism. These efforts have often been regarded by true believers as a threat to religion and the Church. In the early eighteenth century, a professor at Cambridge University was sentenced to jail for claiming that the miracles in the Gospels never happened.[1] The English publishers of Thomas Paine were also imprisoned—for printing his denial of the Bible's truthfulness.

In the mid-eighteenth century, a German professor named Hermann Samuel Reimarus wrote a powerful book distinguishing the Jesus of history from the Jesus of the Gospels. But not until 1778, a decade after his death, was the book published—anonymously so as not to embarrass his family. Reimarus's book, *On the Intention of Jesus and His Disciples,* marks the beginning of the "first quest" for the historical Jesus.

In 1835, another German professor, David Friedrich Strauss of the University of Tübingen, published a two-volume *Life of Jesus* in which he contended that the miracle stories were created by Jesus' followers after his death. The book ruined Strauss's career. He was dismissed from his university post and never held another university teaching position.

The books by Reimarus and Strauss, distressing as they proved to be to their authors, were widely influential, but other authors whose work did not rise to their level suffered similar ignominy. As one modern scholar has written, "Critical study of Jesus and Christian origins seemed to tear apart the fabric of Western culture. . . . To many it seemed that if Jesus did not really walk on the water, then nothing was for certain."[2]

The "second quest" for the historical Jesus was dominated by the great humanitarian, physician, musicologist, organist, and theologian Albert Schweitzer. In *The Quest of the Historical Jesus* (earliest publication 1906), Schweitzer surveyed past efforts and concluded that either Jesus was the eschatological prophet described in the Gospels, preaching the endtime, or we cannot extract any reliable portrait of him at all.

When Schweitzer showed why it was impossible to uncover the Jesus of history, scholarship turned from history to theology—to an attempt to understand the theological meaning of the Gospels rather than their historical underpinnings. In this view, it was not only impossible but undesirable to search for the personality of Jesus. It was Jesus' death on the cross that was meaningful, not his life.

In the last half of the twentieth century, all of this has changed. We are now embroiled in the "third quest." Armed with refined methods of literary criticism and the insights of archaeology, anthropology, and sociology, as well as new texts (especially the Dead

Sea Scrolls), scholars are publishing numerous lives of Jesus that often differ markedly from one another: Jesus is seen as a Jewish revolutionary, a political agitator, a follower of the Cynic philosophy, a magician, an apocalyptic prophet, a popular sage, a holy man or charismatic, a Galilean rabbi, a wily politician, even a trance-inducing psychotherapist, and, of course, a messiah.[3] No consensus has emerged.

Running like a thread through the "third quest," however, is the question of Jesus' Jewishness and its relevance to his message. As one reviewer has observed, nineteenth-century New Testament scholars regarded the life of Jesus as theologically "relevant and therefore not particularly Jewish." On the other hand, theologically oriented scholars who followed Schweitzer in the 1920s and 1930s, such as Karl Barth and Rudolf Bultmann, realized full well that Jesus was "Jewish and therefore [his life] was not particularly relevant" to their theological concerns.[4]

In the "third quest" all of this has changed. Jesus' Jewishness is central. The Harvard University theologian Harvey Cox recently referred to "a widely influential article" that painted seven different "plausible" portraits of Jesus.[5] "They all have one very important thing in common," Cox said. "They are all recognizably Jewish. The Jesus they describe is a participant in one of the many Jewish subcultures of first-century Palestine. The God that Jesus talks about and whose will he tries to make known is not the deity of some generalized theism but the God of Abraham, made known through the covenant with the Jewish people as One, who has active compassion for the outsider and who promises justice and healing to all nations. This Jewish parameter, though one may disagree on its exact boundaries, provides the playing field within which new images of Jesus must be worked out, unless they surrender all claims of being connected to the historical figure whose name they bear."[6]

Thus, Jesus lived and died a Jew at a particular time in Jewish history. As Father Daniel Harrington has written, "Everyone would agree that the historical Jesus must be understood within the context of Judaism."[7] This is where the Dead Sea Scrolls come in. Not only are they by far the most important archive of contemporaneous Jewish documents but, with very few exceptions, they are Jewish religious writings. Though they are often difficult to understand, they are concerned with theological issues, including many of the same issues that concerned Jesus and early Christians. Moreover, the scrolls have not been subject to later editing, as have texts like the Gospels that have come down to us only in later copies.

What the scrolls show is that in almost every respect the message of early Christianity was presaged in its Jewish roots. And even the life of Jesus, as told in the Gospels, is often prefigured in the scrolls.

The beatitudes, for example, familiar from the Sermon on the Mount, have their counterpart in the scrolls:

> Blessed the man who has attained Wisdom and walks in the law of the Most High / . . . [Blessed is he who speaks truth] with a pure heart and who does not slander with his tongue / . . . Blessed is he who seeks (Wisdom) with pure hands and who does not go after her with a deceitful heart . . . *

This passage is found in the Dead Sea Scroll known only by its number, 4Q525.[8] The literary genre to which it belongs is the same as that found in the Gospel of Matthew:

> Blessed are the poor in spirit, for theirs is the kingdom of heaven. / Blessed are those who mourn, for they shall be comforted. / Blessed are the meek, for they shall inherit the earth. / . . . Blessed are the pure in heart, for they shall see God. . . . (Matthew 5:3–12)

That this literary form is not unique to Matthew is hardly surprising to students of the New Testament. Luke, in the Sermon on the Plain, recounts a parallel but slightly different version of

---

*Brackets indicate words or letters that are missing in the ancient manuscript and have been reconstructed by scholars. Parentheses enclose explanatory interpolations.

Matthew's beatitudes (Luke 6:20–26). The apocryphal Gospel of Thomas also contains beatitudes.[9] In Luke and in Thomas, it is "the poor" who inherit the kingdom of heaven. In Matthew, it's "the poor in spirit," a large difference, for the "poor" lack money while the "poor in spirit" lack something very different.

Obviously, the content and even the form of the beatitudes change from composition to composition, but like other aspects of Christian belief and literature, they are not unprecedented. The pre-Christian beatitudes found in the Dead Sea Scrolls are part of the Jewish heritage on which the beatitudes of the Gospels are built.

The concept of the messiah is a more sensitive matter in the Dead Sea Scrolls than the presence of beatitudes. At first, it was thought that the Dead Sea Scroll community believed in two messiahs, the Messiah of Aaron (a priestly messiah) and the Messiah of Israel (a royal or Davidic messiah) and that the double messiahs referred to in these scrolls were distinct from the Christian messiah.

This distinction no longer holds. A recently released Dead Sea Scroll text known as 4Q521, or the messianic apocalypse, reveals a single eschatological messiah with attributes of the single Christian messiah:

> [The hea]vens and the earth will listen to His Messiah. . . . Over the poor His spirit will hover and will renew the faithful with His power. . . . He . . . liberates the captives, restores sight to the blind, straightens the b[ent]. (cf. Psalm 146:7–8) . . . The Lord will accomplish glorious things which have never been. . . . He will heal the wounded, and revive the dead and bring good news to the poor. (cf. Isaiah 35:5–6; 61:1)[10]

I have put in parentheses references to Psalms and Isaiah which this Dead Sea Scroll seems to be quoting, just as the Gospels themselves often do. Both Matthew and Luke echo the same passages in Isaiah and Psalms that appear in 4Q521. Here is the nearly identical language of the two Gospels:

The blind receive their sight and the lame walk, lepers are cleansed and the deaf hear, and the dead are raised up, and the poor have good news preached to them. (Matthew 11:5/Luke 7:22)

While both the Gospel passages and the Dead Sea Scroll text rely on Psalms and Isaiah, there is a difference between the Gospel passages and the Dead Sea Scroll text, on the one hand, and the text of Psalms and Isaiah that they seem to be quoting, on the other. Unlike the texts of Isaiah and Psalms from which the passage is drawn, both the Gospel passages and the Dead Sea Scroll text speak of reviving the dead.[11] This suggests that the Gospels, which are clearly later than the Dead Sea Scroll text, might have used the latter as a source. Or, more likely, both used the same as-yet-undiscovered source, one that referred to reviving the dead. At the very least, the inclusion of the miracle of reviving the dead in both of the Gospels and in the Dead Sea Scroll text emphasizes the common milieu in which they were written.

Another Qumran fragment, dating to about 50 B.C., describes a messianic banquet (1Q28a/1QSa) and seems to speak of God as the father of the messiah, but the text is difficult to decipher. In the three different translations that follow, the parts in square brackets are missing in the text and are reconstructed by the translator:

"This is the assembly of famous men, [those summoned to] the gathering of the community council, when [God] begets the Messiah with them." (Translated by Florentino García Martínez[12])

"When God will have engendered (the Priest-) Messiah, he shall come [at] the head of the whole congregation of Israel with all [his brethren, the sons] of Aaron the Priests, [those called] to the assembly, the men of reknown." (Translated by Geza Vermes[13])

"The procedure for the [mee]ting of the men of reputation [when they are called] to the banquet held by the society of the *Yahad,* when [God] has fa[th]ered the Messiah (or, when the Messiah has been revealed) among them." (Translated by Michael Wise[14])

The critical word in this passage[15] is translated differently in each of the translations ("begets," "engendered," and "fathered").[16] The meaning, however, may or may not be the same. "Engendering," for example, can mean "causing to be born," rather than literally "fathering."[17] Another problem arises because it is not clear who does the begetting or engendering or fathering. Is it God? In the first and third translations, the word "God" appears in brackets, indicating that it is not actually there in the text but has been reconstructed or assumed by the decipherer. In the second translation, the word "God" appears without brackets. Oxford don Geza Vermes, who has computer-enhanced the texts, believes that the letters are actually there in the original manuscript and sees no need to put "God" in brackets.

Assuming he is correct, is this the same God/Son relationship that we find between God and Jesus in the Gospels?

Early Christians clearly saw Jesus as the Son of God who would return in power and glory to rule the earth; however, ambiguities remain. In Mark, when the high priest asks Jesus whether he is "the Messiah [Christos in Greek; *mashiach* in Hebrew], the Son of the Blessed One," Jesus replies, "I am" (Mark 14:62). But in parallel passages in Matthew and Luke, Jesus answers evasively (Matthew 26:64 and Luke 22:67). There is no question, however, that early Christians regarded Jesus as the kind of messiah referred to in 4Q521, a messiah who, as 4Q521 says, controlled "[the hea]vens and the earth." When Jesus quells a storm on the Sea of Galilee, his disciples respond, "Who then is this, that even the wind and the sea obey him?" (Mark 4:41). In Matthew 28:18 Jesus tells some doubters, "All authority in heaven and on earth has been given to me."

The evidence is lacking, however, to show a direct relationship between the theology of the Dead Sea Scroll community and early Christians, and there are enough dissimilarities to make a direct connection doubtful. The similarities may simply show that both grew out of the same Jewish traditions.

In those traditions, the *mashiach* or messiah was originally an earthly and contemporary figure. The word literally means "the anointed one." Kings were in effect crowned by anointing with oil. Upon their ascension to the throne they became "the anointed of the Lord" (1 Samuel 24:6; 26:11, etc.), as when Samuel declares Saul king of Israel and says, "The Lord has anointed you (*meshachakha*) ruler over his people Israel" (1 Samuel 10:1). Priests were also consecrated by anointing with oil.

But when the Babylonians destroyed Jerusalem and burned the Temple of Solomon in 586 B.C., the Davidic dynasty ended, and gradually the term *mashiach* came to refer to the earthly restoration of the Davidic line. After all, God had promised: "I will establish [David's] line forever" (Psalm 89:29). This tradition is reflected in the fact that both Matthew and Luke provide genealogies for Jesus that describe him as a descendant of King David—but through Joseph's line. Although he was clearly a Galilean, Jesus is nevertheless said to have been born in Bethlehem, the birthplace of King David. Critical scholars, however, strongly doubt the historical accuracy of Jesus' genealogy and his birth at Bethlehem. Only Matthew and Luke place Jesus' birth there, where it theologically supports their view that Jesus is the Davidic messiah.

By Jesus' time, however, the concept of the *mashiach* had developed beyond that of an earthly messiah who would restore the glory of the kingdom of David. It also came to mean a divinely sent figure who would return as God's agent and usher in the world to come. The Dead Sea Scrolls reflect this development. A text known as 4Q174 (also 4QFlorilegium), which consists of biblical quotes followed by a few lines of commentary, includes 2 Samuel 7:14: "I will be his father and he will be my son." In Samuel this applies to the Israelite king who becomes the Son of God on the king's enthronement, but in the Dead Sea Scroll commentary that follows this passage, the reference is to a *future* messianic son: "He is the Branch of David who shall arise . . . [to rule] in Zion [at the end] of time."[18]

their induction into office—an early instance of the divine right of kings. Being the son of God signified a monarch's special relationship to God rather than his lack of an earthly father. (Remember that Jesus' genealogy is traced through Joseph.)

Jewish tradition provides an even closer context. God of course is *the* father: "Thou art my father, my God, the rock of my salvation" (Psalm 89:26). Thus we are all sons of God.

God was also Israel's father, the father of the entire nation: "When Israel was a child, I loved him, and out of Egypt I called my son" (Hosea 11:1).

More specifically, Israelite kings were also regarded as sons of God. In Psalm 2:7, the Lord says to the Israelite king, "You are my son; today I have begotten you."

In 2 Samuel 7:14, after proclaiming that he will establish David's royal line for all time, God states, "I will be a father to him [David's descendant] and he shall be a son to me." Indeed, this passage is quoted in one of the Dead Sea Scrolls already discussed (4Q174).

Such instances of sonship are what scholars refer to as adoptionist: God adopts a human being as his son, who henceforth has a special relationship with God. Sonship in this sense has nothing to do with physical descent.

The son of God referred to in the Dead Sea Scroll called 4Q246, however, will arise in the future as a messianic king, an extension anticipated in both 2 Samuel 7 and Psalm 2, whose messianic nuances look to the future for their realization.

But these biblical references describe a divine call rather than a literal parenthood. Moreover, the son attains this status by adoption; there is no suggestion that the son did not have a human father.

In the Gospels of Matthew and Luke (the only two that contain birth narratives), on the other hand, Jesus is the Son of God from the moment of conception. According to some scholars, this is a late development in Christian theology, as can be seen through a careful examination of New Testament texts. The earliest New

Testament texts suggest that only at the resurrection was Jesus considered the begotten son of God, a relationship that was eventually moved back to his baptism and finally to his conception.

Paul's letter to the Romans, written in the mid-fifties, is one of the earliest New Testament documents, composed decades before the earliest canonical Gospel. At the outset it refers to Jesus as "descended from David according to the flesh and . . . declared to be Son of God with power according to the Spirit of holiness by *resurrection from the dead*" (Romans 1:3–4, italics added). This translation is from the New Revised Standard Version, used in most Protestant churches in the United States. The New English Bible translates the first part as follows: "On the human level, he was a descendant of David. . . ." The standard Catholic Bible, called the New Jerusalem Bible, says, "In terms of human nature [Jesus] was born a descendant of David. . . ." Each version then states that Jesus became, or was declared to be, or was proclaimed or designated, the Son of God by or through his resurrection.

Acts 13, which contains a speech by Paul concerning Jesus' resurrection, also indicates that Jesus became the Son of God at that time. Although he has been crucified and buried, he has risen from the dead. That, as Acts tells us, is the "good news. . . . What God promised to our ancestors he has fulfilled for us, their children, by raising Jesus." Then Paul quotes Psalm 2: "As also it is written in the second psalm, 'You are my Son; *today* I have begotten you' " (Acts 13:32–33, italics added). Here again Jesus seems to have become the Son of God by his resurrection.

Other passages, however, suggest that for some Christians Jesus became the Son of God at his baptism by John the Baptist in the waters of the Jordan.[21] In the standard text of Luke 3:22, when John baptizes Jesus, a voice from heaven proclaims, "You are my beloved Son; with you I am well pleased." At this point in the text, the translators of the New Revised Standard Version offer a footnote that states: "Other ancient authorities read [instead], 'You are my Son, today I have begotten you,' "[22] a direct quotation from Psalm 2, as noted above. In Psalm 2, the word "today" applies to the time of the royal accession. Here it is used to indicate that Jesus became the Son of God at his baptism.

In short, Jesus' sonship has been moved back from his resurrection, as reflected in Romans and Acts 13, to his baptism. In the birth narratives, his sonship recedes still further, back to his conception. Although Jesus is regarded as the Son of God both in Mark (the earliest of the canonical Gospels) and John (generally regarded as the latest), neither contains a birth narrative. Moreover, nowhere does Paul in his letters refer to the virgin birth (or, more accurately, the virgin conception).

The Gospels themselves thus suggest an evolution in the meaning of "Son of God," and the Dead Sea Scroll text 4Q246 is part of this development. By the first century the concept already had a long, multifaceted history—it was applied to kings, priests, even to the people of Israel, from people anointed in this world to saviors in the future. In the Dead Sea Scrolls this concept appears as it had evolved shortly before the birth of Jesus.

In the New Testament, we see further development of the concept. Like the people of Israel, early Christians were also sons of God, and became so by being true Christians. In Romans 8:14, Paul tells his listeners, "All who are led by the Spirit of God are sons of God." In Galatians 4:4–7, Paul expands on this idea: "God sent forth his Son, born of woman [Paul never mentions the virgin birth], born under the Law, to redeem those who were under the Law, so that we might receive adoption as sons. . . . [Y]ou are sons. . . . Through God you are no longer a slave but a son."

Jesus' divine sonship thus occurs within a cultural context that is related both to history and to the contemporaneous world in which Jesus lived; to this extent Jesus' divine sonship is by no means unique. As Frank Cross has observed: "[The Qumran material] will trouble the person who has been led by the clergy or by Christian polemics to believe that . . . the titles Jesus held as the Christ or Messiah were unanticipated in Jewish messianic Apocalypticism (or earlier in the Hebrew Bible). In short, I think anyone who has accepted claims of the discontinuity between Christianity and Judaism uncritically, or who has been brainwashed by the perennial tendency of the Christian pulpit to compare Judaism unfavorably with Christianity, may be shocked and may have to rethink his faith."[23]

But for those who understand Jesus' sonship as an unprecedented spiritual relationship to the Father, this context only enriches the possibilities and highlights those special aspects of Jesus' sonship, even to the point of his conception. In short, the Qumran scrolls do not pose a threat to the faith of what Father Joseph Fitzmyer calls a "mature Christian": "Do the Qumran Scrolls," Father Fitzmyer writes, "contain anything that would tend to undermine Christian faith? So far there has been nothing of the sort. Nothing that has been brought to light in the Qumran Scrolls contradicts anything that Christians hold dear. Nothing militates against the 'uniqueness of Jesus,' if that is a concern of the Christian—or better put, of a mature Christian with a non-fundamentalist background."[24]

The New Testament and the Qumran texts employ the same principles of biblical interpretation. For example, both quote the Hebrew Bible as if it applied specifically to their own time. Both also quote biblical texts as if they referred to the end of days, which is now upon us. The prophet Habakkuk declares that the Lord spoke to him and instructed him to write his vision on tablets, large enough "so he may run who reads it" (Habakkuk 2:2). The Qumran commentary on this passage explains that "God told Habakkuk to write down what would happen to the final generation" and that the mysteries were revealed to the Qumran sect's leader, known as the Teacher of Righteousness (Habakkuk Pesher 7). Similarly in Acts 2:16–17, which quotes "the prophet Joel"—or rather misquotes him: "This is what was spoken by the prophet Joel: 'And in the last days [the eschatological meaning is supplied by Acts; Joel actually says "Afterward"[25]] it shall be, God declares, that I will pour out my Spirit upon all flesh.' "

With this quotation Acts explains a contemporary event, the fact that a multitude of Christians from all over the world who were in Jerusalem for the Pentecost began "speaking in tongues," so that each could understand the others in his native language. In other words, the end of days had come and the Spirit had poured over the people.

Themes common to Christianity and the scrolls were probably common as well to many Jewish groups at this time: the messianic expectation; the apocalyptic, eschatological outlook; water (baptismal) rituals; shared property; communal meals. Some of the parallels are vague, others, more precise, and sometimes there are differences between Christian practices and those of the people whose ideas are reflected in the scrolls.

For example, Acts says that after the Pentecost event described above, believers "had all things in common; and they sold their possessions and goods and distributed them to all, as any had need" (Acts 2:44–45; see also Acts 4:32). At Qumran, when a novitiate was finally admitted to full membership, his property was "merged" with that of the community (Manual of Discipline 6:22). Yet both Christian texts and the scroll texts indicate that private property continued to exist among devotees of both groups.

At Qumran, there appears to have been a communal meal at which a priest blessed bread and wine (Manual of Discipline 6:4–6; see also Community Rule 2:11–12). Of course this calls to mind the Last Supper, in which bread and wine also played a prominent part (Matthew 26:26–29; Mark 14:22–25; Luke 22:17–20). It appears that the Qumran meal was meant to be held when the messiah comes. The Last Supper also has eschatological significance. But there are obvious differences. In Matthew, Mark, and Luke, the Last Supper is a Passover meal. The bread and wine have a sacral character—the body and blood of Christ[26]—and this is absent from the Qumran ritual.

The New Testament—particularly the Gospel of John—shares with the scrolls a dualistic theology in which good and evil emanate from two different cosmic sources. History is thus a cosmic struggle between good (light) and evil (darkness). The so-called War Scroll from Qumran describes an apocalyptic battle between the Sons of Light and the Sons of Darkness. The Manual of Discipline admonishes: "Love all the Sons of Light. . . . Hate all the Sons of Darkness. . . . Love all that He has chosen and hate all that He has rejected."[27]

In the Gospel of John, Jesus describes himself as the "light of the world; he who follows me will not walk in darkness, but will have the light of life" (John 8:12; see also John 1:5; 3:19–20). The followers of Jesus are referred to as "the sons of the light" (John 12:35–36). In the parable of the unjust steward, Jesus also speaks of the "sons of light" (Luke 16:8). The Gospels of Luke and John were composed about two hundred years after the Manual of Discipline (Luke about 80 A.D.; John about 100 A.D.; the Manual of Discipline about 100 B.C.).

Many varieties of dualistic doctrines with subtle and often vague differences were circulating at the time, ranging from Neoplatonism to Persian Zoroastrianism to Christian and Jewish Gnosticism. Dualistic theologies are also reflected in such Jewish apocryphal books as Jubilees and the Testaments of the Patriarchs, so while the similarities between the New Testament and the Dead Sea Scrolls do not necessarily imply a direct connection, they do share a worldview.

The Manual of Discipline also speaks of "the Way." The Lord will impart "true knowledge" to those who have chosen "the Way."[28] The closing hymn from the Manual of Discipline places trust in God with these words:

> He will deliver my soul from the Pit
> and will direct my steps to the Way.[29]

In John's Gospel, and elsewhere in the New Testament, "the Way" identifies a new relationship to God; Jesus tells his hearers, "I am the Way, and the truth and the life; no one comes to the Father but by me" (John 14:6; see also Acts 9:2, 19:9, 19:23, 24:22).

Both the Dead Sea Scroll community and early Christians not only considered themselves Jewish but vehemently opposed the Jerusalem Temple and its cult. For the Dead Sea Scroll group, this opposition was only to be temporary (until their own priests could be installed in Jerusalem at the end of days), but for Christianity hostility toward the Temple became permanent. In the words of Yigael Yadin:

> Without a temple, the Essenes [whom Yadin identified with the Dead Sea Scroll sect] developed a way of life that was a kind of substitute for the Temple and worship in it. . . . For the Essenes, the rejection of the Temple was temporary. For them, the Jerusalem priests were illegitimate and the Temple polluted because their own rigid legal interpretations of the Law were not applied. . . . What was a temporary substitute for the Essenes, Christianity adopted as a permanent theology, part of their fixed and final canon. In short, what was for the Essenes an *ad hoc* adaptation to their rejection of the Jerusalem priesthood and Temple, applicable only until the end of days when the Temple would be rebuilt by God according to their own beliefs, became for Christianity a permanent solution. Thus, the historical paradox by which the early Christians could be heavily influenced by a legalistic sect, despite the fact that Christianity itself rejected this legalism.[30]

Jesus may have visited Qumran, or even lived there for a time, but there is no evidence that he did. He was, however, certainly in the vicinity. He was baptized in the Jordan River (Matthew 3:13), a bare three miles away.

After his baptism, Jesus was "led by the Spirit into the wilderness," where he was "tempted by the devil" (Matthew 4:1; Mark 1:12; Luke 4:1–2). The traditional site of the Mount of Temptation is seven miles north of Qumran.

That Jesus may have had some personal association with Qumran, given the similarities between the Dead Sea Scrolls and Christianity, is, however, pure speculation.

On the other hand, a reasonable case can be made that John the Baptist lived, at least for a time, at Qumran. Early in his life, John lived in the Judean desert; according to Luke 1:80, "The child grew and became strong in spirit, and he was in the wilderness till the day he appeared publicly to Israel." This statement appears at the end of the account of John's birth but Luke does not explain how John happened to be living in the wilderness, apparently almost from birth. A possible explanation relates to the Essenes, a sect of Jews who many scholars believe lived at Qumran. According to Josephus, the Essenes would receive the children of other people when they were "still young and capable of instruction" and would raise them according to their way of life.[31] This is how the Essenes managed to perpetuate themselves despite their vows of celibacy. At least two prominent scholars have suggested that perhaps John was adopted and raised as an Essene at Qumran,[32] and was thus influenced by Essene teaching.

As his name implies, John the Baptist emphasized baptism as a rite of purification. So do the Dead Sea Scroll texts (e.g., Manual of Discipline 3:3). John "went into all the region around the Jordan, proclaiming a baptism of repentance for the forgiveness of sins" (Luke 3:3). The waters of the Jordan, where John performed his baptisms, are a stone's throw from where the scrolls were found.

In Matthew 11:18, we are told that John came "neither eating nor drinking." He ate whatever he could find in the desert, mostly locusts and wild honey (Mark 1:6). He "dressed in a rough coat of camel's hair, with a leather belt around his waist" (Mark 1:6). All this fits well with the lifestyle practiced at Qumran.

The opening chapter of the Gospel of Mark explains John the Baptist's role as Jesus' forerunner by quoting from the fortieth chapter of the prophet Isaiah:

As it is written in the prophet Isaiah, "I am sending my herald ahead of you; he will prepare your way. A voice of one crying out in the wilderness: 'Prepare the way of the Lord, make straight his paths.' " (Mark 1:2–3)

The same passage from Isaiah is quoted in the Manual of Discipline to define the Qumran community's life in the wilderness:

> When these become members of the Community in Israel, according to all these rules, they shall separate from the habitation of unjust men and shall go into the wilderness to prepare there the way of Him: as it is written, "Prepare in the wilderness the way of the Lord, make straight in the desert the path for our God." (Manual of Discipline 8:14–15)

While this seems to make a strong case for John's presence at Qumran, there are also countervailing considerations. Although John is prominent in New Testament texts, there is no suggestion that he is an Essene (as many scholars believe the Qumranites were). The Jewish historian Josephus discusses John and his life but does not suggest that he was an Essene, even though he describes the Essenes at length and says that he himself spent time with them. If John had been an Essene, it seems strange that Josephus would omit this fact.

Moreover, John seems to have been engaged publicly in the contentious society of his time; he did not retire to the contemplative life that is implied at Qumran. When "a message came from God to John . . . in the desert" (Luke 3:2), he became the incarnation of the divine voice, calling from the desert to the rest of the world, preaching to all who would listen: "I am the voice of one crying out in the wilderness" (John 1:23), again quoting Isaiah. Perhaps John lived for a time at Qumran and later left the group to preach to all the people. But this is hardly certain.

Another theoretically possible direct connection between the scrolls and Christianity involves the finds from Cave 7. The fragments recovered there are all in Greek, the language of the New

Testament. Cave 7 was discovered by archaeologists, rather than by bedouin, so we can assume that whatever was found there is in scholarly hands and that whatever could be recovered has in fact been recovered. But the finds were sparse—Cave 7 is often referred to as one of the "minor caves." It yielded only nineteen fragments, mostly tiny. Indeed, one of these can hardly be called a text: it consists of imprints on plaster of papyrus on which a few letters may be seen.

Nonetheless, Jose O'Callaghan, a Spanish Jesuit, claims to have identified a number of the Cave 7 fragments as parts of manuscripts of books of the New Testament, including Paul's letter to the Romans, the Gospel of Mark, the Acts of the Apostles, 1 Timothy, 2 Peter, and James. All of these New Testament texts, except perhaps Mark, were composed long after the settlement at Qumran was destroyed by the Romans in 68 A.D.

O'Callaghan's best case is 7Q5, which he identifies as part of the Gospel of Mark. This small fragment contains only nineteen or twenty letters on four or five lines, and only half the letters can be read with certainty. Only one word is complete: *kai,* which means "and." From this, O'Callaghan concludes that the fragment comes from Mark 6:52–53, which describes the disciples' reaction after Jesus stills the stormy waters of the sea.

After the miracle of the feeding of the five thousand with a mere five loaves and two fishes, Jesus' disciples get into a boat. A high wind threatens the boat, but Jesus appears, walking on the water. When he gets into the boat, the sea becomes calm. Then come the two verses (Mark 6:52–53) that supposedly appear on the Greek fragment from Cave 7. The letters below in boldface stand for the only legible ones actually found on the Dead Sea Scroll fragment:

> For they [the disciples] did not understand **a**bout the loaves, but th**eir** hearts were hardened. **And** when they had crossed over, they came to land at Gen**nes**aret and **moo**red the boat.

From these few letters O'Callaghan has reconstructed this short text.

There are other problems as well. An Oxford expert in Greek paleography, C. H. Roberts, dates the fragment between 50 B.C. and 50 A.D. Mark was written around 70 A.D. Qumran was destroyed in 68 A.D., so it is extremely unlikely that 7Q5 was written after that date. In short, 7Q5 was almost certainly written before Mark was composed, so it cannot be a copy of Mark.

Another, even more serious problem is that there is not enough room for the words "to land" between "and" and the "nes" in Gennesaret. O'Callaghan argues, however, that this particular text omitted the words "to land," though all ancient manuscripts of this text contain these words.

Finally, O'Callaghan's solution depends on the identification in the second line of an incomplete letter as a Greek *nu*. Many experts regard this as either highly unlikely or impossible.

Thus, the scrolls do not have a direct connection with Jesus or early Christianity but they do provide a vastly important context. From them we get a direct glimpse into the world out of which Christianity grew. This was the soil. Here are the roots. For those who want to understand the history of Christianity, the scrolls are exciting and enriching. For those who see Christianity and Christian doctrine as something entirely new and unrelated to its Jewish milieu, the scrolls are threatening.

CHAPTER 6

AN ESSENE LIBRARY?

Everything in the previous chapter assumes that the scrolls predate the Christian Gospels, and in fact they do. The earliest Gospel, Mark, was written in about 70 A.D. The scrolls, on the other hand, were written between about 250 B.C. and 68 A.D.

The scrolls can be dated in a number of ways, some more general, some more specific. The pottery in the caves where the scrolls were found, for example, can be dated by shape to this period. Carbon-14 testing can also be used.

Since the radioactivity of carbon 14 declines over time at a known rate, the age of organic materials can be determined by measuring the amount of radioactivity remaining in carbon-14 atoms found in them. The test requires the destruction of a certain amount of material, however—several grams in the early 1950s (only a few milligrams with new techniques now available). Reluctant to destroy even several grams of the scrolls, the authorities limited the initial carbon-14 tests to the linen in which the scrolls from Cave 1 were wrapped.[1] The date obtained was 33 A.D. plus or minus two hundred years. This too confirmed the general period of the scrolls.

When scholars first saw the scrolls, they immediately followed Albright and dated them to about 100 B.C., based on a comparison of the script with that of the Nash Papyrus, a small papyrus fragment containing the Ten Commandments, the oldest biblical text known at that time, which he dated to about 150 B.C.

Characteristics of handwriting, like styles of pottery, change and develop over time. Based on changes in the script—the shape and stance of the letters, their relationship to a line, the order and direction of the strokes, and other such clues—a relative chronology can be developed. That is, the expert paleographer can conclude that one particular handwriting specimen is earlier or later than another. Then, when absolute (as opposed to relative) dates are secured for some exemplars, the others in the series can be assigned dates within the range of the absolute dates.

Several members of the scroll publication team developed this kind of paleographical expertise in the 1950s, but the outstanding accomplishment in this regard belongs to Harvard's Frank Cross. His seminal study (published in 1961) is probably the most frequently cited scholarly paper in Dead Sea Scroll scholarship. It is called "The Development of the Jewish Scripts,"[2] and it is a 70-page article with 186 footnotes. In it, he discusses each letter of the Hebrew alphabet, one by one, in its various forms (formal, semiformal, cursive, and semicursive) in each relevant period (Archaic [250–150 B.C.], Hasmonean [150–30 B.C.], and Herodian [30 B.C.– 70 A.D.]).

In this way expert paleographers have dated the various Dead Sea Scroll texts, often within a range of fifty years or so. To test the accuracy of paleographic dating, more than a dozen scroll fragments have recently been carbon-14-tested using the refinement known as AMS (Accelerator Mass Spectrometry), which requires only a minuscule specimen. The results not only confirm the age of the scrolls, they show that paleographic dating is reliable within an even narrower range than carbon-14 dates.[3]

Although the scrolls have been securely dated, their date does not reveal who wrote them. For this scholars have turned to two sources—first, to an analysis of the content of the scrolls with reference to what we know from other ancient sources about Judaism at this time; and, second, to the nearby ruins of Qumran, which on the face of it would seem to have some relationship to the scrolls.

Almost at the outset, the publication team concluded that the scrolls were a library of the early sect of Jews known as Essenes. The evidence, however, is inconclusive. We know about the Essenes mostly from the first-century Jewish historian Josephus (c. 37–95 A.D.). They are also described by Philo, Josephus's slightly earlier Jewish contemporary in Alexandria, who is best known as a philosopher. The Essenes are also mentioned by the Roman geographer Pliny the Elder and, fleetingly, in a few other works.

Josephus identifies four different Jewish movements of his day. The major ones are the Pharisees and Sadducees. The third group is the Essenes. The fourth movement Josephus identifies simply as the "Fourth Philosophy."[4] Although the Essenes are a smaller group than the Pharisees or Sadducees, Josephus describes them at greater length, perhaps because he considered them somewhat exotic—or perhaps because he himself began the initiation process into the group, but then withdrew.[5]

According to both Josephus and Philo, the Essenes numbered about four thousand. Josephus tells us they were to be found "in large numbers in every town."[6] Indeed, in Jerusalem, they apparently lived in an identifiable enclave, as indicated by the existence of an Essene Gate to the city.[7]

The descriptions indicate they were a close-knit group: Whenever they traveled, they carried nothing with them except arms, as a protection against highwaymen. For the rest, they depended on their fellow Essenes. "On the arrival of any of the sect from elsewhere, all the resources of the [Essene] community are put at their disposal, just as if they were their own; and they enter the houses of men whom they have never seen before as though they were their most intimate friends."[8]

One strange omission: Josephus gives no indication that the Essenes have repaired to the wilderness or that they have a center in the desert. He tells us only that they live in towns. He does say that "they live by themselves,"[9] but the context seems to indicate that they inhabit particular sections of the many towns where they live.

They do have a community, however. And in many respects the characteristics of this community are the same as those described in the scrolls. To become a member of the group requires a detailed probationary period. Only after a year is the applicant "allowed to share the purer kind of holy water, but is not yet received into the meetings of the community."[10] Then "his character is tested for two years more, and only then, if found worthy, is he enrolled in the society."[11]

Essene society is rigorously hierarchical. "They do nothing without orders from their superiors."[12] But they are also democratic: "They elect officers to attend to the interests of the community."[13]

They are communitarian. Their goods are held in common: "The individual's possessions join the common stock and all, like brothers, enjoy a single patrimony."[14]

As might be expected, "They despise riches."[15] Because all their property is held in common, "you will not find one among them distinguished by greater opulence than another. . . . You will nowhere see either abject poverty or inordinate wealth. . . . There is no buying or selling among themselves, but each gives what he has to any in need."[16]

They pray—before the sun comes up and at night. They purify themselves by bathing in cold water. They eat in silence.

They also "display an extraordinary interest in the writings of the ancients."[17] A new member swears "carefully to preserve the books of the sect."[18]

The Essene attitude toward marriage is either confused or complicated. The usual solution is to say that some were celibate (perhaps those at Qumran), while others were not. Thus Josephus tells us that "they disdain marriage."[19] To maintain their numbers, "they adopt other men's children, while yet pliable and docile."[20]

"Another order of Essenes," however, do marry, but only for purposes of procreation.[21] A prospective wife must first go through a
three-year probationary period to demonstrate her ability to have
children, though it is not clear how. Only then does the marriage
take place. Intercourse during pregnancy is forbidden in order to
show "that their motive in marrying is not self-indulgence but the
procreation of children."[22] This latter attitude is especially significant in relation to the scrolls because a small fragment among the
scrolls provides that "whoever has intercourse with his wife for
lust, which is against the rule, he shall depart and never return."[23]

Much has been made of the fact that only three or four of the
excavated graves at Qumran were those of women and children,
but it is hard to draw any conclusions from this. Varying interpretations can be given to the paucity of women and children in the
graves, especially given the complexity of Essene attitudes toward
marriage and children.

The Essenes have other peculiar customs. They apparently have
a particular aversion to stool. On the Sabbath, they refrain from
defecation. The rules for disposing of stool at other times are carefully delineated. Indeed, the first thing an applicant for membership is given is a small shovel.[24] He is instructed to dig a trench a
foot deep before defecation, then to wrap a mantle around himself
so as not to be exposed. After defecation, he is to "replace the excavated soil in the trench."[25] In addition, he is admonished to do
all this in a "retired spot."[26] After this exercise, he is to wash his
hands.

Since metal is likely to have survived, we would like to know if
the excavation of Qumran produced any small shovels. Indeed, a
considerable number of metal objects are known to have been excavated at the site (in addition to at least one bronze inkwell) and
taken to Belgium by the two scholars who are supposed to be
writing the final report on the excavations at Qumran, Robert
Donceel and his wife, Pauline Donceel-Voûte. As I write, the
École Biblique is trying to get the objects back.[27] Whether shovels

or parts of shovels are among them is not known. Some maintain that a mattock from Qumran should be interpreted as such a shovel.

Because of their somewhat ascetic lifestyle, the Essenes are said to "live to a great age—most of them to upwards of a century."[28] Physical anthropologists can determine the age of a person at death by an examination of the bones; unfortunately, the bones excavated at Qumran in the 1950s are nowhere to be found and may never be found.

In general, Josephus finds the Essenes "masters of their temper, champions of fidelity [and] very ministers of peace."[29] Although "they avoid swearing," new members are required "to swear tremendous oaths,"[30] he writes, so it is hard to make much of this prohibition in identifying the group referred to in the scrolls. Moreover, the required oath, although extremely high-minded, is not specific enough to provide a key to identification in the scrolls. Thus, the oath requires the swearer to "practice piety toward the Deity . . . hate the unjust and fight the battle of the just . . . keep his hands from stealing and his soul pure from unholy gain."[31] Such an oath would be appropriate for any Jewish group at the time.

As to the character of the Essenes: "They make light of danger, and triumph over pain by their resolute will. Death, if it comes with honor, they consider better than immortality."[32]

As for their beliefs, they hold that "the soul is immortal and imperishable."[33] Such a belief was common to many groups at the time, however. Josephus tries to draw distinctions among the Essenes, Pharisees, and Sadducees regarding their attitude toward Fate: The Essenes believe that "Fate is mistress of all things, and that nothing befalls men unless it be in accordance with her decree. . . . [They are] wont to leave everything in the hands of God."[34] The Sadducees "do away with Fate, holding that there is no such thing and that human actions are not achieved in accordance with her decree, but all things lie within our own power."

The Pharisees are in between: "Certain events are the work of Fate, but not all; as to other events, it depends upon ourselves whether they shall take place or not."[35] This is so general as to be of little help in identifying any particular text as Essene. Josephus himself seems confused; elsewhere he tells us that the Pharisees "attribute everything to Fate and to God."[36] While he qualifies this, the distinctions among the beliefs of various competing Jewish groups remain subtle, if not downright vague and uncertain.

Josephus makes almost no reference to the Essenes' relationship to the Jerusalem Temple. The scrolls, however, seem to make clear that there was a sharp break between the scroll people and the Jerusalem priesthood.

There is another omission in Josephus. He says nothing about the Essene calendar. The scroll sectarians followed a different calendar from the one used in the Jerusalem Temple. That means that the scroll sectarians and the main groups of Jews observed holidays and festivals, including Yom Kippur, the most sacred day of the year, at different times. This is a critical division. Surely, if the Essenes used a different calendar, Josephus would have mentioned this in his lengthy description of their customs and beliefs, but he does not. Neither is there any hint of an unusual Essene calendar in any other extant ancient sources. If the Essenes didn't have a different calendar, they were not the people of the scrolls.

Philo makes many of the same observations as Josephus. The Essenes lead a communitarian life. "No one's house is his own in the sense that it is not shared by all. . . . they all have a single treasure and common disbursements; their clothes are held in common and also their food through their institution of public meals."[37] "What one has is held to belong to all and conversely what all have one has."[38]

Like Josephus, Philo tells us that they "live in many cities of Judea and in many villages and grouped in great societies of many members."[39] Also like Josephus, Philo makes no mention of isolated communities in the desert or away from cities and villages. But Philo also says that Essenes do *not* live in cities: "The first thing about these people is that they live in villages and avoid the cities because of the iniquities which have become inveterate among city dwellers."[40] So which is it? Do they live in cities or don't they? What about Jerusalem? I call attention to this seeming contradiction because it illustrates how difficult it is to fit the pieces of the puzzle together. We are trying to relate ancient authors like Philo and Josephus to the texts of the scrolls and then to the archaeology of Qumran. We are looking for a coherent, consistent picture. Yet we can't even put together all the pieces of a single author, Philo.

Philo is very clear that the Essenes are celibate. "They eschew marriage . . . For no Essene takes a wife."[41] Yet the scrolls contain community rules regarding women and children. This is often explained by saying that there were marrying Essenes and celibate Essenes. The latter, like the inhabitants of Qumran, lived in the desert; the former, according to this effort at harmonization, lived in cities and towns. Philo supposedly speaks only of those who live in cities and towns—and they, he tells us, do not marry. To add to the confusion, the graves of a few women and children have been excavated at Qumran. Compare Philo: "No Essene is a mere child, nor even a stripling or newly bearded."[42]

Philo also speaks of the Essenes' "abstinence from oaths."[43] Yet the scrolls detail an elaborate oath required of applicants for membership.

Similarly with slaves: "Not a single slave is to be found among them," says Philo.[44] Yet the scrolls contain rules regarding the treatment of slaves.

As we would expect, Philo describes a frugal, virtuous, good-tempered, devoted, moral, and pious people. Alas, the Essenes were surely not the only group of people who could be characterized in this way. So these characteristics are not of much help in identifying the scrolls with the Essenes.

Given what we know of the Essenes from Josephus and Philo, can we establish a relationship between the scrolls and the Essenes from the evidence of the scrolls themselves?

Neither the word "Essene" nor any of its variants appear in the scrolls,[45] nor does the name of any other Jewish groups that were competing with each other at the time. It would be easier if some of the scrolls identified their doctrines as Essene (or something else), but they do not.

Some of the scrolls were clearly written elsewhere—probably Jerusalem—and brought to the site. We know this because some of the scrolls were written (that is, copied) before the site was established.

Moreover, at least half the scrolls are not sectarian in their contents; that is, they do not reflect the views of any particular group of Jews, let alone the Essenes, but rather are characteristic of Judaism generally. This is true of the over two hundred biblical scrolls. It is also true of many other Qumran texts. In most cases, however, the surviving fragments are simply too small to reveal whether or not they reflect the views of a particular group of Jews.

Nevertheless, a number of the scrolls do seem to express a particular outlook, including antagonism to another group, probably the group that controlled the Jerusalem Temple. Scholars call the texts with a particular religious, social, and organizational outlook sectarian documents. Those who believe the Dead Sea Scrolls reflect the views of the Essenes refer to the sectarian documents as Essene texts and refer to the people who wrote the scrolls as Essenes. Those who are less sure or who want to use a more neutral term refer to them simply as sectarian texts and refer to the people whose views they reflect as the Qumran sect.

Perhaps the most clearly sectarian document is the scroll known as the Manual of Discipline, which appears to contain the laws of a particular Jewish community. The most complete copy of the Manual of Discipline was found in Cave 1 and was one of the scrolls photographed by John Trever at the American School of Oriental Research. Millar Burrows, then director of the school, published and first named the document. The text reminded him, a devout Methodist, of a book in the Methodist Church tradition with a similar name. Hence, he called it the Manual of Discipline, illustrating how the background of a researcher can subtly creep into and affect the interpretation of a text.

The ancient Hebrew name of the text appears to have been Serekh ha-Yakhad, the Community Rule. In the most recent authoritative text, it is called the Rule of the Community,[46] as distinguished from a supplement to this text called, among other things, the Rule of the Congregation.

The importance of a given document to the Qumran community is suggested by the number of copies that have been recovered. In the case of the Manual of Discipline, at least ten other copies have been recovered, mostly from Cave 4, but all except the copy from Cave 1 are extremely fragmentary—there is just enough to demonstrate that they are the same document.

The Cave 1 copy of the Manual of Discipline contains eleven columns (almost the entire text) and fills twenty pages of Geza Vermes's frequently used English translation.[47] It has been called "a constitution of the Qumran community."[48]

It describes the rules and rites for admission into the Covenant of the community, the annual renewal of the Covenant, the rules for communal life, the assembly or council of the community, and the penalties for violation of the community's rules. It also contains some theological tenets of the community and a hymn in which the community praises the creator.

It is a unique, previously unknown text. "There are," Geza Vermes has written, "to my knowledge, no writings in ancient Jewish sources parallel to the Community Rule [Manual of Discipline], but a similar type of literature flourished among Christians between the second and fourth centuries, the so-called 'Church Orders' represented by the Didache, the Didascalia, the Apostolic Constitution, etc."[49]

In many respects the Manual of Discipline does indicate a community much like the Essene community described by Josephus, although there are also differences. It also resonates with other Jewish literature and, as Vermes remarks, with later Christian doctrine. Moreover, sometimes it is not clear whether the text de-

The Manual of Discipline, also known as the Rule of the Community and the Community Rule, contains rules and regulations for a devout separatist Jewish group.

scribes a real community in the present time or an eschatological, visionary community at the end of time.

The community it describes is both strictly governed and strictly hierarchical: "Each man shall sit in his place: the Priests shall sit first, and the elders second, and all the rest of the people according to their rank. . . . The man of lesser rank obey(s) his superior."[50] "Whoever has murmured against the authority of the Community shall be expelled and shall not return."[51]

Membership in the community is by examination. The novitiate must wait a year until he is admitted to "the pure Meal of the Congregation . . . nor shall he have any share of the property of the Congregation (during that year)."[52] If he passes a subsequent examination, which tests not his knowledge but his adherence to the moral and ritual laws of the community, he is admitted to the next stage. But even then, "He shall not touch the Drink of the Congregation until he has completed a second year."[53] At the end of the second year, he is again examined.

At the end of the first year, the novitiate gives the community bursar all his property and earnings, which are registered to his account but cannot be spent for the Congregation.[54] At the end of the second year his property and earnings are merged with the community's funds.

"These are the ways that all of them shall walk. . . . They shall eat in common and pray in common and deliberate in common."[55] A third of every night is to be spent reading Scripture, studying the Law, and praying.

The Assembly of the Congregation has its equivalent of *Robert's Rules of Order:* "No man shall interrupt a companion before his speech has ended, nor speak before a man of higher rank."[56] Other rules govern daily intercourse: "Let no man address his companion with anger, or ill-temper, or obduracy, or with envy."[57]

"Let no man accuse his companion before the Congregation without having first admonished him in the presence of witnesses."[58]

Sanctions are also provided: For deliberately lying, penance for six months. For deliberately insulting a companion unjustly, penance for a year and exclusion from the community.[59] For falling asleep during the Assembly of the Congregation, penance for thirty days. For failing to care for a companion, penance for three months. For interrupting a companion while he is talking, penance for ten days. For appearing naked before a companion, six months; for exposing oneself as a result of sloppy dressing, thirty days.[60]

One peculiar rule is especially interesting because it also appears in Josephus's description of the Essenes. The Manual of Discipline provides: "Whoever spits in an Assembly of the Congregation shall do penance for thirty days."[61] In Josephus's description of the Essenes, he tells us, "They are careful not to spit into the midst of the company."[62] This seems like a curious prohibition to include in the laws of a community. Would more than one community have such an explicit statement of such a law? Surprisingly, the answer is yes. As one scholar has pointed out, the Jerusalem Talmud prohibits spitting at prayer-time.[63]

As mentioned earlier, a rigorous dualism runs through much of the Manual of Discipline:

> He (God) has created man to govern the world, and has appointed for him two spirits in which to walk until the time of His visitation: the spirits of truth and falsehood. Those born of truth spring from a fountain of light, but those born of falsehood spring from a source of darkness. All the children of righteousness are ruled by the Prince of Light and walk in the ways of light, but all the children of falsehood are ruled by the Angel of Darkness and walk in the ways of darkness. The Angel of Darkness leads all the children of righteousness astray. . . . But the God of Israel and His Angel of Truth will succour all the Sons of Light.[64]

And "the Priests shall bless all the men of the lot of God. . . . And the Levites shall curse all the men of the lot of Satan."[65] The curses are pretty terrible: "May He deliver you up for torture at the hands of the vengeful Avengers. May He visit you with destruction. . . . Be cursed without mercy. . . . Be damned in the shadowy place of everlasting fire. May God not heed when you call on Him, nor pardon you by blotting out your sin. May He raise His angry face towards you for vengeance. May there be no Peace for you."[66]

But the characteristics of the righteous man are indeed inspiring: "a spirit of humility, patience, abundant charity, unending goodness, understanding and intelligence . . . (He) trusts in all the deeds of God and leans on His great lovingkindness."[67]

God will not suffer evil forever. An apocalyptic vision gives hope for the future: "God has ordained an end for falsehood, and at the time of the visitation He will destroy it forever. Then truth, which has wallowed in the ways of wickedness during the dominion of falsehood until the appointed time of judgment, shall arise in the world forever. God will then purify every deed of man with His truth. . . . Like purifying waters He will shed upon him the spirit of truth. . . . Until now the spirits of truth and falsehood struggle in the hearts of men and they walk in both wisdom and folly. . . . For God has established the two spirits in equal measure until the determined end, and until the Renewal."[68]

In the meantime, the Covenanters are to separate themselves "from the congregation of the men of falsehood and . . . unite . . . under the authority of the sons of Zadok, the Priests who keep the Covenant."[69] Zadok and his sons, descendants of Aaron, were the sole priests in the Jerusalem Temple from the time of Solomon until the Babylonian destruction in 586 B.C. When the Temple was rebuilt (the Second Temple), the descendants of Zadok resumed their hallowed position as high priests, but, as explained in the introduction to this book, under the Hasmoneans they were ousted and replaced with Hellenized Jews. Many scholars trace the origins of the Qumran sect to this displacement of the Zadokite priesthood. In the Manual of Discipline, and elsewhere in the scrolls, the Qumranites emphasize the sole legitimacy of the Zadokite priesthood.

The Covenanters are to "separate from the habitation of ungodly men and . . . go into the wilderness to prepare the way of Him."[70] The text then quotes the famous passage from Isaiah 40:3, "Prepare in the wilderness the way of the Lord, make straight in the desert a path for our God." This of course is the verse identified and quoted in all four Gospels (Matthew 3:3; Mark 1:2–3; Luke 3:4; John 1:23). In Matthew and Luke this verse from Isaiah is part of John the Baptist's charge to his followers: "Repent, for the kingdom of heaven is at hand." In the Gospel of John, the Baptist quotes this passage to define his mission.

There is also much in the Manual of Discipline that reflects mainstream Jewish thought and observance. Listen to these moving words from the closing hymn:

> I will enter the Covenant with God
> and when evening and morning depart
>   I will recite His decrees.
>
>   . . . . .
>
> I will bless His Name.
> I will praise Him before I go out or enter,
>   or sit or rise
> And while I sit on the couch of my bed.
>
>   . . . . .
>
> I will bless Him for His exceeding wonderful deeds
>   at the beginning of fear and dread.
>
>   . . . . .
>
> I will meditate on His power
>   and lean on His mercies all day long.
> I know that judgment of all the living is in His Hand,
>   and that all His deeds are truth.[71]

One of the most beautiful prayers recited daily in synagogues around the world, part of Israel's best-known prayer, the Sh'ma, comes from Deuteronomy 6 and includes these words—not so different from the words of the Manual of Discipline just quoted:

You shall love the Lord your God with all your heart and with all your soul, and with all your might. And these words which I command you this day shall be in your heart. You shall teach them diligently to your children, and you shall speak of them when you sit in your house and when you walk by the way, when you lie down and when you rise up.

Or listen to Psalm 119 and compare it with the quotation from the Manual of Discipline:

> I will meditate on your precepts,
> and fix my eyes on your ways.
> I will delight in your statutes;
> I will not forget your word.
> . . . . .
>
> My heart stands in awe of your words.
> I rejoice at your word.
> . . . . .
>
> I hate and abhor falsehood,
> but I love your law. (vv. 15–16, 161–63)

Or forget about comparisons and just listen to the soaring lines of this hymn that closes the Manual of Discipline:

> He that is everlasting
>   is the support of my right hand;
> the way of my steps is over stout rock
>   which nothing shall shake;
> for the rock of my steps is the truth of God
>   and His might is the support of my right hand.[72]

This, then, gives a fair picture of the single most important text in support of the Essene hypothesis, though it is the evidence of factor after factor in document after document on which the Essene case fully rests. One such text is the so-called Damascus Document.

The Damascus Document is unusual for several reasons, not the least of which is that it was found not in the wilderness of Judah, but in Cairo, and a half century before the scrolls were discovered on the northwest shore of the Dead Sea.[73]

In December 1896, Solomon Schechter, a Reader in Talmud at the University of Cambridge in England, set sail for Egypt in the hope of obtaining for his university some old manuscripts from the Ben Ezra synagogue in Fostat, a suburb of Cairo. Like many synagogues, the thousand-year-old Ben Ezra synagogue had a *genizah,* or storage room for sacred but worn-out texts. A *genizah* is supposed to be only for temporary storage, until the texts can be properly buried. For some unknown reason, however, the texts in the Ben Ezra *genizah* were never buried. For centuries documents accumulated there. And not just sacred documents, but every imaginable sort of secular document as well.

Before Schechter's visit, documents surfacing on the antiquities market were traced to the *genizah*; antiquities dealers were regularly bribing the keepers of the synagogue to obtain them. Schechter wanted to empty the place and came armed with appropriate introductions from his university, as well as a letter from Britain's Chief Rabbi to the Grand Rabbi of Cairo. *Baksheesh* also helped.

The entrance to the *genizah* was through an opening in the wall high above the women's gallery upstairs. The *genizah* itself was a dark, windowless, airless space where every movement raised plumes of centuries-old dust. Schechter reports that he almost suffocated, but he persisted. Within two months he was able to remove thirty large bags of documents. Threatened with ill-health, he departed having almost, but not quite, emptied the *genizah*.

The Cairo Genizah documents, as they are now known, include over 140,000 texts—an enormous collection that paints an extraordinary picture of Jewish life in medieval times. Our concern here, however, is with only two of these.

Among the documents that Schechter brought back to Cambridge were two copies, designated A and B, of what he called a "Zadokite Work." Scholars agree that A (the much more com-

In 1897, Solomon Schechter (shown here surrounded by boxes of genizah *documents) found copies of a "Zadokite Work" among documents in the Ben Ezra synagogue* genizah. *Copies of this work, now known as the Damascus Document, were found fifty years later at Qumran.*

plete copy—eight parchment leaves written on both sides) dates to the tenth century, and B (only one long parchment leaf of two columns) dates to the twelfth century. But these are the dates when these manuscripts were copied, not the date of the text's composition. The Hebrew in which they are written resembles biblical Hebrew and reflects none of the developments in the language after the Roman destruction of the Temple in 70 A.D. Schechter correctly surmised that the text must have been composed before the destruction of the Temple.

Schechter also recognized that the text appeared to be that of a group of Jews who separated themselves from the mainstream of their coreligionists and regarded themselves as the True Israel. The members of this community appear to have been led by priests who are "sons of Zadok," the line of priests, descendants of Aaron, established by Solomon and replaced in the second century B.C. by Hasmonean rulers. Hence, the name Schechter gave to the document, "A Zadokite Work."

In many ways, Schechter was prescient. Because the text refers to several unknown works, he concluded: "The Sect must also have been in possession of some Pseudepigrapha now lost." He even posited the likelihood of a Manual of Discipline: "This might suggest that the Sect was in possession of some sort of manual containing the tenets of the Sect, and perhaps a regular set of rules of discipline."[74]

A half century later, scholars examining the fragmentary texts from Qumran identified the same text found in the Cairo *genizah* among the Dead Sea Scrolls. And not simply a single copy, but at least ten copies (eight in Cave 4, one in Cave 5, and one in Cave 6). Obviously this was a very important work in the Qumran collection.

Whose precepts did the Zadokite Work reflect? Long before the discovery of the Dead Sea Scrolls this was a matter of intense scholarly interest, especially because one scholar, the Custodian of Hebrew Manuscripts at the British Museum, George Margoliouth, related the work to the early Christian community. A front-page *New York Times* headline on Christmas Day, 1910, said of the work: "DESCRIBES PERSONAGES BELIEVED TO BE CHRIST, JOHN THE BAPTIST, AND THE APOSTLE PAUL." If anything was needed to focus scholarly attention on whose doctrine was embedded in this text, this headline sufficed.

In 1922, Louis Ginzburg, then the doyen of American Rabbinic scholars and a professor at the Jewish Theological Seminary in New York, summarized responsible scholarship analyzing the document and added his own. Ginzburg called his study *An Unknown Jewish Sect.*[75] Both Schechter and Ginzburg of course knew the descriptions of the Essenes in Josephus and Philo, as did other scholars. But even those scholars who considered the question concluded that the Zadokite Work was not an Essene document, although it emphasized ritual purity, the avoidance of oaths, and strict Sabbath observance. R. H. Charles, who edited a standard work on the Apocrypha and Pseudepigrapha in 1913, dismissed in a single sentence the possibility that the Zadokite Work was an Essene document. "The Zadokites were not Essenes," he said.[76] A main reason for this view was that the Zadokite Work contained laws relating to animal sacrifice and the Jerusalem Temple, whereas the Essenes had supposedly rejected animal sacrifice.

Since the discovery of the Qumran scrolls, however, the Zadokite Work has been reinterpreted: It does not reject sacrifice *per se,* only offerings of unqualified priests and offerings that hide evil and injustice.[77] Thus, the Zadokite Work, which was not regarded as an Essene document before the discovery of the scrolls, has now become one of the major supports for the Essene hypothesis.

The work as a whole, including the Qumran fragments, is now known as the Damascus Document and the common scholarly siglum for the copies from the Cairo Genizah is CD, which stands for the Cairo Damascus [Document], a title based on at least seven references to Damascus in the work. It appears that the members of the sect fled there and established a new covenant: "[They] entered the new covenant in the Land of Damascus."[78] Unfortunately, the text breaks off at the end of this line. Whether the reference to Damascus represents only a symbolic flight, perhaps a code word for Babylon, or an actual historical event is unclear. Scholars have argued both ways. Or it could be a code word for Qumran. The question is especially important in tracing the history of the Essenes—if the document is indeed an Essene composition.

The Damascus Document is divided into two sections. The first is called the Admonition and sometimes the Exhortation. It is not easy reading, a detail that accounts of its contents usually fail to tell the reader. One recent commentary describes the Admonition/Exhortation as a "review of Israelite history focusing upon its past and future punishment, as well as upon God's gracious salvation of a portion of the people."[79] Here is a brief sample of the more easily understandable contents of the text:

> God . . . hid his face from Israel and from his sanctuary, and gave them up to the sword. But . . . he left a remnant and did not give them up to destruction. . . . A Man of Mockery arose who sprinkled upon Israel waters of falsehood. . . . The first ones who entered the covenant became guilty through it; and they were given up to the sword, having departed from God's covenant. . . . The Sons of Zadok are the chosen ones of Israel, those called by name, who stand in the end of days. . . . (Their successors) worshiped the Ashtoreth, and . . . continuously polluted the sanctuary. . . . The penitents of Israel . . . depart(ed) from the land of Judah and dwell in the land of Damascus . . . (and) entered into the New Covenant in the land of Damascus. . . . Those who guard (the precepts) are the poor of the sheep. These will escape at the time of the visitation. But those who remain will be handed over to the sword when the Messiah of Aaron and Israel comes.[80]

The Admonition/Exhortation thus contains references to a New Covenant entered by a select group of Israelites led by de-

Fragments of the Damascus Document found in the Qumran caves.

scendants of the biblically appointed priest Zadok. The priests who controlled the Temple have polluted it. At the end of days, the Messiah will come, destroying most, but vindicating the members of the New Covenant.

The second part of the Damascus Document is a series of statutes or laws. With the help of the additions to CD from among the Qumran texts, we now know that the laws constituted about two-thirds of the complete text. These laws are concerned mostly with strict Sabbath observance, the purity of priests, marriage, oaths, and other such matters. One law that particularly caught my aging eye prohibited anyone over sixty from serving as a judge: "No longer shall anyone stand from sixty years and upward to judge the congregation, for through human failing his days have become few."[81] Another law appears to prohibit sexual intercourse in Jerusalem: "Let no man lie with a woman in the city of the sanctuary to defile the city of the sanctuary with their pollution."[82] This is far stricter than the law of Pharisees or Sadducees.

The most authoritative edition of the Damascus Document notes that its penal code "corresponds very closely to that of the Rule of the Community [the Manual of Discipline], both in the list of offenses and the nature of the penalties," but then significantly hedges this statement: "CD's laws conflict with some of what is usually assumed regarding the Qumran Community on the basis of the Rule of the Community [the Manual of Discipline]."[83] For example, the Manual of Discipline seems to reflect a community of celibate men; the laws in the Damascus Document contain regulations concerning marriage, women, and children. The Manual of Discipline describes a community with commonly held property; the Damascus Document assumes that the group's members have their own private income. The Manual of Discipline prohibits slaveholding; the Damascus Document regulates slavery.

The evidence that the Damascus Document is an Essene work is ambiguous at best.

More broadly, are the Dead Sea Scrolls in general an Essene library? A clear majority of scroll scholars answer yes. They not only identify the sectarian documents among the scrolls as Essene, they also identify the ruins of Qumran as the remains of an Essene settlement. A minority of scholars—and they tend not to be in the mainstream of Dead Sea Scroll research—have argued against the Essene connection. These scholars tend to look not at the convergence between the scrolls and Essene life and doctrine as described by Josephus and Philo, but at the differences.

On the basis of the scrolls alone, therefore, the case is a close one. It is time, then, to look at the ruins of Qumran. Do they shed any light on the matter?

CHAPTER 7

THE ARCHAEOLOGY OF QUMRAN

After five seasons of digging at Qumran (between 1951 and 1956), Père Roland de Vaux thought he understood the site quite well.

His interpretation, however, was unmistakably affected by his interpretation of the scrolls, which he took to be an Essene library. De Vaux believed Qumran to be the home of the Essenes, an isolated religious community living in the desert awaiting the eschaton, the end of days. His interpretation was also affected by his own background as a Dominican monk living in a communal monastery.

When de Vaux came upon a long room at Qumran with some inkwells and large plastered objects, he interpreted the objects as the desks on which the scrolls had been written. The room itself was the "scriptorium,"[1] a term used for the room in medieval monasteries where monkish scribes copied manuscripts.

When he discovered an even larger room adjacent to a smaller room with over a thousand common dishes and goblets, he interpreted the larger room as the dining room, or "refectory"[2] (another room in a medieval monastery), where the sectarians ate their meals together.

When he excavated nearly fifty graves in the huge cemeteries adjacent to the site (which held over twelve hundred individual graves) and found that only three or four were of women and children and the rest of men, he interpreted this as evidence that the inhabitants were celibate, a confirmation of Pliny the Elder's statement that the Essenes "live without women, renouncing love entirely."

When he traced the elaborate water system with its cisterns and five *miqva'ot,* or ritual baths, he understood the latter as confirmation of the importance of ritual purity to the site's inhabitants.

Reading Pliny's reference to Ein Gedi, an important oasis twenty miles south of Qumran, as "lying below" (*infra hos*) an Essene settlement, de Vaux identified Qumran as the Essene settlement to which Pliny was referring.

In short, everything seemed to fit.

Unfortunately, de Vaux died in 1971 without writing a final report on his excavation. So his archaeological conclusions could not be checked by others.

In 1987, amid mounting concern over the failure to publish the scrolls, the École Biblique et Archéologique Française, the French Dominican school in Jerusalem on whose behalf de Vaux had conducted his excavations, engaged the Belgian scholar Robert Donceel to write a final report based on the photographs, drawings, plans, field notebooks, and artifacts that de Vaux had left. Donceel's wife, Pauline Donceel-Voûte, joined the project, and eventually took over—"usurped" is the word one of the fathers at the École Biblique used to me in describing this. Mme. Donceel denies the charge, saying that she provided her husband with assistance only when the École itself failed to provide him with promised help, and that she has been "in the limelight" only because she speaks better English than he.

In any event, the Donceels arrived at radically different conclusions from de Vaux's. They interpreted the site not as an isolated religious commune but as a "villa rustica," a winter villa much like

Directly behind the Qumran settlement, in the knobby spur, are Caves 4 and 5.

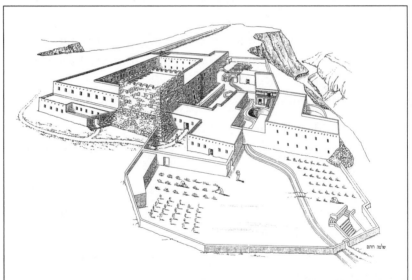

*An artist's reconstruction of the settlement at Qumran, suggesting that the rectangular
building with the tower constituted the initial settlement and the structure outside was
added later. The tower in the center of the drawing will help to orient it
to aerial photographs of the site.*

OPPOSITE: *Roland de Vaux's plan of the Qumran settlement has both posed and answered
questions for archaeologists. It clearly shows the extensive water system at the settlement, the
fault line from an earthquake in 31 B.C., a tower with its protective glacis, and several rooms
that are key to de Vaux's theories about the settlement, such as the dining room, the pantry, a
study room with benches lining the walls, and the so-called scriptorium. But the plan does not
indicate a wall, lately discovered and marked as a proposed reconstruction here, that would have
completed a square core structure; some archaeologists believe that this was the original core of
the settlement. The walls in the central area are thin and come together at odd angles, which
suggests that they may have been added later, and that the area was once an open courtyard.*

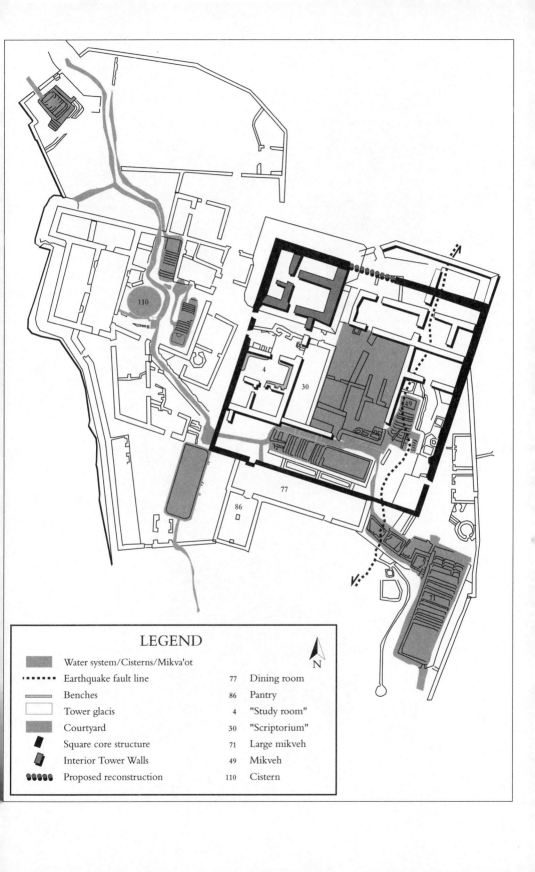

LEGEND

N

▨ Water system/Cisterns/Mikva'ot			
▪▪▪▪▪ Earthquake fault line	77	Dining room
═══ Benches	86	Pantry
▭ Tower glacis	4	"Study room"
▨ Courtyard	30	"Scriptorium"
◣ Square core structure	71	Large mikveh
◢ Interior Tower Walls	49	Mikveh
●●●●● Proposed reconstruction	110	Cistern

PHOTO COURTESY OF THE ISRAEL ANTIQUITIES AUTHORITY

*Three inkwells (one bronze and two ceramic) recovered in the Qumran excavations
(two in the so-called scriptorium) may suggest that scrolls
were copied at the settlement.*

THE SCHØYEN COLLECTION MS 1655/2

*A bronze inkwell supposedly found at Qumran
by bedouin around 1950 was sold by Kando
to a Norwegian collector.*

those that wealthy Jerusalemites built in the early years of this century near Jericho (seven miles north of Qumran) 'to escape the winter chill of the Holy City.

In one respect the Donceels are like de Vaux. Nearly a decade after they began work, they still have not published what archaeologists call a final report. They now concede that they will never write one. "It is not on the program," Mme. Donceel told me. But they did publish a few articles in which they contend that the luxury goods found by de Vaux in his excavation preclude interpretation of the site as an impoverished, or at least ascetic, religious community. The room that de Vaux thought was the scriptorium, they designate a triclinium, an elegant Roman-style dining room. What de Vaux regarded as desks they say are reclining benches that lined the walls of the dining room.

Their conclusion that the site is a villa rustica has not met with favor in the archaeological community—to put it mildly. Many archaeologists feel that their expertise—especially that of Mme. Donceel (her specialty is mosaics; none were found at Qumran)—is not adequate to the task. One of the École Biblique fathers responsible for supervising the publication called their conclusions "stupid." The École Biblique and the Donceels are, as of this writing, not speaking.

As the situation deteriorated, the École Biblique decided to wait no longer and to publish some of the raw material from de Vaux's dig—538 excavation photographs, 48 plans keyed to the photographs, and de Vaux's summary of each locus of the excavation.[3] This partial publication allowed other scholars to review de Vaux's work for the first time.

The judgment has been devastating: "The excavation of Khirbet Qumran was not conducted according to the accepted rules of stratigraphy. . . . [This is] the inevitable conclusion arising from de Vaux's field journals," writes Yizhar Hirschfeld, a highly regarded Israeli archaeologist.[4] This is about as harsh a criticism of an excavation as can be rendered. Nothing is more important in an excavation than to dig stratigraphically, to separate the layers from one another, so that each can be dated and interpreted independently.

American archaeologist Jodi Magness was similarly critical: "Despite the wealth of new information presented in this volume, it remains difficult to reevaluate the archaeology of Qumran. . . . [V]ital information such as section drawings . . . is not provided. . . . Since most of the rooms at Qumran clearly had more than one occupational phase, as indicated by architectural changes and the presence of two or more floors, the lack of this information makes it impossible to reconstruct the sequence accurately."[5]

While stratigraphic methods have certainly been refined since the 1950s, when de Vaux dug, they were well established even then. The first stratigraphic excavation was made, surprisingly, by Thomas Jefferson in the late eighteenth century when he excavated an Indian burial mound in Virginia. The technique was introduced to Palestine in 1890 by the British archaeologist Sir Matthew William Flinders Petrie, digging at Tell el-Hesi. While his methods were still somewhat crude by modern standards, they were later refined by a series of excavators, including George Reisner and Clarence Fischer, digging at Samaria, and culminating in the work of the mistress of stratigraphy, Dame Kathleen Kenyon, at ancient Jericho, a bare seven miles north of Qumran. She was excavating there at the same time de Vaux was working at Qumran. And the two regarded each other as close colleagues.

In a stratigraphic excavation, isolating debris layers is the key to understanding the history of the site. The École Biblique publication makes clear that de Vaux did not do this. His locus numbers do not distinguish between layers; one locus may include, for example, several floor levels. The same locus number is assigned to material above and below an ash layer. Instead of using locus numbers to identify discrete archaeological spaces, de Vaux's locus numbers often appear merely as an inventory of rooms and other spatial areas.

Moreover, de Vaux committed another archaeological sin: He excavated almost the entire site, leaving little for other archaeologists to excavate later in order to check his results or to dig with the improved methods that the future inevitably brings.

The major part of the site left unexcavated at Qumran is the cemeteries. There would be much to learn from a modern excavation of even a few of these graves. But political conditions in Israel make it impossible to do this now. The ultra-Orthodox have effectively banned the excavation of Jewish graves.[6]

Even the artifacts that de Vaux did find are unavailable for study by outside scholars. As Robert Donceel recently noted, "Except for the few dozen artifacts used to illustrate his preliminary reports and his only, relatively short, synthesis, the finds were left unpublished."[7] Donceel tells us that the finds included stoneware, abundant blown glassware, metal objects (mostly tools[8]), wood, reeds, palm leaves, and over twelve hundred coins (almost all of which have now been lost[9]). The pottery included fineware, such as "painted Jerusalem" plates, Hellenistic blackware, Roman *terra sigillata*, delicately shaped cups and bowls, and rimmed plates. None of this is currently available to help us interpret the site. We have only the Donceels' word that it exists. One scholar has recently expressed a "crying need for the complete publication of the excavation evidence."[10] For now, however, we must interpret the site with what we have, not with what we would like to have.

The first question is whether the site has any connection with or relation to the scrolls. Is the proximity of the site and the scrolls simply happenstance? If the Donceels are right, the answer is yes.

But the Donceels are not the only scholars who would dissociate the scrolls and the site. Professor Norman Golb of the University of Chicago believes the scrolls were brought from Jerusalem to the Judean wilderness for safekeeping when Jerusalem was threatened by Roman legions. As previously noted, the First Jewish Revolt against Rome began in 66 A.D. and effectively ended with the destruction of the so-called Second Temple and the burning of

Jerusalem in 70 A.D. According to ancient literary sources, the Romans destroyed the region around Jericho in 68 A.D. The destruction of Qumran is generally thought to have been carried out by the Roman legions at the same time. In Golb's view, Qumran was a Judean military fortress which, like Jerusalem, was destroyed in battle with the Romans.[11]

Two Australian scholars, Alan Crown and Lena Cansdale, argue that Qumran was really a commercial entrepôt, a rest stop for people involved in the vigorous Dead Sea traffic transporting bitumen (asphalt), salt, and other commodities, as well as for pilgrims and other travelers.[12] Because of its high salt content, the Dead Sea can carry ships with heavier loads than can less saline waters. More important, the Dead Sea blocks cross-country routes from the Mediterranean coast to Transjordan and beyond. In ancient times, traffic had to either skirt the Dead Sea (at that time the water level was sixty-five to eighty feet higher than it is today because so much water is now taken from the Jordan River, which feeds it) or use a shortcut—the surface of the Dead Sea itself. This shortcut was especially critical for material coming from or going to Jerusalem; the valleys east of Jerusalem lead directly to the Dead Sea area. Qumran served the needs of this traffic, according to Crown and Cansdale. The site had nothing to do with the scrolls, they say.

Until recently, most scholars agreed with de Vaux—that Qumran was the home of an isolated religious community—and the majority of scholars still back de Vaux. But this interpretation is increasingly subject to debate.

It is nevertheless widely recognized that, as Philip Davies puts it, "the excavators were led to certain expectations from the [ancient] literature. Accounts by the historian Josephus and Pliny the Elder about the Jewish sect of the Essenes and the contents of the Community Rule (1QS) [The Manual of Discipline] gave a prior testimony to the ancient inhabitants."[13] In other words, what the excavators expected to find, they found.

Their expectations may also have been molded by their own religious backgrounds. Davies continues, "Both de Vaux and Milik, as well as many other early commentators on Qumran, were Catholic priests. Otherwise, how could the site be described as a monastery? . . . Had the scrolls not been found in the nearby caves, would the Qumran ruins have been interpreted as such? . . . Whether there was ever such a thing as a Jewish monastery [before the third century A.D.] I simply don't know, but the excavated structures were interpreted with this idea in mind."[14]

Of course a major building block in de Vaux's position is the belief that the scrolls themselves are an Essene library. But can the scrolls be connected with Qumran? The first and most obvious connection is that the scrolls were found very near the site. While Cave 1 is almost a mile north of Qumran, a number of other caves with inscriptional materials, especially Cave 4, are almost part of the site. The easiest entry to Cave 4 is from the site, over a finger of marl terrace barely two hundred yards from the Qumran wall. On the other hand, Cave 4 can also be entered from the wadi. Though this entry seems forbidding, I had little trouble negotiating it. The sandstone is extremely friable and easily provides a foothold. In any event, the proximity of Cave 4 to the ruins of Qumran suggests a connection, but it is hardly conclusive.

The pottery found in the caves and at the site also suggests a connection. Examples of the peculiarly shaped jars in which some of the scrolls were stored in the caves were also found at Qumran. This pottery obviously came from Qumran, and de Vaux actually found the kiln where much of the pottery was fired. But does the fact that whoever placed the scrolls in the caves used pottery from Qumran establish the kind of connection we are talking about? Perhaps the pottery was simply purchased from a nearby vendor. Moreover, the pottery in itself does not indicate that the settlement was an isolated religious community, despite the fact that it is, for the most part, rough, inelegant ware.

What about the scriptorium?

De Vaux's notion that the objects he found in the room were writing desks (or tables) was questioned long ago, even before the Donceels declared the tables benches. It now seems clear that de

Vaux not only hastily concluded that the objects were desks but also arranged to have them displayed in a way that fit the hypothesis. The artifacts he interpreted as desks are trapezoidal objects made of mud-brick and rubble covered with a plaster shell. Originally each stood less than eighteen inches high—pretty low for a writing desk. The desk I am sitting at stands twenty-eight inches above the floor. We know the original height of the Qumran "desks" because on one of them a portion of the plaster has survived from top to bottom, curving where it merges into the floor surface.[15] In the museum exhibit featuring these "desks," however, they were mounted on metal frames, as a result of which the surface of the "desk" stood twenty-six inches above the ground, a bare two inches below the height of my writing desk.

The objects on which de Vaux believed the scribes sat were similarly elevated. The height of these "benches" varied between about eight and ten inches. In the museum exhibit, however, the "bench" was mounted so that it stood over thirteen inches high. It was later shown from a reconstructed model that it would be almost impossible to write on the trapezoidally shaped desks while sitting on the supposed benches. Were he to sit on such a low bench, the scribe's knees would be above the desk. "He would be most uncomfortably doubled over trying to write on the [supposed desk], his arms necessarily encircling the obstructing knees. . . . There is no conceivable posture of the scribal knees and feet that would permit the table to stand sufficiently close for writing."[16]

Moreover, it is very unlikely that scribes used writing tables at this time. In Byzantine paintings, the evangelists are shown seated, writing on their laps. They are never shown writing on tables. Although these paintings were made hundreds of years later, "it would be contrary to logic," a scholar has noted, "to argue that such a convenience [a writing desk], once contrived, might have been forgotten or discarded."[17]

The museum exhibit that presented these objects as desks has long been dismantled, although a photograph of the exhibit is frequently used even now; indeed, we have reprinted it here. As pre-

Caves 4 and 5 (side by side in the cliffs in the center of the photograph).

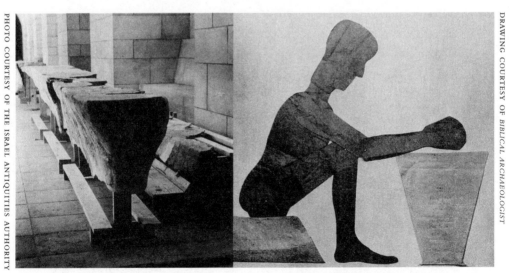

Few scholars would now defend the reconstruction of these puzzling installations as desks, as pictured here in the Rockefeller Museum.

Scribes would have had to sit in an impossibly awkward position to use the "writing desks" in the "scriptorium.".

viously noted, what de Vaux regarded as desks, the Donceels interpreted as benches in a Roman-style triclinium, or dining room.
Like many of the Donceels' suggestions, this has not held up, however. These supposed triclinium benches are only a foot and a half
wide. "This is far too narrow," a prominent archaeologist has
noted, "for a sofa or bed of any kind, let alone for that of a
triclinium. A triclinium bed was made for comfortable reclining
and, occasionally, for accommodating more than one person."[18]
At the only other site in Israel where a triclinium has been found,
the benches are nearly six feet wide.[19] In addition, these strange
installations at Qumran taper down, so that the base is sometimes
as narrow as seven inches. This would hardly make a stable sofa
or bed.

This furniture remains a puzzle. One scholar has suggested that
they are seats on which the scribes sat.[20] Another argues they were
indeed tables, but not for writing; perhaps the scribes kept their
inkwells and pens here.[21] Still another suggestion is that the objects
were tables used to prepare the skins for writing by cutting rule-
lines vertically or horizontally.[22]

Since the objects seem clearly not to be reclining sofas, it is unlikely that the second-story room from which they fell (they were
found on top of a destruction layer that seemed to have come from
the collapse of the floor above) was a triclinium. But was the
room, even without desks, a scriptorium? True, de Vaux found
two inkwells in the room. But do two inkwells necessarily indicate
a scriptorium? To confuse matters further, he found a third inkwell
in an adjoining room. Moreover, at least three other inkwells that
have surfaced on the antiquities market are supposed to have come
from Qumran.[23] Yet not a single fragment of a leather or papyrus
manuscript was found in the excavation, let alone in the supposed
scriptorium. Strange? Other organic materials were found in the
excavation, including wood, reeds, and palm leaves.

Conversely, if the scrolls had come from the settlement at Qumran, we would expect to find among them more mundane, nonlit-
erary documents, such as contracts, letters, bills of sale, leases,

The room de Vaux identified as the scriptorium.
On the rubble of the collapsed second floor he found two inkwells,
from which he concluded that the scrolls were copied here.

court documents. Similar documents have been found in other caves up and down the Jordan Valley, placed there by local refugees in time of strife. Did the Qumranites have no such documents? Why were few, if any, found in the Qumran caves if the scrolls were placed in the caves by people living at Qumran?

The large room that de Vaux called a refectory or dining room does seem to be a place where a large group of people ate from rather rough pottery tableware. Does this indicate an isolated religious community? Could it instead have served travelers and pilgrims on their way to or from Jerusalem? Pottery of finer quality was also found at the site. Could this have been for the pleasure of those who could afford better?

De Vaux divided the occupation of the site into five principal phases:

The earliest occupation was during the Iron Age, in about the eighth or seventh century B.C. De Vaux dates a round cistern (locus 110) to this period. The site was abandoned and then reoccupied only in the second century B.C. (Period 1a). This small settlement greatly expanded in the first century B.C. (Period 1b). Even de Vaux admits that the distinction between Period 1a and Period 1b is unclear.[24] Many archaeologists reject the distinction entirely.[25] And knowledgeable archaeologists now argue that the site was settled not as early as 150 B.C. but more likely about 100 B.C. or even later.[26]

In 31 B.C. an earthquake devastated the area. The extent of damage at Qumran is, again, hotly disputed.[27] According to de Vaux, Qumran was abandoned as a result of the earthquake, to be reoccupied only in 4 B.C. (Period 2). Many scholars now believe, however, that there was little, if any, break in occupation.[28] The site was destroyed in 68 A.D. by the Roman army on its advance toward Jerusalem.

The idea that the site was destroyed in 68 A.D. is based largely on the account in Josephus, rather than on de Vaux's excavation. Josephus tells us that on the Roman equivalent of June 20, 68 A.D., the future emperor Vespasian reached Jericho, where he was joined by Trajan, father of the future emperor of that name, then one of Vespasian's generals and commander of the Tenth Legion. Most of the inhabitants of Jericho had fled. Those who remained were put to death.[29] Vespasian camped at Jericho, as troops were gradually poised at various points around the country in preparation for the final assault two years later on Jerusalem.[30] Roman arrowheads found in the excavation of Qumran support the conclusion that the site succumbed in 68 A.D.[31] And the latest date on coins from the site also supports a Roman destruction at this time.[32]

Thereafter, the site was occupied briefly, according to de Vaux, by a detachment of Roman soldiers surveilling the Dead Sea and perhaps, again briefly, during the Second Jewish Revolt (132–35 A.D.), either by Jewish rebels or by Roman soldiers.

Interest in the site naturally focuses on the periods contemporaneous with the scrolls. In the absence of a final report that provides enough information for an archaeologist to draw reasonably reliable conclusions, the best speculation I have heard concerning the site's development is that (as yet unpublished) of Israeli archaeologist Yizhar Hirschfeld. He believes that initially the site was occupied by a squarish fortress-type structure, which can be easily identified on the plan (see page 109); its multistoried tower still stands in the northwest corner of the site. The tower provided security to the inhabitants in case of attack and architecturally expressed the owner's dominion over the area.

One factor strongly suggesting, at least to me, that the initial phase of the second century B.C. settlement at Qumran involved only the square fortress-type building is a comparison with a similar structure at nearby Ein Feshkha, a mere two miles south of Qumran on the shore of the Dead Sea. This contemporaneous settlement was undoubtedly affiliated with Qumran (a wall may actually have connected the two sites).[33] Unlike Qumran, however, Ein Feshka is watered by several small springs, as well as one large spring. It probably subsisted mostly on agriculture, date palms, port facilities, and bitumen. The major structure at Ein Feshkha is almost a twin of the proposed initial squarish structure at Qumran.

The Ein Feshkha structure has a central courtyard, which, on first impression, seems not to be the case at Qumran. Where we expect to find the central courtyard in the squarish structure at Qumran we find instead walls forming interior spaces (loci 23–25, 32–37). But unlike the other walls of the Qumran structure, which are straight, of uniform width, and at right angles to one another, the walls where one would expect to find the Qumran courtyard are of various widths and sometimes come in at odd angles, as can be seen on de Vaux's own plan. Often they don't form enclosed spaces (rooms).[34] In short, it looks as if these walls were added later.

Surely there is nothing in the Ein Feshkha structure suggesting that it was the home of a religious community. De Vaux was nevertheless able to see such an indication in the architecture of the site: "This building [at Ein Feshkha] was clearly not a private residence, but was suited to the needs of a religious community," he wrote.[35] Again, what he wanted to find, he found.

Hirschfeld sensibly argues that the buildings outside the square fortress at Qumran were added sometime after the fortress was built. Such fortified outposts were common at the time, according to Hirschfeld, and were not necessarily military. Later, during the reign of Herod the Great, says Hirschfeld, when the outbuildings were added, the entire complex served as an administrative settlement for Herod's governor during a period of peace and stability. The plan of the site in this phase can hardly be interpreted as a military installation. Is it possible that the site became an Essene settlement only in a later phase—after the earthquake, at which time the buildings outside the square fortress were added?[36]

What about the extensive water system with elaborately connected cisterns and *miqva'ot* (ritual baths)? Do these establish de Vaux's contention that the site was a religious commune? One

The tower in the northwest corner of the core structure at Qumran. A glacis at the base provides greater stability.

The fault line in this miqveh *may have been caused by an earthquake in 31 B.C., leading to a temporary abandonment of the site.*

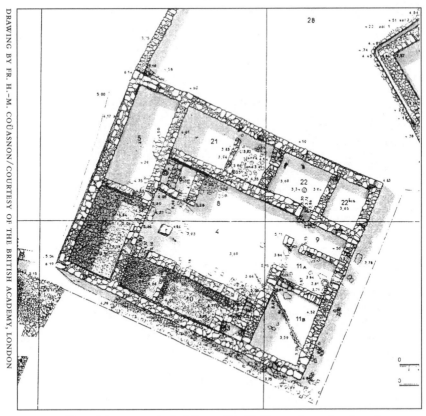

Plan of the rectangular building at Ein Feshka similar to the plan of the core building at Qumran.

scholar, Bryant Wood, assuming that two hundred people lived at Qumran, actually computed the amount of water needed for normal living and bathing and compared this with the amount of water available at Qumran. He even calculated how much the donkeys would drink and how much water would be lost by evaporation. He concluded: "More than twice the required amount [of water] was available,"[37] and therefore he believes there was much ritual bathing at Qumran.

Yizhar Hirschfeld, however, comes to the opposite conclusion: "This is a considerable quantity of water," he admits, "but not unusual in comparison to the quantities of water that were collected at other desert fortresses in the region. . . . Actually, the water capacity at Qumran is small relative to the water capacity of other desert fortresses."[38]

But suppose that there was a lot of ritual bathing going on at Qumran. This would certainly be consistent with its identification as an Essene site. Josephus and others indicate that the Essenes purified themselves in ritual baths. However, other Jews also used ritual baths; Jerusalem at this time was pockmarked with them.

There is no question that Qumran was a Jewish site. The only inscriptional materials found in the excavation of the site itself were some ostraca, pieces of pottery used as notepaper. Most of these ostraca are in Hebrew and contain Jewish names. In short, the site was occupied by Jews; about this there is no contention. Thus, even the presence of ritual baths is not conclusive evidence of an isolated religious community, but simply indicates the presence of a Jewish community.

Since there are no springs at Qumran and the rainfall is less than four inches a year—and in some years not even that—all of which occurs within ten to twenty days,[39] one might wonder how Qumran actually got so much water (one hundred thousand liters a year, according to one estimate).[40]

The answer is: carefully collected runoff. The Wadi Qumran, which the site overlooks to the north, runs into the Dead Sea.

Looking up the wadi with the sea behind, one can easily imagine water flowing through it two or three times a year for millions of years, creating a sandy floor as the sandstone marl wore away. The wadi aprons out as it approaches the sea; from a height, one can still see the patterns of the water flow in the desert sands. But this sandy wadi ends abruptly less than half a mile in from the shore. There a hiker will hit the high, hard, vertically ascending limestone cliffs. Water doesn't seep easily into these limestone formations; when it rains, much of the water flows over the limestone surface toward the sea, dropping off toward the end of the Wadi Qumran in a giant cascade onto a lower level, where it forms a pool; when the pool fills, the water continues down into the wadi and eventually into the Dead Sea.

The water system at Qumran siphons water from this natural pool into a channel that curves around the cliff and into the site. Through this aqueduct, the water fills the cisterns one by one, supplying the site with abundant water in the midst of the desert wilderness—an elaborate engineering feat indeed.

The cemeteries adjoining the Qumran site also raise questions. As noted earlier, of the approximately fifty graves that were excavated, only three or four were those of women and children. Does this indicate the celibacy of the community? The presence of some women and children, it could be argued, shows just the opposite.

The number of individual graves raises another puzzling question: How does it happen that so many people—over twelve hundred individual graves are carefully laid out in closely ordered rows—are buried here? Each of the tombs is marked by an oval-shaped heap of stones on the ground surface, often with a larger stone at either end. With one exception, the tombs are all oriented north/south. Each grave consists of a rectangular cavity between four and six feet deep, at the bottom of which another cavity was dug, usually in the eastern wall, creating an underground shelf where the body was laid on its back, head pointing south, with hands at the sides or folded over the pelvis. The lower side-cavity where the body was laid was then sealed with mud bricks or stones and the rest of the grave shaft filled in. Finally, the cairn was added on top.

Cemeteries of this magnitude and order suggest a highly organized administration over a long period of time, but if two hundred people worked and lived at Qumran at any one time, that was a lot.[41] Why, then, so many graves? Do the cemeteries suggest that a religious group controlled the site? The lack of any typical military grave goods seems to rule out contingents of soldiers. (The carefully arranged rows of individual burials rule out the suggestion that the graves were the result of a military confrontation.)

Finally, the reference in Pliny the Elder saying that Ein Gedi lies below (literally, "underneath these," *infra hos*) an Essene settlement is also not conclusive. Those who rely on this statement take it to mean that Ein Gedi lies south of an Essene settlement, and it does lie south of Qumran. In ancient times, however, "below" did not mean "south." The ancients had words for north, south, east, and west, and Pliny used them—but he did not use "south" here.[42]

There is general agreement among scholars who have studied the problem that *infra hos* does not mean "south of." There is less agreement as to precisely what it does mean in this context. According to the Australian scholars Crown and Cansdale, "When Pliny said 'below,' he meant just that, at an altitude lower than something else."[43]

Several scholars have studied the problem, with inconclusive results,[44] but more than one suggestion points to a site higher up in the cliffs above Ein Gedi for the location of the Essene settlement Pliny refers to, rather than at Qumran. I discussed the problem with Professor Glen Bowersock of the Institute for Advanced Study in Princeton, formerly chairman of the Classics Department at Harvard University. Like other experts, Bowersock agrees that *infra hos* does not indicate "south of." "[Crown and Cansdale]

Traces of a waterfall can be seen in this photo of limestone cliffs behind the settlement. A few floods each year provided the settlement with abundant water.

Small heaps of stones mark each grave in a large cemetery adjoining the Qumran settlement.

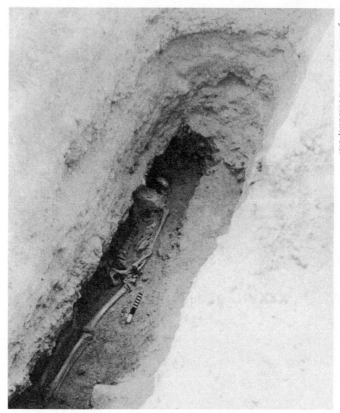

A skeleton in situ *on a shelf at the bottom of a Qumran shaft tomb.*

Nearly twelve hundred graves, each marked by a stone cairn, are arranged in neat rows in the Qumran cemeteries.

seem to me absolutely right in denying that *infra* means 'south' in the crucial phrase," he wrote me.[45] But Bowersock also rejects the idea that it means literally "below"—at least not here. "I do not believe, as of now, that the word is used here or (I suspect) any-where in geographical contexts to describe relative elevation. Of course, in other contexts it can be so used (e.g., 'I am standing below the window.')."[46]

Most likely, he told me, *infra* indicates location relative to a body of water.[47] As it happens, Bowersock is studying the problem as it arises in a Greek context. *Infra,* or "below" (and the Greek equiv-alent), probably indicates relative position in relation to a sea or a river flow; the closer position is *infra.*[48] In his helpful letter, Bow-ersock wrote, "I suspect that the traditional terms for Egypt (Upper and Lower Egypt) point to the solution: Upper Egypt is southern Egypt, Lower is northern. The reason is distance from the sea on a north-south axis."

If the Dead Sea is the referent body of water in the passage from Pliny, then he is saying that Ein Gedi is *infra,* lower, or nearer the sea, than the Essene settlement.

On the other hand, if the Jordan River is the referent, south would indeed be lower, downstream, for the Jordan (unlike the Nile) flows north to south.

Whether Pliny uses *infra* to express relative altitude or relative distance from the Dead Sea, he seems to be saying that the Essene settlement is located in the cliffs above Ein Gedi, and this would rule out Qumran. But if the referent is the Jordan River (as de Vaux himself suggested[49]), then Qumran might still qualify. De Vaux also notes, correctly, that after Ein Gedi, Pliny refers to Masada ("*inde,* on leaving this, Masada").[50] Pliny seems to be de-scribing sites going from north to south. This, too, seems to sug-gest that the Essene settlement lies north of Ein Gedi.

The location of Ein Gedi is well known: It lies at the bottom of the cliffs near the Dead Sea shore twenty miles south of Qumran. De Vaux knew of the possibility that *infra hos* might refer to an Essene settlement in the cliffs above Ein Gedi, but he was not aware of any site that would fit this description.[51] So he chose Qumran, a conclusion he naturally favored, as he had excavated it. He admits, however, that the "particular passage in Pliny is not *in itself* decisive."[52] Only the scrolls themselves will make the point.

Contrary to de Vaux, there are some archaeological remains above Ein Gedi, which the local kibbutzniks call "the Essene village."[53] Excavation might well disclose whether these remains meet the requirements of Pliny's description.[54]

Another factor: Over 1,200 coins were found in the Qumran excavations. By comparison, a mere 144 were found at Ein Feshkha. Does this suggest that Qumran was a commercial center, rather than the site of an austere religious community?[55]

In the Qumran buildings, no space can be identified as a synagogue. But according to Philo, on the Sabbath the Essenes "proceed to sacred spots which they call synagogues."[56] Contrary to a common assumption, there were many synagogues in Palestine before the destruction of the Temple. The Gospels tell us Jesus attended the synagogue in Capernaum. Paul, according to his letters, which date to before the destruction, went from synagogue to synagogue in the diaspora. The Talmud mentions that even while the Temple stood there was a synagogue on the Temple Mount, and there were surely many more in the city itself. A plaque from one of these Jerusalem synagogues (the Theodotus inscription) has been recovered in an excavation, and archaeologists have uncovered at least three synagogue buildings from before the Roman destruction of the Jerusalem Temple. Two of the three are at wilderness sites not far from Qumran—at Herodion and at Masada.

There is no indication that Qumran had a synagogue. A circular area in the room de Vaux called the refectory was paved, in contrast to the rest of the floor, which was plastered, but this is hardly enough to mark the room as a synagogue, and even de Vaux did not claim otherwise.[57]

Although Masada was originally built by Herod the Great as a mountain fortress/palace, it was later occupied by a militant Jewish faction during the Great Revolt against Rome (66–70 A.D.). Indeed, these Jews held out until 73 or 74, though Jerusalem fell in 70, and they remodeled the synagogue at the site. Moreover, there is no question that the building was used for this purpose, at least during its later phase, during the revolt, because scrolls (or scroll fragments) were found buried under the floor of the synagogue. Here, apparently, was the synagogue's *genizah,*[58] or repository for worn-out sacred texts.

One of these Masada scroll fragments is known as the Songs of the Sabbath Sacrifice. A copy in more complete condition has also been found at Qumran. It is curious that the text would turn up at both places. The Jews who defended Masada were a fiercely militant group. The Essenes were said to be pacifists. In his description of the Essenes, Philo says: "As for darts, javelins, daggers, or the helmet, breastplate or shield, you could not find a single manufacturer of them, nor, in general, any person making weapons or engines or plying any industry concerned with war."[59] The Songs of the Sabbath Sacrifice is sometimes identified as one of the sectarian documents that seem to relate the scrolls to the Essenes. If so, what was it doing at Masada? How can a text that was used by these militants serve as evidence of an Essene connection?

All in all, considering only the archaeological evidence, if it weren't for the proximity of the scrolls to Qumran we would never think of Qumran as the site of an isolated *religious* community— and certainly not as the home of the Essenes.

CHAPTER 8

AN UNCERTAIN CONCLUSION

Whether Qumran was an Essene settlement and whether the Dead Sea Scrolls are an Essene library remain vexed questions. My own conclusion, despite many misgivings, is that it probably was an Essene settlement with an Essene library.

In 1966, Frank Cross unequivocally concluded that Essenes inhabited Qumran and were responsible for the scrolls. Here are his words:

> The scholar who would "exercise caution" in identifying the sect of Qumran with the Essenes places himself in an astonishing position: He must suggest seriously that two major parties formed communalistic religious communities in the same district of the desert of the Dead Sea and lived together in effect for two centuries, holding similar bizarre views, performing similar or rather identical lustrations, ritual meals, and ceremonies. He must suppose that one [the Essenes], carefully described by classical authors [like Josephus and Philo], disappeared without leaving building remains or even potsherds behind; the other [the inhabitants of Qumran], systematically ignored by the classical sources, left extensive ruins, and indeed a great library. I prefer to be reckless and flatly identify the men of Qumran with their perennial houseguests, the Essenes.[1]

In 1992, a leading younger Dead Sea Scroll scholar, James C. VanderKam of the University of Notre Dame, wrote that "most scholars would agree with Frank Cross's forceful statement."[2]

I admire Cross and VanderKam, but I must agree with Oxford don Martin Goodman, who has recently remarked, "The Essene hypothesis of Qumran origins is much less probable than is usually proposed."[3]

VanderKam maintains that the Manual of Discipline is "the most important Qumran text" in deciding these questions. Yet the introduction to the most recent authoritative edition of the Manual of Discipline (which this edition calls the Rule of the Community) does not even suggest the possibility that it is an Essene document.[4]

VanderKam bases his "identification of the Dead Sea Scroll community as Essene . . . primarily on two kinds of data: (1) evidence from the Roman geographer Pliny the Elder, and (2) the contents of the scrolls themselves as compared with Josephus' and others' descriptions of Essene beliefs and practices."[5]

But, as we have seen, Pliny's reference to Ein Gedi as "lying below" (*infra hos*) an Essene settlement is ambiguous. VanderKam states, "The only place on the west side of the Dead Sea north of Ein Gedi where archaeological remains of a communal center were found is Qumran."[6] Recognizing that some scholars have argued that "lying below" actually refers to altitude rather than direction and that Pliny is actually saying that there is an Essene settlement above—at a higher altitude than—Ein Gedi, VanderKam says that "there was no settlement at that location." In this he errs. As mentioned earlier, there are ancient remains above Ein Gedi—the so-called Essene Village—that have never been excavated.

Moreover, we don't know all the sites in the area. The only recent archaeological survey was done by a dedicated, knowledgeable, well-meaning archaeologist named Pesach Bar-Adon, who, however, did not proceed according to modern surveying principles. As Martin Goodman has noted, "Numerous other sites could emerge at any time in areas still insufficiently explored."[7]

Here are my conclusions:

1. Given the caves' propinquity to the site, the scrolls are almost surely associated with Qumran, but they did not necessarily belong to the inhabitants of the site. With the cooperation of the people who lived at Qumran, the scrolls may have been brought to the area from elsewhere for safekeeping.

The three inkwells de Vaux found, however, do suggest that at least some of the scrolls were copied at the site. Several more inkwells that have appeared on the antiquities market are said to have come from Qumran (perhaps stolen by workers or somehow obtained by John Allegro, one of the original members of the publication team, from an antiquities dealer). It would be hard to find another contemporaneous site with so many inkwells.[8]

In the winter of 1996 a Hebrew ostracon (an inscribed potsherd) was discovered at Qumran, and it has just been deciphered by Harvard's Frank Cross and Esther Eshel of Hebrew University.[9] Cross and Eshel interpret it as a transfer by an applicant for membership in the community, pursuant to his oath. According to Cross and Eshel, it records a gift of a slave and an estate (a house, plus fig and olive trees) by a neophyte of the sect to the *yahad,* the word for "community" that the scrolls use for the close-knit membership group associated with the texts. If the interpretation by Cross and Eshel is correct, this is powerful evidence linking the site to the scrolls. But their interpretation has already been challenged. They themselves cautiously say their reading "seems to be without serious objection," but they indicate that only one of the three Hebrew letters (the last) that compose the word "is certain." At least one prominent Israeli scholar, Ada Yardeni, has proposed a different reading.[10]

In any event, to me it seems extremely unlikely that a relatively small wilderness settlement like Qumran would have its own exclusive library of more than eight hundred scrolls, the equivalent of as many books, but that many have been found there, and probably at least as many have not survived. This would have been an enormous library in ancient times. It is unlikely that this library was the permanent possession of the inhabitants of Qumran.

That the scrolls were not written at Qumran is also suggested by the extremely large number of scribal hands represented among the surviving manuscripts. While no systematic study has yet been made, scholars have identified only three scribal hands that appear in more than one scroll. Together, those three wrote fewer than a dozen scrolls.[11] Undoubtedly these numbers will increase with further study, but nonetheless, the fact that hundreds of scribes produced these documents tends to refute the notion that they were produced at Qumran.

The area around Qumran, the Judean wilderness, has always been a place of refuge and hiding—for people, treasure, and documents. David fled to this arid wilderness—to Ein Gedi, to be precise—pursued by King Saul, who, when he had to relieve himself, entered the very cave where David was hiding; David, however, refrained from killing the Lord's anointed, but cut off the hem of Saul's cloak as he defecated to prove that he could have killed him if he had wanted to (1 Samuel 24). Even closer to Qumran than Ein Gedi is the so-called Cave of the Treasure, where, thousands of years before David's time, unidentified Chalcolithic people hid a treasure of finely worked bronze and ivory artifacts, including crowns, scepters, and standards.[12] Long after David's time Bar Kokhba warriors of the Second Jewish Revolt (132–35 A.D.) left some of their most important wartime correspondence in a nearby cave.[13] Samaritan refugees fleeing the armies of Alexander the Great in the fourth century B.C. hid in a cave in the Wadi Daliyeh north of Jericho; they were apparently discovered and then asphyxiated by a fire set at the mouth of the cave, which left their skeletons and worm-eaten documents to be discovered in the 1960s by the same tribe of bedouin that initially discovered the

Dead Sea Scrolls.[14] These are not the only examples, but they are enough to make the point that it is not unusual to find documents brought from elsewhere hidden in these caves.

2. The ruins of Qumran are probably those of an isolated religious community. The most persuasive evidence for this is the very long room (70 by 15 feet) adjacent to a pantry containing over a thousand crude, unpainted, undecorated plates and bowls that have no pretensions to elegance. The room (Locus 77) must have been a dining room.

Then there are the cemeteries—over twelve hundred graves, each carefully marked with a discrete oval cairn. With very few exceptions, these graves have the same characteristics, which certainly suggests religious uniformity.

How are the dining room and the cemeteries to be interpreted? Perhaps the dining room was there to serve travelers passing through. Perhaps the graves were needed for the inhabitants of the site over hundreds of years. Perhaps it was the cemetery for the entire area. Perhaps other sites had cemeteries like this, but they have not survived—or been found. However, these ideas are speculative. The most likely explanation is that the dining room and the graves suggest a communal habitation. The fact that there are no apparent residential areas within the confines of the settlement means that most of the inhabitants probably lived in tents or caves. Indeed, very recent excavations seem to confirm this. What appears to be evidence for tent pegs has been found near the site, as have paths leading to caves in which the inhabitants may have lived.[15] All this suggests that Qumran was a religious community of some kind, whose members ate together in modest surroundings, rather than a manor house or a commercial entrepôt or a villa rustica.

In 1997 a Dead Sea Scroll exhibit in Utah displayed a unique bronze altar said to have come from Qumran, which is now in the hands of a private collector.[16] The altar is listed in the exhibit as

Father Josef T. Milik with thousands of pots and goblets in the pantry adjacent to the Qumran dining room.

having been purchased from Kando by John Allegro, who was in Jerusalem at the time of the excavations. It is a strange-looking object that is without parallel and may well be a fake, yet it must at least be mentioned, for if it is genuine and does come from Qumran, it too suggests that Qumran was a religious settlement.

That the site was likely to have been a communal religious settlement does not, however, necessarily identify it as Essene. The site is consistent with such a conclusion, but does not require it. In the end, the Essene hypothesis must rest on the scrolls.

3. Some of the scrolls were written a century before the earliest post–Iron Age settlement at Qumran was established and must have been brought from elsewhere. Others, such as the biblical scrolls, are obviously not Essene documents.

The Essene hypothesis ultimately rests on those documents that have been identified as sectarian, that is, as reflecting a consistent, identifiable religious viewpoint.

There is in fact some convergence between the scrolls and the description of the Essenes in Josephus and Philo, in matters both large and small—for example, the rule forbidding spitting, to which Josephus refers. But there are also obvious divergences. For example, Josephus tells us that the Essenes held their property in common, whereas the Damascus Document (14.13) says that the sectarians should give two days' earnings each month for the poor, the sick, and the orphaned. The Essenes are supposed to have been peace-loving, yet a violent military confrontation is described in the so-called War Scroll (see Chapter 10). They are supposed not to have owned slaves, yet the Damascus Document (12.10) says that they cannot *sell* their servants to Gentiles.

Much of the convergence between the scrolls and the ancient descriptions of the Essenes relates to characteristics that are shared by many other Jewish groups—an initiation process for membership, the role of fate, predeterminism, asceticism, an apocalyptic outlook. The ancient sources refer to numerous Jewish groups about which little is known—the Zealots, the Sicarii, nascent Christians, Judeo-Christians, Hasidim, the Therapeutae, the Boethusians, the Hellenes, the Herodians, the ascetic Judaism of Bannus, the Samaritans, and so on. Doubtless there were many other such groups about whom we know nothing, not even their names. A Rabbinic source tells us that there were at least twenty-four groups of heretics within Judaism before the Roman destruction of the Temple in 70 A.D.[17] Each of these groups regarded itself as embodying the true meaning of scripture and as preserving the true heritage of ancient Israel. The features supposedly identifying the scrolls as Essene could also be characteristic of some other group of Jews, known or unknown.

Neither Josephus nor Philo nor any other ancient author tells us that the Essenes used a different calendar and observed Jewish holidays on a different day from other Jews. If the Essenes did observe Jewish holidays on a different date, that would be a defining characteristic of extraordinary importance. Yet no hint of this is found in the ancient descriptions of the Essenes. But the scrolls make it abundantly clear that the sect did indeed have a different calendar—a solar calendar unlike Judaism's standard lunar calendar.

Moreover, the sectarian scrolls themselves do not refer to their group as Essenes.

Finally, we must be careful not to read into the ancient sources or the scrolls something that isn't there. For example, neither Josephus nor the scrolls say that Essenes lived in the wilderness. Though they separated themselves from other Jews, they did not necessarily leave Jerusalem or other towns where they lived.

Judaism was deeply splintered at this time; some Jewish groups have left no trace. The viewpoints of other Jewish groups, those we know about, overlapped considerably. For example, both the Manual of Discipline and the Gospels quote Isaiah on the subject of going into the desert to prepare a way for the Lord; yet we can't conclude from this that the scroll community included early Christians who had a communal redoubt in the wilderness.

Martin Goodman has put the matter well: "The Dead Sea sectarians had many important preoccupations in common with other contemporary Jews, such as biblical interpretation, eschatology, *halakha* [religious law] and purity; the similarities should not surprise, since all forms of first-century Judaism derived ultimately from the Torah and were subjected to similar cultural and social influences. . . . The details which have led scholars to identify the Qumran sectarians with other Jewish groups can be most plausibly explained by the common origin of all such groups in first-century Judaism."[18]

Yet, if we must identify the Dead Sea Scrolls with any known group, the Essenes do seem the closest. I once asked the late Jonas Greenfield of Hebrew University whether he would agree that the scrolls were, if not Essene, at least Essenic. "Well," he replied, "Essenoid."

Kyle McCarter of Johns Hopkins University has suggested another way of concluding that the sectarian scrolls might be attributed to the Essenes: by excluding other known groups. The apocalyptic character of the scrolls, for example, eliminates the two major groups Josephus refers to, the Pharisees and the Sadducees (even though, like the Sadducees, the Qumran sectarians were of priestly descent).[19]

For all these reasons, if I had to pick one group with whom to associate the scrolls, it would be the Essenes—but I am by no means sure of this conclusion. One way some scholars are creating a little "wiggle room" in support of the Essene hypothesis is by suggesting that the people from Qumran might have been a kind of Essene group who were not quite like the Essenes described by the ancient authors.

4. If the library was brought to Qumran, as seems likely, given the variety of scribal hands and the number of documents, there is little doubt that it came from Jerusalem. Jerusalem was obviously the place, a day's walk from Qumran, where a library of this mag-

nitude would be maintained. The most likely date when the scrolls may have been taken to the caves for safekeeping is sometime after 66 A.D., when Jerusalem was threatened by the First Jewish Revolt against Rome.

Norman Golb of the University of Chicago argues that the scrolls were in fact the Temple library.[20] But the documents themselves fairly refute this idea. There is not a single Pharisaic or Sadducean document in the collection, and these were the two most prominent groups controlling the Temple hierarchy during the period of the scrolls. Indeed, the scrolls express frequent opposition to the Jerusalem Temple.

I believe the library belonged to another group, perhaps the Essenes of Jerusalem (who lived near the Essene Gate)—or perhaps some other group whom we cannot identify.

That there are other possibilities cannot be denied. But none carries much conviction. We are left with mere speculation. Anyone can play the game. The uncertainties will remain—until, perhaps, new evidence surfaces.

CHAPTER 9

UNDERMINING
THE JEWISH BIBLE

The Dead Sea Scrolls include the oldest copies of biblical
books ever discovered. Some two hundred different biblical
manuscripts have been identified among the scrolls, the earliest
from the mid-third century B.C., the latest from the mid-first century A.D. A Qumran fragment from the book of Daniel, the latest
of the Hebrew scriptures, dates to the late second century B.C.,
barely fifty years after it was composed, closer to the date of the
original autograph than any other text of the Hebrew Bible ever
discovered.

Yet the subject of the scrolls' relationship to the biblical text is
often ignored. For one thing, fragmentary biblical texts can be
much more easily reconstructed than previously unknown texts
because complete copies of biblical texts serve as a kind of template onto which missing parts of fragmentary biblical scrolls can
be fitted.

Although the biblical texts among the Dead Sea Scrolls are a
thousand years older than the oldest extant Hebrew Bible, they indicate that, all in all, modern copies are amazingly accurate. There
are relatively few discrepancies between the Qumran biblical texts
and later ones. Nevertheless, numerous relatively minor changes—

and some not so minor—have been incorporated into new Bible translations as a result of comparisons with Dead Sea Scroll biblical texts.

In one case an entire paragraph has been recovered from a Qumran manuscript—from the opening of Chapter 11 of the First Book of Samuel, which recounts a siege by the Ammonite king Nahash of the Israelite city of Jabesh-Gilead. The standard Hebrew text gives no reason for this Ammonite attack and reveals only that the Israelites asked for terms of surrender. Nahash's terms were harsh; he would relieve the siege and permit the Israelites to live only if they agreed to let him gouge out the right eyes of their men. No reason is given for this cruelty. The Hebrew text of Samuel found among the Dead Sea Scrolls is fragmentary, but it explains why the Ammonite king Nahash decided to attack Jabesh-Gilead and why he imposed such cruel terms for surrender rather than death.

Ammon lies east of the Jordan, in land allotted to the Israelite tribes of Reuben and Gad. Nahash regarded this land as his. The added material from the Qumran text explains that he viewed the Israelite inhabitants as rebels, for whom blinding was standard punishment in ancient times.[1] When Nahash recaptured this land from the Israelites, he imposed this conventional punishment, according to the Qumran text. Although gouging out only the right eye would not actually blind the Israelites, it would handicap, if not disable, them as fighters. Swordsmen, archers, and slingers without depth perception would not pose much of a military threat.

According to the Qumran text, seven thousand Israelites escaped from Nahash and fled west across the Jordan to Jabesh-Gilead, where Nahash attacked them, demanding the same punishment for them as for their brethren east of the Jordan.

When the first Israelite monarch, King Saul, learned of the attack on Jabesh-Gilead and Nahash's barbarous terms, he mustered other Israelite tribes and successfully relieved the siege of Jabesh-

Gilead, thereby consolidating recognition of his incipient monarchy, which, in the end, sealed the Ammonites' fate as well.

This passage may have been omitted from the Hebrew text of the Bible as a result of what scholars call homeoteleuton—a lapse in which the scribe's eye jumps from one appearance of a word to a later appearance of the same word, omitting everything in between. The name Nahash not only is the first word in the omitted passage (which we can now insert at the beginning of Chapter 11 or the end of Chapter 10) but also appears at the beginning of Chapter 11; the standard Hebrew text begins "Then Nahash . . ." The ancient scribe may have written "Nahash" in the omitted passage, raised his eyes, and returned to the text he was copying, but focused on the second "Nahash" a paragraph later, thereby omitting everything in between.[2] The erroneous text was then copied over and over until it became part of the standard Hebrew text.

The New Revised Standard Version, the popular Protestant translation of the Bible, has already included this errant paragraph at the end of 1 Samuel 10. The paragraph, which incidentally has no verse number in this translation, reads as follows: "Now Nahash, king of the Ammonites, had been grievously oppressing the Gadites and the Reubenites. He would gouge out the right eye of each of them and would not grant Israel a deliverer. No one was left of the Israelites across the Jordan whose right eye Nahash, king of the Ammonites, had not gouged out. But there were seven thousand men who had escaped from the Ammonites and had entered Jabesh-Gilead."

Then the next chapter begins: "About a month later, Nahash the Ammonite went up and besieged Jabesh-Gilead . . ." A footnote tells us that the authoritative Rabbinic text known as the Masoretic Text, or MT, omits the first four words of this sentence.

Even before the discovery of the Qumran texts, scholars could have suspected that something was missing here. The first time Nahash is mentioned in the Hebrew Bible (MT), he is introduced simply as "Nahash the Ammonite," an unusual form for the first mention of a king. In the four books of Samuel and Kings, when-

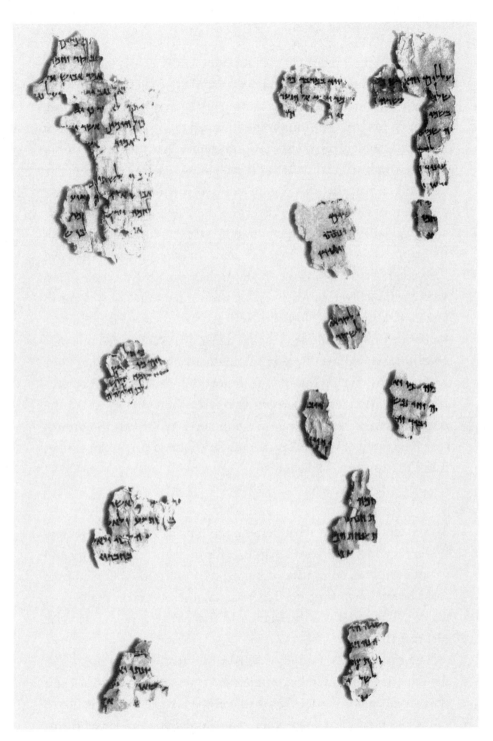

This Hebrew fragment from the book of Samuel corresponds to the version of Samuel in the Greek Septuagint (LXX) rather than the Masoretic Text (MT), showing that the translators of the LXX used a Hebrew text that varied from the standard MT.

ever a reigning foreign king is introduced, it is as "X, king of Y."[3] With the addition of the lost paragraph from the Qumran text, Nahash is properly identified as king at the first reference to him: "Nahash, king of the Ammonites" (literally king of the children of Ammon), which provides strong evidence that the passage from Qumran was originally part of the Hebrew text.

Another hint that this was an omitted part of the Hebrew text comes from Josephus, who describes the background of Nahash's attack on Jabesh-Gilead, including the fact that he had gouged out the right eyes of the Israelites east of the Jordan who had "rebel[led]" against his rule. Nahash then pursued the Gileadites, who presumably escaped, west of the Jordan, attacking them in Jabesh-Gilead. There, Josephus writes, Nahash offered them surrender terms that included having their right eyes gouged out. According to Josephus: "It was for them to choose, whether they preferred the cutting out of a small portion of the body, or to perish utterly." Evidently Josephus's copy of the Bible included the missing passage recovered from Qumran, which tends to confirm that the newly discovered paragraph was indeed part of an earlier, if not the original, biblical text.[4]

In the tenth century, what became the official text of the Hebrew Bible, together with vowel markings for the consonantal script and various kinds of notes, was produced by a group of scribes known as Masoretes, working in Tiberias, on the shore of the Sea of Galilee. The result was the Masoretic Text (MT), now the standard Hebrew Bible.

The earliest extant copy of MT, dating to the tenth century, is the famous Aleppo Codex, housed since about 1400 in an Aleppo synagogue, whose custodians had refused to make it available to modern scholars.[5] In 1947, when rampaging Syrian mobs set fire to the Aleppo synagogue to protest the United Nations decision to partition Palestine, part of the Aleppo Codex was burned. Part, however, was somehow saved and, years later, smuggled out of Syria into Israel.[6] These pages (294 leaves out of 380) are now housed in the library of Hebrew University in Jerusalem.

Because the Aleppo Codex was unavailable, modern scholars have relied mostly on a copy of the Hebrew Bible that is about a century later than the Aleppo Codex. Dating to about 1005, the Leningrad Codex is textually very close to the Aleppo Codex and even shows signs that it was corrected in accordance with the Aleppo Codex, or another manuscript very much like it. The Leningrad Codex is housed in the state library of St. Petersburg. It is the oldest complete copy of MT that has survived the centuries. As such, it is the base text for the famous critical edition of the Hebrew Bible known as Biblia Hebraica (BH), which is now being prepared in its fifth edition.[7]

Each edition of BH contains an elaborate scholarly apparatus that lists the thousands and thousands of variations in different manuscripts of the text. From them the editors choose a reading to incorporate into their own text.

Early Hebrew manuscripts are not the only source for determining the best reading. As early as the third century B.C., the Torah, or Five Books of Moses, was translated from Hebrew into Greek for Greek-speaking Jews in Alexandria. Soon thereafter, the rest of the Hebrew Bible was also translated into Greek. According to a document known as the Letter of Aristeas, Ptolemy II (Philadelphus) ordered the translation for his Alexandria library, but it was probably ordered by Alexandrian Jews. The Letter of Aristeas goes on to say that the high priest in Jerusalem dispatched seventy-two scholars—six from each tribe—to make the translation; the scholars completed their work on the Five Books—the Pentateuch—in seventy-two days. According to a legend recounted by the Jewish philosopher Philo, who lived in Alexandria, the seventy-two scholars translated in isolation, but each produced an identical manuscript. The result of their labors is known as the Septuagint (LXX for short).

The extant copies of the Septuagint are much older than the Aleppo and the Leningrad Codices, the oldest copies of the Masoretic Text. The three most famous copies of LXX, dating to the fourth and fifth centuries, are the Codex Sinaiticus and Codex Alexandrinus, both now in the British Library, and the Codex Vaticanus, in the Vatican library.

However, the Septuagint manuscripts have always been suspect as a source for the basic Hebrew text. LXX is, after all, a translation, and it is often unclear whether variations from MT are attributable to the translation or to the Hebrew text from which the Greek text was translated. There are also some gross differences between LXX and MT. The book of Jeremiah, for example, is nearly 20 percent longer in LXX, though the additions may be secondary, made after the Greek text was composed and circulated. The Septuagint version of Esther includes an extensive series of what scholars call Additions. In Genesis, the LXX includes an additional generation between Adam and Noah. It includes a psalm not found in MT.

Greek translations also include entire books that were not included in the Hebrew Bible, apocryphal books such as Judith, Tobit, the Wisdom of Solomon, and Ecclesiasticus. (Since the Roman Catholic Church based its canon on Greek translations, these books are part of its canon but are called deuterocanonical.)[8]

A third stream of manuscripts—in addition to MT and LXX—has been preserved by the Samaritan community, for whom only the Pentateuch is canonical. The Samaritan Pentateuch is very close to the Pentateuch of MT—differing in only six thousand readings![9] The Samaritan Pentateuch has generally been marginalized as a textual source because the differences are often thought to be late, secondary, and/or, more important, changed to reflect Samaritan theology. Since the seventeenth century, scholars have known of a somewhat different edition of Exodus in the Samaritan Pentateuch, but it was generally dismissed as insignificant for text-critical purposes. Then a copy turned up at Qumran—in the

The Leningrad Codex, dated to about 1005 A.D., is the oldest complete copy of the Masoretic Text (MT) of the Bible.

The three-column Codex Vaticanus, from the fourth or fifth century, is one of the oldest copies of the Septuagint version of the Bible.

paleo-Hebrew script used before the Babylonian exile,[10] the same script that the Samaritans have retained (in a modified form) for their holy writings to this day. The Qumran manuscript of Exodus closely follows the Samaritan version[11] and now establishes that two editions of Exodus were circulating in Judaism at the turn of the era, one proto-Samaritan and the other proto-MT.

Until the discovery of the Dead Sea Scrolls, these three streams of manuscripts—MT, LXX, and the Samaritan Pentateuch—were all that scholars had to determine the basic text of the Hebrew Bible. True, there were some biblical quotations in the New Testament (in Greek) and in Rabbinic literature, but these were of relatively little help. The paucity of sources often led to a textual dead end. What choice was to be made, for example, when both LXX and the Samaritan Pentateuch vary in precisely the same way from MT, as is the case with about nineteen hundred variations?

With these limited and late sources, it was also very difficult if not impossible to uncover earlier stages of textual development or even to understand the relationship of the various manuscript traditions to one another.

The scrolls from Qumran now provide an abundant source of materials with which to approach these questions. Approximately a quarter of the Dead Sea Scrolls are biblical manuscripts, which include fragments of every book of the Hebrew Bible except Esther.[12]

One result has been to give somewhat more authority to the Greek Septuagint, even though it is a translation. Based on the Hebrew biblical fragments among the Dead Sea Scrolls, it appears that the differences between LXX and MT are often attributable not to the fact that the LXX is a translation, but rather to the fact that the LXX translators were working from a somewhat different Hebrew base text. This in effect increases the reliability of the Septuagint. (The same situation, but to a lesser extent, applies to the Samaritan Pentateuch.) When there is a variation between the standard Hebrew *textus receptus,* on the one hand, and the Septuagint, on the other, scholars are now readier to accept the reading of the Septuagint. Or they might prefer a reading found only in a Qumran text or in the Samaritan Pentateuch. In short, as the chief editor of the scrolls, Emanuel Tov of Hebrew University, writes, the biblical texts from Qumran have "taught us no longer to posit MT at the center of our textual thinking."[13]

A particularly dramatic example involves Deuteronomy 32, a famous poem placed in the mouth of Moses in which he recalls the "days of old," when the Lord divided the land among the nations, fixing the boundaries of peoples. In MT, he fixed these boundaries according to "the sons of Israel" (*b'nai yisrael,* in Hebrew): "When the Most High apportioned the nations, when he divided the sons of man, he established the borders of the peoples according to the number of the sons of Israel" (Deuteronomy 32:8). But there was no Israel at the time the boundaries of nations were established and Moses is speaking here to the children of Israel before they reach the Promised Land, while they are still wandering in the desert. The "days of old" are thus far earlier than the existence of Israel.

The Septuagint text differs significantly at this point. It mentions "sons of God" (*huioi tou theou,* in Greek), rather than "sons of Israel," which makes more sense, but smacks of polytheism: Each of the world's peoples is allotted to a divine son—Chemosh gets the Moabites, Qos gets the Edomites, Milkom gets the Ammonites, Ba'al gets the Canaanites, and so forth, while Yahweh* takes care of the Israelites, his chosen people.[14]

Was the Hebrew text changed sometime between its composition and the earliest surviving texts from the tenth and eleventh centuries A.D., presumably to remove the embarrassing reference to "sons of God"? Or is the pristine Hebrew text to be preferred over a Greek translation?

Recent archaeological finds at the remote northern Sinai site of Kuntillet 'Ajrud (Horvat Teman) have revealed an ancient travelers' way station that housed a kind of chapel in which were found some

---

*Yahweh is the Israelite God's personal name, consisting of four Hebrew letters, YHWH, known as the tetragrammaton.

large storage jars, painted and inscribed, dating to about 800 B.C. An inscription on one of the jars refers to "Yahweh of Shomron (Samaria) and his Asherah." Another mentions "Yahweh of Teman and his Asherah." Though a few scholars maintain that Asherah refers to a tree or some other cult symbol, most agree that Asherah refers to a particular pagan goddess. Yahweh and his consort may even be pictured in one of the paintings, although this is a more controversial matter.[15]

Closer to the center of Israel, at a site called Khirbet El-Qom, a mere twelve miles west of Hebron, a contemporaneous inscription has been recovered that reads, "Be blessed by Yahweh my guardian and by his Asherah."[16]

If Yahweh had a consort, why not children? Most scholars agree that monotheism was a relatively late development in Israelite religious history. As a leading Israeli archaeologist, Amnon Ben-Tor, once told me, "Yahweh had a very hard time at first [establishing his exclusivity]." When the First Commandment states, "Thou shalt have no other gods before [or beside] me," does this mean that Yahweh is the only god or that Yahweh is the chief god, as the text may imply? In the words of the highly regarded *HarperCollins Bible Dictionary*, "This commandment does not deny the existence of other gods, but it demands total allegiance on the part of Israel to its own God."[17]

So a strong case can be made that the better text is the LXX, with "sons of God," even though it is a translation, rather than the Hebrew text's "sons of Israel."

On the other hand, the Hebrew text plainly speaks of the "sons of God" when it means to do so, as in the passage at the beginning of Genesis, Chapter 6, where, when the "sons of God" (*b'nai ha-elohim*) see how beautiful the daughters of men are, they sleep with them and beget giants. The phrase "sons of God" appears elsewhere in the Bible as well, particularly in Job and Psalms. In Job 38:7, the sons of God (*b'nai ha-elohim*) shouted for joy at the creation, apparently having been there to watch the spectacle. So the

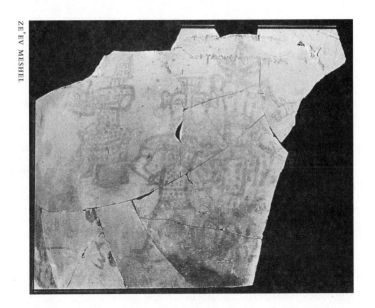

An inscription and drawing on a pithos, or storage jar, found at Kuntillet 'Ajrud.
The inscription refers to Yahweh and his Asherah. Some scholars believe
the drawing includes Yahweh and his consort.

authors of the Hebrew text did not hesitate to refer to the sons of God when that is what they meant.

These were the arguments pro and con before the discovery of the Dead Sea Scrolls. The argument has now been settled by a tiny scrap of leather from Cave 4 at Qumran that comes from a scroll of Deuteronomy, Chapter 32, and contains the crucial words "sons of God." So there was a Hebrew text of Deuteronomy from about the turn of the era that, in the critical passage, referred not to the "sons of Israel" but to the "sons of God"—evidently, the original text which was later altered in MT.

The original—as we now know it—has a power that is lost when the text is emended. In its original formulation, Yahweh chose Israel as his own portion, while other, lesser gods were assigned to other nations.

The New Jerusalem Bible, the New English Bible, and the New American Bible, among other translations, use the phrase "sons of God" in Deuteronomy 32:8, while the New Jewish Publication Society translation skirts the problem by adopting neither "sons of God" nor "sons of Israel": "[The Most High] fixed the boundaries of peoples in relation to Israel's numbers." Other translations use other circumlocutions, both here and elsewhere where the text refers to "sons of God," such as Genesis 6:2. There the New American Bible has "the sons of heaven." The New Jewish Publication Society translation has "divine beings," although a footnote states that others translate these words "sons of God."

A final example illustrates the effect of the Qumran scrolls on biblical textual criticism. It comes from Chapter 6 of the second book of Samuel, which describes King David as he brings the Ark of the Covenant to Jerusalem. Leading the procession, he dances wildly, leaping and whirling before the crowds, perhaps exposing himself, as he is girded (only?) in a linen ephod, an apron or loincloth. David's wife Michal, we are told, "despised" him for this gross behavior. In a line dripping with sarcasm, she confronts him: "Didn't the king of Israel do himself honor today—exposing him-

*This tiny scrap of leather found in Cave 4 contains the crucial words "Sons of God"
from Deuteronomy 32:8.*

self today in the sight of the slave girls of his subjects, as one of the riffraff might expose himself!" David replies: "I will dance before the Lord and dishonor myself even more, and be in *my own* [italics added] low esteem; but among the slave girls that you speak of I will be honored."

This semi-official Jewish translation (from the latest Jewish Publication Society version) is based on MT; a footnote, however, states that the Septuagint reads "your," where MT reads "my own." The Septuagint reading ("your low esteem"), rather than the Masoretic Text ("my own low esteem"), seems to make sense as the preferred reading. A number of other English translations—for example, the New American Bible, the New Jerusalem Bible, and the Revised English Bible—all read "your" instead of "my own." Given the greater reliability the Qumran texts have given to the Septuagint, textual critics can now be confident that the Septuagint version is, at this point in the text, the better one.

Almost all of the more than two hundred biblical manuscripts from Qumran are fragmentary—a scrap here and a scrap there. Nevertheless, the materials are enough to analyze the *kinds* of biblical manuscripts (text types, in the scholarly jargon) contained in the corpus. Frank Cross has divided the biblical scrolls into three categories: those that seem to resemble most closely MT tradition, those that resemble the Greek LXX (of which we now have, for the first time, parts of its Hebrew base text), and those that resemble the Samaritan tradition. Although there are differences within each of these manuscript traditions, they may in general be regarded as proto-Masoretic, proto-Septuagintal, and proto-Samaritan. Cross traces the origins of the three text types to different locales: The proto-Masoretic developed in Babylonia, the proto-Septuagintal in Egypt, and the proto-Samaritan in Palestine. Some of the biblical manuscripts among the Dead Sea Scrolls, however, cannot be placed in any of these categories.

Cross's tripartite division of biblical texts has been challenged by another great Dead Sea Scroll scholar, the chief editor of the scroll publication team, Emanuel Tov of Hebrew University. "Most of the [biblical] texts," he says, "are *sui generis*."[18] "They do not share any major textual, linguistic or scribal characteristics."[19] As Cross observes, "[Tov] carefully avoids the language of filiation, families, types."[20] Cross describes the differences between Tov and himself as the difference between "splitters" and "clumpers."[21] In evolutionary biology, splitters see a new species in every individual. Clumpers bunch minor variations within a single species. "Tov is a splitter. I am a clumper," says Cross.[22]

Whoever is right, one thing is clear—a variety of texts was accepted at Qumran.

Tov has identified biblical texts he believes were written at Qumran that tend to modernize biblical spelling and language. This, says Tov, reflects "a free approach to the biblical text."[23] Surprisingly, especially given the Qumranites' stringent religious rules, these manuscripts contain many careless mistakes, sloppy handwriting, and untidy corrections.[24] Apparently, the transcribers were not yet imbued with the holiness of the exact transmission of the text.[25] Whoever was responsible for the biblical texts among the Dead Sea Scrolls was apparently unconcerned that the text was not standardized. We are at a time before the biblical text had become *the* biblical text.

The Bible often contains its own dissent—or at least variations not only in details but in larger issues as well. Deuteronomy, for example, as its name implies, is a second telling of the law—and in many ways a different telling from the one provided in the preceding books. Thus, we find the Ten Commandments repeated in Deuteronomy 5 with some significant variations from the first telling in Exodus 20.

The Bible presents another retelling of history in the two books of Chronicles. Chronicles starts again with Adam, but its viewpoint is different from what went before. For example, it praises some kings who were earlier condemned, and vice versa. In such earlier books as Samuel and Kings, David is spelled with three He-brew letters, with no vowels. In Chronicles (and some later prophets), it is spelled with four Hebrew letters; a vowel (*Y* or *yod*) is inserted before the final *D* to indicate the precise pronunciation. Whoever decided on the books to be included in the canon was quite willing to include these variations.

A further retelling of biblical history is contained in the book of Jubilees, an apocryphal book, several copies of which were found at Qumran, often referred to as an example of a "Rewritten Bible."[26] Perhaps because Jubilees was not written until about 150 B.C., it was not included in the Bible and has been relegated to the Apocrypha, although it may well have been regarded by some as holy scripture in its time and is still regarded as canonical (or deuterocanonical) by Roman Catholics and some other Christian denominations.

With the help of the Dead Sea Scrolls, we can determine ap-proximately when the text of the Hebrew Bible became at least relatively fixed.

When the Dead Sea Scrolls surfaced on the antiquities market, professional archaeologists and Arab tribesmen began to explore caves in other wadis, including those south of the Wadi Qumran. Thus nineteen biblical scrolls were found in two other wadis—Nahal Hever[27] and Wadi Murabba'at. These manuscripts, too, are sometimes considered Dead Sea Scrolls though they date some-what later than the Qumran materials and were apparently hidden in the caves during the Second Jewish Revolt against Rome, also known as the Bar Kokhba revolt (132–35 A.D.). All nineteen of these later biblical scrolls are closely related to the Masoretic Text,[28] whereas the biblical scrolls from Qumran vary widely; some are closely related to MT, others to the Septuagint, still others to the Samaritan Pentateuch, and some to none of the above.

Between 70 A.D., when the Romans destroyed Jerusalem, and 135 A.D., when they suppressed the Bar Kokhba revolt, the text of the Bible became almost completely standardized—a process that seems to have begun even before the Roman destruction of the Temple and was apparently largely completed by the time of the Second Jewish Revolt.[29]

A Greek manuscript of the Twelve Minor Prophets discovered in Nahal Hever displays a systematic revision of the text toward the proto-MT.[30] The scribal corrections analyzed in the Qumran scrolls, however, cannot be characterized this way. Emanuel Tov, who has studied these "scribal interventions" (mostly corrections in an already existing text), tells us that "MT did not yet have such an authoritative status that texts would be corrected to it. . . . [T]o the best of my knowledge we do not know of any convincing example of a Hebrew text [from Qumran] which has been corrected towards MT."[31] To the contrary, in several instances involving spelling and language differences, the corrections have "remove[d] that text even more from MT."[32] Nevertheless, the majority of biblical texts from Qumran are already proto-Masoretic. The process of standardization appears already to have begun, or at least the proto-MT was the preferred text, judging from the comparative number of exemplars at Qumran.

Canonization of the text is different from standardization. Canonization refers to the adoption of particular books as authoritative or holy. The processes of standardization and canonization proceeded independently, although often at much the same time.

The Torah, or Pentateuch, or Five Books of Moses, was probably canonized when the exiles returned to Israel from Babylonia in the fifth century B.C., as the Bible itself implies when Ezra, whose ancestry is traced to Aaron, the high priest, is described as "expert in the Law of Moses" (Ezra 7:6). Ezra appointed judges who knew this Law and how to apply it. "Let anyone who does not obey the Law of your God . . . be punished" (Ezra 7:26).

The Talmud says, "When Israel forgot the Torah, Ezra came up from Babylon and reestablished it; and when Israel once again forgot the Torah, Hillel the Babylonian [first century A.D.] came up and reestablished it."[33] This may suggest that Hillel was involved in the canonization process not only of the five books of Moses but of subsequent books as well.

That the New Testament frequently refers to "the Law and the Prophets,"[34] indicates that by the end of the first century collections of each of these categories must have been recognized as authoritative.

Until recently, scholars attributed the final canonization of the Hebrew Bible to the so-called Council of Yavneh, in which the Rabbinic sages met at the end of the first century A.D., after the Roman destruction of Jerusalem, to decide which books should constitute the Hebrew Bible. The best recent scholarship, however, concludes that there was no council as such.[35] At most, the Yavneh sages confined their consideration to marginal books, such as Ecclesiastes and the Song of Songs, which were included, and Ben Sira, which was ultimately rejected.

That the Rabbinic canonization was not the only one, however, is indicated by the Septuagint, which contains a number of books—such as Tobit, Judith, the Wisdom of Solomon, Ecclesiasticus, and the first two books of the Maccabees—which were not included in the Rabbinic canon. Judaism and Protestant Christianity now assign them to the Apocrypha. In the Roman Catholic tradition, they are called deuterocanonical.

Before the discovery of the Dead Sea Scrolls the apocryphal book of Enoch (more precisely, 1 Enoch) was known only in an Ethiopic translation. Now as many as twenty fragmentary copies of the Aramaic original have been found at Qumran, which suggests that Enoch and perhaps other books now considered apocryphal were regarded as authoritative Scripture at least by some groups. Allusions to Enoch occur at least fourteen times in the New Testament; the New Testament Letter of Jude quotes from Enoch as having the authority of inspired Scripture (Jude 14–15). In some copies of the Ethiopic Bible Enoch is included in the canon.

Jubilees, the so-called Rewritten Bible, was apparently considered authoritative at Qumran: At least fifteen copies of this book have been identified, an immediate indication of the importance the Qumran sectarians attached to it. To this day, it is considered canonical by the Abyssinian Church in Ethiopia.

The Dead Sea Scroll text known as MMT (discussed more fully in Chapter 10) indicates that there were other collections of presumably holy or authoritative books at Qumran. MMT refers to "the book of Moses and the books of the Prophets and (the writings of) David [and the events of] ages past."[36] The allusion to writings of David may refer to the psalms; Luke speaks of "the Law and the Prophets and Psalms" (Luke 24:44). But what are the writings of the events of ages past? Elsewhere in MMT we find reference to "the laws and the judgments and the purity regulations and . . . the ordinances of Israel."[37]

One measure of the authority of the various books that ultimately became part of the Hebrew Bible is the number of copies recovered from the Qumran caves. The most popular "biblical" book at Qumran was Psalms—fragments from thirty-nine copies have been found. The books of the Torah follow: Deuteronomy (thirty-six copies), Exodus (seventeen copies), Genesis (fifteen copies), Leviticus (thirteen copies), and Numbers (eight copies). Among the prophets, Isaiah clearly was the most popular (twenty-two copies). (The most popular books at Qumran—Psalms, Deuteronomy, and Isaiah—were also popular among early Christians; these three books are the most frequently quoted books of the Hebrew Bible in the New Testament.) The Qumranites were apparently little interested in history, at least as far as we can tell from the number of copies of the historical books. Only one copy of Chronicles and one of Ezra/Nehemiah were found; two copies of Joshua; three of Judges and Kings; and four of Samuel.

In short, the biblical texts from Qumran were still fluid; reflecting neither a fixed text nor a fixed canon.[38] Different textual traditions were accepted. Some books that were eventually not included were considered authoritative. The Bible itself refers to at least half

*The text known as MMT contrasts the stringent religious laws of the Qumran sect
with those of their opponents.*

a dozen books, perhaps once considered authoritative, that have not survived—such as the Book of Jashar (Joshua 10:13 and elsewhere), the Book of the Wars of Yahweh (Numbers 21:14), the Chronicles of the Kings of Judah and Israel (1 Kings 14:19 and elsewhere), and the Acts of Solomon (1 Kings 11:41). Despite the fact that the Qumran manuscripts come from a time when neither text nor authority was fixed, however, they are nevertheless remarkably close to the texts that were finally included in the canonized Bible.

CHAPTER 10

ILLUMINATING JUDAISM

The scrolls emphasize a hitherto unappreciated variety in Judaism of the late Second Temple period, so much so that scholars often speak not simply of Judaism, but of Judaisms.[1] This is exemplified in the Judaism of the Qumran sectarians. Whether they were Essenes or some other kind of Jews, their religious literature as preserved in the scrolls reveals this rich variety.

Frank Cross has observed that Rabbinic Judaism—the Judaism the rabbis developed after the Roman destruction of the Second Temple in 70 A.D.—in its earliest literature presents itself not as a post-destruction creation but as something "monolithic, going back relatively unchanged, if not to Sinai, at least to the Second Temple period."[2] This traditional view of Jewish history is clearly challenged by the Dead Sea Scrolls.

As Cross explains: "Before the ascendancy of the Pharisees and the emergence of Rabbinic orthodoxy after the fall of the Second Temple [in 70 A.D.], Judaism was more complex and variegated than we had supposed.[3] The apocalyptic strain in Judaism was much stronger and more widespread than historians of Judaism have thought. . . . Many scholars, both Jewish and Christian, prefer to downplay apocalyptic elements in their traditions."[4]

"Apocalyptic," from the Greek word for revelation, is used as a noun as well as an adjective, and describes literature that discloses heavenly secrets in visions. This literature, full of veiled references, often focuses on great historic crises. The world is in the grip of warring forces, of good and evil, of God and a Satanic opponent, heading for final judgment. The end of days or the end of time is near, signaled by current events when their meaning is properly understood (eschatology). Apocalyptic is thus closely related to eschatology. Since the messiah, too, is about to appear, apocalyptic is also closely related to messianism.

The book of Daniel—with its secret visions, prophecies transmitted to Daniel and interpreted by angels, a promise of the resurrection of martyrs who will "shine like the stars" (Daniel 12:3), and the conviction that history is now reaching its climax—is the prime example of apocalyptic literature in the Hebrew Bible. In the book's best-known vision, "one like a son of man" comes "on the clouds of heaven" (Daniel 7:13). In the New Testament the title "Son of man" is adapted and applied to Jesus as the Messiah. Daniel is the latest book in the Hebrew Bible, composed in about 150 B.C., later than some of the Dead Sea Scrolls.

In the New Testament, Revelation, often referred to as the Apocalypse, is a similarly apocalyptic book and describes the visions received from Christ by someone named John. According to these visions, persecution of faithful Christians will be followed by punishment of the nations and by the triumph of God and his followers. The final cosmic battle will occur at a place called Armageddon (a Greek form of Har, or Mount, Megiddo).

A similar battle is envisioned in the most prominent example of apocalyptic among the Dead Sea Scrolls, the War Scroll, sometimes called the Scroll of the War of the Sons of Light Against the Sons of Darkness. Its siglum is 1QM; it was among the original bedouin discoveries in Cave 1; the *M* stands for *milchamah,* the Hebrew word for war. As its name suggests, the scroll describes a war at the end of time between the forces of good, led by God, and the forces of evil, led by Belial, a Satan-like figure. Because the end of days or time is involved, scholars describe the subject as apocalyptic eschatology.

The nineteen surviving columns of this scroll, which has been only partially preserved, describe the preparations for battle and the battle itself, rather than why the battle occurred or what is supposed to happen after the battle. The text also includes a few moving prayers, but the battle's broader significance is obscure. In this sense, the War Scroll is disappointing.

This much, however, is clear: "This shall be a time of salvation for the people of God, an age of dominion for the members of His company, and of everlasting destruction for the company of Belial/Satan . . . His (God's) exalted greatness shall shine eternally to the peace, blessing, glory, joy and long life of all the Sons of Light" (I.4–5, 9). On the other hand, the war itself will be terrible: "It shall be a time of [great] tribulation for the people whom God shall redeem; of all its afflictions, none shall be as this, from its sudden beginning until its end in eternal redemption" (I.13).

The text describes in great detail the army of God and the ministering angels, the dress of the combatants, the trumpets they are to blow, the standards they are to carry, the necessary purification in preparation for battle, and the formations they are to march in. The battle tunics are to be "embroidered with blue, purple and scarlet thread." The shields will be of "bronze polished like mirrors." No man shall go down to battle who is impure. The latrines must be two thousand cubits (a cubit is about a foot and a half) outside the camp "so that no indecent nakedness may be seen in the surroundings of their camps" (VII.8).

"The priests shall sound a sustained blast on the trumpets for battle array." Then a priest shall rise and speak to the people, quoting Deuteronomy 20:2–4: "Hear, O Israel! You are about to join battle this day against your enemies. Do not fear! Do not let your hearts be faint, do not be alar[med and do n]ot tremble before them. For your God goes with you to fight for you against your enemies that He may deliver you."

Satan is called the Angel of Malevolence, as well as Belial. His rule "is in darkness." "The Prince of Light," on the other hand, was appointed by God from ancient times "to come to our support."

"O God of Israel, who can compare with Thee in might? Thy mighty hand is with the poor." He will "destroy evil" and "bring Darkness low and magnify Light . . . to stand forever, and destroy all the Sons of Darkness."

The outcome is foreordained:

> Their kings shall serve you
>> and all your oppressors shall bow down before you;
>> [they shall lick] the dust [of your feet].
> Shout for joy, [O daughters of] my people!
> Deck yourselves with glorious jewels
>> and rule over [the kingdoms of the nations!
> Sovereignty shall be to the Lord]
>> and everlasting dominion to Israel.

The War Scroll is only one of many sectarian manuscripts from Qumran that exhibit apocalyptic, eschatological, and/or messianic aspects. The Temple Scroll, though far different, is another, and helps us understand many aspects of the scrolls community. One section of the Temple Scroll (among five major sections, although this one takes up nearly half the scroll) describes a visionary temple from which the scroll takes its name. Instead of describing how to wage an eschatological war, the Temple Scroll describes how to build an eschatological temple—presumably one that will replace the illegitimate temple in Jerusalem and last forever. As Father Joseph Fitzmyer, a leading scroll scholar at Catholic University of America, has noted, the temple of the Temple Scroll emphasizes the role the sanctuary is "to play in the eschaton,"[5] that is, in the messianic age. Another scholar has described the envisioned temple as "quasi-utopian,"[6] an imaginative reconstruction of an ideal time.

The Temple Scroll was composed sometime in the second century B.C., before Herod's great rebuilding of the modest Second

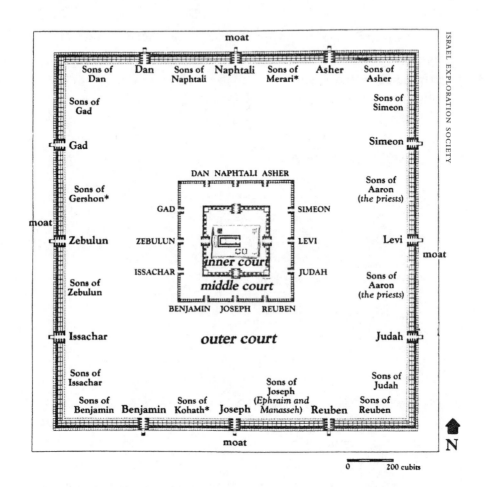

A plan of the eschatological temple described in the Temple Scroll.

Temple constructed by the exiles when they returned from Babylonia. But even Herod's magnificent rebuilding could not compare with the imaginary temple compound described in the Temple Scroll. It consists of three concentric square courtyards—an outer courtyard, a middle courtyard, and an inner courtyard in which the temple itself stands. Each side of the outer courtyard is approximately half a mile long and has three gates, or twelve altogether, each named for one of the twelve Israelite tribes. The wall of the middle courtyard also has twelve gates, similarly situated and named. The compound covers about the same area as the Old City of Jerusalem does today. Magen Broshi has remarked, "By comparison with the temple described in the Temple Scroll, the Herodian Temple was a miniature."[7]

The visionary temple would extend from about the middle of the present Old City eastward across the Kidron Valley all the way to the Mount of Olives—an impossible location, given the steep valley followed by the abrupt rise high above the present Old City. This kind of extravagant vision is typical of apocalyptic literature.

The Temple Scroll's description of the temple compound is apparently related to several other fragmentary Dead Sea Scroll texts that describe the New Jerusalem.[8] In these, an angelic surveyor measures the houses—their rooms, windows, lattices, stairs, and doors—as well as the streets of the new city, giving a guided tour of eschatological Jerusalem to the narrator, who reports what he saw in the first person.

The Temple Scroll also describes in great detail the furniture and utensils of the temple, the sacrifices offered, and the festivals observed there, as well as the laws of the city of the temple. A number of the festivals described in the Temple Scroll are previously unattested in ancient literature, including a New Wine festival, a New Barley festival, a New (Olive) Oil festival, and a Wood Offering festival. The scroll also includes descriptions of more familiar festivals such as the Day of Atonement (Yom Kippur) and the Feast of Tabernacles (Sukkot).

Still another scroll contains Sabbath songs to be sung in the heavenly temple. Sometimes called the Angelic Liturgy, the songs describe the angelic priesthood, give an account of the worship performed on the Sabbath in the heavenly sanctuary, and invoke angelic praise. The editor of the text has called it "a quasi-mystical liturgy designed to evoke a sense of being present in the heavenly temple."[9]

> Praise the most high God (*elohim*), O you high among all the gods (*elim*) of knowledge.
>
> Let the holy ones of the gods (*elohim*) sanctify the King of glory, who sanctifies by his holiness all his holy ones.
>
> Princes of the praises of all the gods (*elohim*), praise the God (*elohim*) of majestic praises. . . .
>
> For he [is the God of gods] (*el elim*), of all the Princes on high, and the King of king[s] of all the eternal councils.[10]

This visionary eschatology and apocalyptic upheaval are usually associated with Christianity, not Judaism. According to John Collins, a leading authority on the subject, "Apocalyptic ideas played a crucial role in the formation of early Christian beliefs. . . . The genre generally declined in Judaism after the first century A.D. but flourished in Christianity down to the Middle Ages."[11]

Yet when these scrolls were written, eschatology, apocalypticism, and messianism were very much a part of mainstream Judaism, and it was from Jewish forms of these categories that the Christian forms developed. According to Frank Cross, "Many conservative Jews are uneasy about these continuities. In light of their experience with Christianity, they would like to push Christianity as far away from Judaism as possible."[12]

When I suggested to Cross that in Judaism apocalypticism did not really survive the Roman destruction of the Temple in 70 A.D., he took from his shelf a copy of Gershon Scholem's widely influential *The Messianic Idea in Judaism* and pointed out an early passage: "I must preface a word intended to correct a widespread misconception. I am referring to the distortion of historical circumstances, equally popular among Jewish and Christian scholars, which lies in denying the continuation of the apocalyptic tradition in Rabbinic Judaism." Scholem laid the fault at the feet of the "great Jewish scholars of the nineteenth and early twentieth centuries who to a great extent determined the popular image of Judaism. In view of their concept of a purified and rational Judaism, they could only applaud the attempt to eliminate or liquidate Apocalypticism from the realm of Judaism. Without regrets they left the claim of apocalyptic continuity to a Christianity which, to their minds, gained nothing on that account. Historical truth was the price paid for [this] prejudice."[13] The discovery of the blatant apocalyptic in the scrolls supports Scholem's position.

The scrolls also make clear the variety of Judaisms that were being practiced before the Roman destruction of the Temple. The Qumran community was fanatically opposed to the Temple and its authorities, so much so that they used a different calendar—so the holiest days of the year were observed at different times by the two groups. The scroll sectarians also had festivals that were, so far as we know, not part of the calendar of Temple Judaism at all.

The historical complexity that this introduces sensitizes us to the many other kinds of Judaism that are only hinted at in the surviving literature, whether their followers be Essenes, Boethusians, Hasidim, Herodians, or still others who have left no record. And all this is in addition to the two Jewish groups we know more about—the Pharisees and the Sadducees. As Lawrence Schiffman of New York University has remarked, this was "an era characterized by several competing approaches to Judaism, each claiming a monopoly on the true interpretation of the Torah."[14]

The Qumran literature also reflects an extraordinary concern for ritual purity—perhaps an odd combination with rampant apocalypticism. But this was a time in Judaism when the concern for purity was at its height. According to an early Rabbinic text, "Purity broke out in Israel [at this time]."[15]

Purity is sometimes associated with cleanness and impurity with uncleanness, which leaves a mistaken impression. Purity is a mat-

ter not of physical cleanness but of ritual cleanness, which is required for contact with the divine; this in turn is achieved by engaging in holy, sacred activities, especially in the Temple, which is
why purity is enjoined especially on the priests. But at least in theory, the Temple was accessible to all Jews. Indeed, three times a
year they were (supposedly) required to make a pilgrimage there.
For a holy nation, a kingdom of priests, the purity requirements of
the priesthood were incumbent upon all Jews: "You shall be to me
a kingdom of priests and a holy nation" (Exodus 19:6).

There is considerable archaeological evidence of the extent to
which purity requirements were adhered to by the Jewish populace in general. Ritual baths are found by the dozens, especially in
the Jerusalem area, during the period almost precisely contemporaneous with the scrolls, say 250 B.C. to 70 A.D.—but not nearly so
many before or after.

Although there is some dispute as to whether the installations at
Qumran are *miqva'ot,* the abundance of them at other sites where
observant Jews lived at this time strongly argues that the installations at Qumran were indeed *miqva'ot.*

Stone-manufacturing industries flourished at the turn of the era
around Jerusalem, and one reason was surely that stone vessels, unlike glass and pottery vessels, were not subject to ritual impurity.
Thousands of stone cups, as well as straight-walled bowls, jars with
lids, and even plates, have been found in archaeological excavations in houses of rich and poor, indicating that the popularity of
stone vessels was not based on a fashion that only the wealthy
could afford, like the costly painted pottery known as Jerusalem
ware. Moreover, almost no stone vessels have been found in areas
centered on Hebron, which were inhabited by Idumeans, or
Samaria, inhabited by Samaritans. In short, stone vessels have been
found in over sixty sites known to have been inhabited by Jews,
but almost never in non-Jewish areas.[16]

Apparently, stone vessels were not subject to impurity because
stone is natural, unadulterated by human transformation, such as
the firing of clay—an inference supported by the fact that unfired

earthen vessels are also not subject to impurity, according to Rabbinic law.

The emphasis on purity is typical of other restrictions. For example, no depictions of human beings or animals have been found in Jewish areas at this time, whether poor or very wealthy, not even in Herod's magnificent palace-fortresses, such as Masada. This is in contrast to the situation both earlier and later. Indeed, a few hundred years later, even synagogues were highly decorated with human and animal forms. In the late Second Temple period, however, the Second Commandment's prohibition against images was very strictly interpreted. Later, it was applied only to images that were idolatrous.

Another peculiarity of this period was the use of ossuaries, boxes that held human bones. About a year after initial burial, when the flesh of the deceased had decayed and fallen away, the bones were collected and carefully placed in small limestone boxes, often beautifully carved and decorated, with the person's name scratched on the outside. Perhaps the custom was related to the increasingly widespread belief in physical resurrection in the messianic age. In any event, ossuaries from the time when Qumran was inhabited by the sectarians are found only in the Jerusalem area. The Qumranites did not practice secondary burial—all the burials at Qumran are primary burials.

What accounts for the strict rules of purity, the strict interpretation of the Second Commandment's prohibition of images, and the stringent application of the laws in general at the end of the Second Temple period remains a puzzle, but there is no doubt that this was the case.

Some of the differences between the Temple Jews, who followed Pharasaic interpretation of the law, and the stricter Qumran sectarians are set forth in the famous document known as MMT.*

MMT is a difficult text in three parts: (1) a calendrical section; (2) a section of laws; and (3) an epilogue that discusses the separa-

---

*Miqsat Ma'aseh ha-Torah, variously translated as "Some Precepts of the Torah" or "Some Works of the Law."

tion of the sect from those who disagree with their laws. The first section confirms the nature of the sectarian calendar, a 364-day year of 52 weeks, unlike the lunar calendar followed in the Jerusalem Temple. As we have seen, the Qumran sectarians did not observe holy days at the same times as did those who followed the calendar of the Jerusalem Temple.

The beginning of MMT is missing, so we don't know if there was some sort of introduction to the calendrical material. The break in subject matter after the calendrical material is so abrupt that the calendrical material may simply be a completely separate document of which only the end has survived. In any event, it is the last two sections of MMT that concern us here. The middle section consists of about twenty religious laws (*halakhot*), mainly involving ritual purity. The last section explains that "we have [written] to you so that you may study (carefully) the book of Moses and the books of the Prophets and (the writings of) David." Emphasizing the importance of the purity laws, the text explains, "We have separated ourselves from the multitude of the people [and from all their impurity]."[17]

In the decade between the time when Elisha Qimron of Ben Gurion University and John Strugnell revealed the existence of MMT and the time when they published the text, scholars were told that MMT was a letter of the Teacher of Righteousness to the Wicked Priest, a reference to the high priest of the Jerusalem Temple.[18] This is a claim that Qimron and Strugnell no longer make. MMT is not a letter. And it is not clear who the first-person speaker is, or what group he was addressing. But the form in which the laws are stated is clear: We do this (good thing); but others do that (bad thing).[19]

It is difficult, however, to understand why these picayune distinctions were so important—indeed, so important that they seem to account for the separation of the sect from the Jewish mainstream.

Yet the thrust of MMT's laws is clear. As Ya'akov Sussman of Hebrew University has written, "All the *halakhic* rulings in MMT are stringent."[20] Take the law regarding what I call the Backward-

Jumping Impurity Up a Stream of Liquid. To understand this law, start with a pitcher of water, both the pitcher and the water being pure. Now pour some of the water into another vessel that is impure. Clearly, the water in the second vessel is now impure by virtue of its contact with an impure vessel. But what about the water still in the pitcher? And what about the pitcher itself? Did the impurity of the water in the second vessel render the water remaining in the pitcher (and the pitcher itself) impure? The Qumran sectarians, subscribing to the strictest possible interpretation, said yes. That is the ruling in MMT. Other Jews, presumably the Pharisees, said no.

Surely the occasion for the application of a law like the Backward-Jumping Impurity Up a Stream of Liquid would arise rarely, if ever. Yet that is the kind of issue that separated the Qumran Jews from other Jews.

Another example: According to Numbers 19:7, priests contract ritual impurity (paradoxical though it may seem) by the process of manufacturing the sacred ashes of the red heifer, which are used in solution to remove other kinds of impurity.[21] In short the ashes of the red heifer purify the defiled and defile the pure. The rabbis too were puzzled, and according to one Rabbinic text, even Solomon, the wisest of men, was baffled by the seeming paradox.[22] The rabbis declared that the defilement caused by the preparation of these purifying waters was an example of the kind of law for which there is no rational explanation, except that God said it (*hukkot*).

In any event, priests must bathe in the *miqveh* to remove the impurity contracted through the manufacture of the ashes of the red heifer. But is their impurity eradicated when they emerge from the *miqveh* or only with the setting of the sun on that day? Here, the Torah seems explicit: Numbers 19:7–10 says that the purification bath becomes effective only at sunset, and according to MMT, the Qumran sectarians abided by the strict construction of the text. MMT also suggests that the Pharisees found a way around this restriction, ruling that the priest would become pure immediately upon emerging from the ritual bath.

Presumably, the same dispute would arise with respect to all the categories of impurity removed by bathing in a *miqveh*. In Rabbinic law this is known as the problem of the *tebul yom,* literally, "one who has immersed himself on that day." Is a person purified on emergence from the *miqveh* or only at the end of the day? The Qumranites invariably adopted the stricter rule. To many people today, such differences in the interpretation of the laws may seem unimportant. But to the Qumranites and to Jews in general at the time, they were crucial. These laws were not metaphors for leading the good life but were necessary applications of divinely ordained Jewish law. Unless you understand that, you will not understand the world of Qumran. The Talmud says that "the impurity of a knife was more important to Israel [at this time] than murder."[23] The Jerusalem Talmud refers to this, in its own words, "disparagingly,"[24] that is, critically. But for the Qumran sectarians, purity was of paramount importance.

Professor Lawrence Schiffman of New York University claims that the sectarian laws of the Qumran sect so closely resemble Sadducean *halakhah* as to indicate either that the Qumranites were not Essene but Sadducean or that the term "Essene" must be redefined to include a number of breakaway groups, at least one of which originated from among the Sadducees.[25] Other scholars contest this, arguing that a few laws shared by the Sadducees and the Qumran sectarians are not enough to support Schiffman's claim, since most laws of most Jewish groups were the same.

In any case, MMT makes clear that what divided the Qumran sectarians from other Jews was not ethics or politics, whether external or internal, or even theological doctrine, but the laws of ritual observance, mainly the laws of purity.

Since MMT also indicates, polemically, some of the laws of the Qumranites' opponents—presumably the Pharisees, who controlled the Jerusalem Temple—scholars are able to trace the sources of Rabbinic Judaism to a period before the Roman destruction of the Temple. All forms of modern Judaism are heirs of Rabbinic Judaism, which emerged in the centuries after the destruction of the Temple in 70 A.D. Rabbinic Judaism has traditionally been governed by an exceedingly complex, nuanced, and detailed legal and ethical structure, codified in the Talmud and expanded in a vast corpus of other works. According to the rabbis, the Talmud, known as the Oral Law, in contrast to the Written Law—that is, the Bible—partakes of the same level of sanctity as Written Law. Indeed, according to the rabbis, the Oral Law was given to Moses on Mount Sinai at the same time as the Written Law. The earliest documentary expression of the Oral Law is the Mishnah, compiled in about 200 A.D., which forms the core of the Talmud. The Mishnah and a new kind of commentary called Gemara make up the Talmud, of which there are two versions, the Jerusalem Talmud, from about 400 A.D., and the Babylonian Talmud, about two hundred years after that. The latter is both more complete and more authoritative. It's the Babylonian Talmud, developed in the diaspora, that is studied in *yeshivot* around the world, including Israel, to this day.

But how did this elaborate structure of rules and regulations, which is already highly developed in the Mishnah, come into being? Between the latest book of the Hebrew Bible (Daniel, about 150 B.C.; the rest is more than a century older) and the earliest text in the Rabbinic corpus (the Mishnah, about 200 A.D.) there is a tremendous gap, which, until the discovery of MMT, had baffled scholars who were looking for the sources of the Oral Law. As talmudist Ya'akov Sussman writes, "One stands awed by the remarkable phenomenon of a fully developed halakhic system, governing all aspects of life and crystallized to its most minute details, which emerges fully formed in the [Mishnah]. . . . How did all this evolve?"[26]

With the help of MMT and similar texts, scholars may now begin to trace the roots of Rabbinic Judaism in pre-destruction Israel. According to Schiffman, much of post-destruction Rabbinic *halakhah* can already be found in pre-destruction Pharisaic Judaism, as revealed in polemical texts like MMT.

The scrolls do more than clarify the sources of Oral, or talmudic, Law. The Qumran corpus also contains biblical commentaries, which, like modern commentaries, quote and comment upon the written text. These are the earliest known antecedents of modern running commentaries.[27] But the Qumran commentaries (called *pesharim*) are of a special kind: The commentator interprets such prophetic books as Isaiah, Hosea, Nahum, and Habakkuk as if they were addressing and explaining contemporary conditions. The Bible thus becomes an encrypted explanation of current events in which biblical prophecy is fulfilled in the life of the Qumran community—a practice not unlike the use of prophecy in the New Testament.

The Dead Sea Scrolls *pesharim* quotes, for example, Habakkuk 2:15: "Woe to him who causes his neighbors to drink, who pours out his venom to make them drunk that he may gaze on their holy days,"[28] followed by this commentary: "Interpreted: This concerns the Wicked Priest (presumably the high priest of the Jerusalem Temple) who pursued the Teacher of Righteousness to the house of his exile that he might confuse him with his venomous fury."[29] In this way the biblical text is made relevant to the present.

Another kind of Jewish biblical interpretation is called *midrash,* an imaginative expansion and elaboration of the biblical text, often building on a word or phrase on the assumption that the meaning of the text is virtually inexhaustible. One of the original intact scrolls from Cave 1, known as the Genesis Apocryphon, retells and amplifies the stories of Genesis in this way. Unfortunately, the scroll was in the worst shape of all the intact scrolls recovered from this cave and much of it cannot be reconstructed. But enough has survived (together with other fragmentary copies from Cave 4) to give us the general drift of most of the stories. Noah, for example, was such a brilliant child that his supposed father suspected that someone else—perhaps an angel—had impregnated Noah's mother. Midrashic interpretations like this can be found in a number of Qumran texts. Although these expansions have no basis in history, they enrich the biblical text on which they expand, creating a living, continuously developing tradition.

Sometimes a Qumran text will try to harmonize conflicting biblical passages. For example, the Temple Scroll resolves the conflict in how war booty is to be distributed. In 1 Samuel 30:24–25, combatants and noncombatants are to share equally. Numbers 31:27, however, prescribes a lesser amount to be withheld from combatants for the levitical (priestly) share. The Temple Scroll provides a complicated formula by which the apparently conflicting biblical provisions can be conformed with one another.[30] The Temple Scroll presents itself as divine law, in some ways the Qumran sect's Torah. Its nature as a holy book is emphasized by the fact that in many passages God speaks in the first person; in the parallel version in the canonical Torah, God is referred to in the third person. The Temple Scroll, for instance, states: "The priests, the sons of Levi, shall come forward, for I have chosen them to minister to me and to bless by my name" (63:3). The parallel passage in the Bible uses the third person: "The priests, the sons of Levi, shall come forward for the Lord (Yahweh) your God has chosen them to minister to him and to bless by the name of the Lord (Yahweh)" (Deuteronomy 21:5).

That the Qumran community probably recognized as Scripture a book that was not included by Temple Jews once again emphasizes the varieties of Judaism that competed for favor at the end of the Second Temple period. All this changes, however, after the destruction of the Temple in 70 A.D., when only two forms of Judaism survive the cataclysm. One, Christianity, eventually dominates Western civilization after separating itself from its forebears. The other, Rabbinic Judaism, is the ancestor of all branches of modern Judaism.

CHAPTER 11

TREASURE SEARCH — THE COPPER SCROLL

E verything about the Copper Scroll is mysterious or controversial, or both. As its name implies, it consists not of animal
skin or papyrus, like the other Dead Sea Scrolls, but of copper—a
thin sheet, just short of 8 feet (2.4 meters) long and 12 inches
(.3 meters) from upper edge to lower edge, made of smaller sheets
of copper foil riveted together. As we saw in Chapter 2, the scroll
was found by archaeologists rather than bedouin, on a ledge at the
back of Cave 3, separate from the other fragmentary scrolls and artifacts found there, an important factor, as we shall see. When discovered, in March 1952, it consisted of two separate rolls, which
formed a sequential text listing sixty-four sites where hoards of
treasure were buried—huge amounts of gold and silver, cultic vessels and vestments, and scrolls. But all that became known only
after the copper rolls were opened.

Even before that was accomplished, however, letters hammered
in with a stylus were recognizable from the reverse as Hebrew
script. But the badly oxidized copper fairly crumbled at the touch,
and initial efforts to open the copper rolls failed.

Not long after he arrived in Jerusalem from England in late au-
tumn 1953 as a member of the publication team, John Marco Al-

*Archaeologists discovered these two rolls of copper
(actually part of the same scroll) on a ledge inside Cave 3.*

legro suggested to Lankester Harding, then still head of the Jordanian Antiquities Department, that since it was proving so difficult to unroll the Copper Scroll, it should be sent to Manchester, where Allegro had been teaching. There, he urged, experts might have more success. When he made the suggestion, Allegro had not yet inquired whether any experts were available in Manchester who would be willing to undertake the task. The advantage of Manchester, Allegro suggested, was that he would be able to "sound out the possibilities and supervise the work."[1] Though the publication of the Copper Scroll had been assigned to J. T. Milik, not to Allegro, Harding nonetheless agreed to the idea, but it was not until 1955 that Harding received permission from the Jordanian government to send one of the two rolls to Manchester.

Allegro did not have much luck involving experts at the University of Manchester in his project. They showed little interest and treated him "curtly."[2] He then approached a firm that specialized in manufacturing grinding wheels, but it lacked the machines necessary to the task. A colleague suggested he try the Manchester College of Science and Technology. There he succeeded. As Allegro watched, Dr. H. Wright Baker, a professor of mechanical engineering who described himself modestly to Allegro as a "mere plumber," undertook the task, cutting the scroll layer by layer, producing twenty-three hemispherical slices from the two rolls. The second roll arrived in Manchester in early January 1956 and the work was completed by the middle of that month.

Although Baker made every effort to cut the scroll in the margins so that none of the inscribed letters would be destroyed, this proved impossible. Worse still, the fresh cuts started the process of oxidation all over again. In the words of Kyle McCarter of Johns Hopkins University, who is preparing a new edition of the scroll: "The places touched by the saw in England exhibit an oxidation pattern. Centuries in the caves did minimal harm, but somehow the insult of the modern tool has started a process of deterioration along the cuts. By comparing the new photographs with those taken in the 1950s, one can see that a fair amount of material has been lost—in some sample locations a full centimeter—on both sides of each saw cut."[3]

Nevertheless, when the scroll was opened, it could be read. And John Allegro was the first person to read it. From the outset, he was fascinated with its seemingly realistic descriptions of sixty-odd sites where huge amounts of treasure lay buried. Was the list real or was it fiction? Allegro contended it was real.

Allegro's colleagues on the publication team, especially de Vaux and Milik, stoutly maintained that the list was mere folklore and described nothing real.

More than scholarly objectivity lay behind their position, however. By this time, Allegro was at odds with the other members of the publication team. In early 1956, Allegro gave three broadcasts on BBC radio in which he suggested that the leader of the Qumran sect, the Teacher of Righteousness, was a messianic figure who had been crucified, suggesting that the New Testament account of Jesus' crucifixion, in the words of one journalist, was nothing more than "a mythologized, hand-me-down version of the Dead Sea Scroll original."[4] As Allegro described the reaction to his broadcasts: "Something I said about the possibility of the Essene leader's having been crucified apparently stirred the imagination of some elements of the press and caused alarm in religious circles."

The notion that the Teacher of Righteousness was crucified was sheer speculation if not pure invention. Allegro's infuriated colleagues in Jerusalem took the extraordinary step of denouncing Allegro in a letter to the London *Times* signed by Milik, de Vaux, Strugnell, Skehan, and Starcky: "We are unable to see in the texts the 'findings' of Mr Allegro. We find no crucifixion of the 'teacher,' no deposition from the cross, and no 'broken body of their Master' to be stood guard over until Judgment Day. Therefore there is no 'well-defined Essenic pattern into which Jesus of Nazareth fits,' as Mr Allegro is alleged in one report to have said."

Allegro's claim that the Copper Scroll was a list of real buried treasure appeared to his colleagues to be another effort by him to create an unjustified sensation in the press.

When the Copper Scroll could not be unrolled, Professor H. Wright Baker of the College of Technology at Manchester cut the two rolls, layer by layer, into twenty-three semicircular strips.

The Copper Scroll, now cut into strips, is displayed in the Amman Archaeological Museum.

John Allegro, a member of the original scroll research team, led a search for the treasure of the Copper Scroll.

As soon as the scroll was opened, Allegro made a transcript and a translation, and later he was able to continue his study when the treasure was publicly displayed. A detailed study of the text was necessary if any of the sites where the treasure was buried were to be located.

In the summer of 1956, the Jordanians replaced Lankester Harding with one of their own as head of the Antiquities Department, and Allegro quickly developed a close relationship with the new director, who, unlike Harding, was in no way devoted to de Vaux. Allegro was delighted with the change: "The new Director of Antiquities offered me every facility for continuing my study of the text. I was also enabled to make two complete sets of photographs of the face of the scroll. This was a long and tedious process, for the curve in its surface meant that each segment had to be photographed many times in slightly different positions."[5]

In 1959 Milik published a preliminary translation of and commentary on the Copper Scroll in French,[6] followed soon thereafter by an English version.[7] In 1960 Allegro published his own book on the Copper Scroll, which included his translation of the text.[8] This was followed two years later by Milik's *editio princeps.*[9] All this focused public attention on the scroll's contents and on the question of whether the buried treasure it described was real or fictional.

Though it is often unclear whether a particular hoard mentioned in the scroll is gold or silver, and sometimes the unit of measurement is not given, estimates of the buried gold and silver described in the scroll vary from almost sixty tons to about two hundred tons. In fact, no one knows the modern equivalents of *talents* and *minas*; it's possible that a *talent* weighs something between twenty-five and seventy-five pounds. Despite the uncertainties, however, there is no question that the total amount described is substantial, a minimum, based on the lowest estimate, of one hundred twenty thousand pounds—worth roughly a third of a billion dollars in today's market. The upper estimate would be about a billion dollars.

Largely because of the huge quantities of buried treasure recorded, the vagueness of the locations, and the poor quality of the inscription, Milik and de Vaux claimed that the treasure was fictional, perhaps in part to discourage treasure hunters as well as disparage Allegro. As early as 1956, shortly after the Copper Scroll had been cut open, Milik wrote, "It almost goes without saying that the document is not an historical record of actual treasures buried in antiquity. The characteristics of the document itself, not to mention the fabulous quantity of precious metals and treasures recorded in it, place it firmly in the genre of folklore."[10] In the press release announcing the contents of the scroll, the publication team described it as merely "a collection of traditions about buried treasure."[11]

Superficially, this seemed a reasonable position, in view of examples such as these:

> On Mount Gerizim under the stairs of the higher underground cavity, a box and its contents and 60 talents of silver.

> At the mouth of the spring of Bet-Sham (Beth-Shean?), vessels of silver and vessels of gold, of offering and silver. In all 600 talents.

> In the great underground duct of the sepulchral chamber towards the house of the sepulchral chamber. The whole weighing 71 talents and 20 minas.

Today, however, most scholars agree with Allegro that the scroll describes actual treasure. The chief reason for this opinion is the form of the document, which provides no evidence that the list is fanciful but simply lists site after site in literal terms, without any narrative setting whatever.

Moreover, a number of locations are described in unusually realistic detail. For example, one site mentions Bethsaida, where offering vessels are buried "in the reservoir where you enter the small pool." Many sites appear to be listed in geographical order. Most of the sites are located in Jerusalem and environs and in the Jericho-Qumran area.

Some scholars have suggested that the site descriptions are intended simply as reminders to officials who knew the precise locations where the treasure was buried and needed only to be given the sometimes vague descriptions in the scroll as keys to recall. Or further directions might be given in a second copy of the scroll, referred to in the text concerning the final site in the list: In the final site, located "in the underground cavity which is in the smooth rock north of Kokhlit whose opening is towards the north with tombs at its mouth," there is "a copy of this writing and its explanation and the measurements and the details of each item."

As one scholar has said, "No writer could fail so exceedingly if the intent had been to produce a romance of hidden, glorious temple treasure. We read nothing of a golden menorah . . . much less of an ark of the covenant—those items which would have been highlighted if this were a folktale as Milik proposed."[12]

That the list is preserved on a copper plaque—which may not have been intended to be rolled like a scroll, but may have been mounted on a wall of a treasury[13]—indicates its importance and the need for permanence. This is not the stuff of fairy tales, a view buttressed by the announcement at the end of the list that a second copy is available elsewhere with more details. As Kyle McCarter has argued, "It is extremely difficult to imagine that anyone would have gone to the trouble to prepare a costly sheet of pure copper and imprint it with such an extensive and sober list of locations unless he had been entrusted with hiding a real and immensely valuable treasure and wanted to make a record of his work that could withstand the ravages of time."[14]

Nor is the great value of the treasure necessarily fanciful. Ancient literature contains many references to vast treasures obtained in military adventures or held in communal treasuries or as tribute imposed on conquered nations. Compared with these, the treasure listed in the Copper Scroll is not impossibly large. Herodotus says that the annual income of the Persian kings was nearly forty tons of gold, which is about two-thirds of the low estimate for the

Copper Scroll—and that's just for one year. The treasure Alexander the Great found at Persepolis and Susa has been estimated at the equivalent of over four times the highest estimate of the gold and silver described in the Copper Scroll. Pompey exacted tribute of ten thousand talents, presumably of gold, when he conquered Jerusalem in 63 B.C.[15] According to 1 Chronicles 22:14, King David left his son Solomon funds with which to build the Temple, including one hundred thousand talents of gold and a million talents of silver. As one authority has stated, "The sums listed in the Copper Scroll are not beyond the realm of reason, [although] they are, to be sure, very, very large. . . . We can no longer consign the Copper Scroll to the category of fantasy literature on the grounds that the figures it contains are too large to believe."[16]

In 1959 and 1960,[17] with financial support from a London tabloid, Allegro conducted a search for the sites where the treasure presumably had been buried. He began with this description: "In the fortress which is in the Vale of Achor, 40 cubits under the steps entering to the east: a money chest and its contents, of a weight of 17 talents."

Allegro translates the Hebrew *horebbah* as "fortress."[18] Vermes, on the other hand, leaves *horebbah* untranslated, while two other scholars, Michael Wise and Florentino García Martínez, read the word as *horveh* and translate it "ruin." Allegro and others have probably correctly identified the biblical valley of Achor as the northern border of Judah (modern name: el-Buqei'ah). Overlooking the valley, six miles west of Qumran, there is a Hasmonean *fortress,* which may be why Allegro uses that translation instead of "ruin." In Arabic the site is called Khirbet Mird. It is generally identified as ancient Hyrcania. According to Josephus, in 31 B.C. Herod the Great rebuilt a Hasmonean fortress that stood here.

Admitting that "there are a number of fortifications in the area," Allegro nevertheless decided that the "fortress" referred to in the Copper Scroll "can hardly be other than [Hyrcania or Khirbet Mird]."[19] There Allegro and his team concentrated on the easily identified Herodian masonry, especially what appeared to be walls enclosing the fortress, but they were unable to find the "eastern entrance" and thus were "unable to define the treasure site 'forty cubits under the steps entering to the east.' "[20]

Undaunted, Allegro tried the next site, described as "In the sepulchral monument, in the third course of stones: 100 bars of gold," which he supposed to be "in the vicinity" of the first site. The word that Allegro translates as "sepulchral monument" others translate simply as "tomb" or "sepulcher."[21] Allegro probably chose "sepulchral monument" because he located an installation overlooking the valley that "at first sight appears to be a look-out post. . . . But closer inspection shows it to be more monumental in character." This Allegro then refers to as a "monument." His surveyor "thought that it could well have been a funerary monument, and certainly there was no difficulty in determining the 'third course of stones.' "[22]

Allegro's group had brought with them what he described as "metal and cavity detectors of the most advanced type," but they were unable to locate the place in the wall where the treasure might be buried. In the end they decided not to "destroy the whole monument on the off-chance that it might be the treasure cache of the copper scroll."[23]

From Hyrcania, Allegro proceeded to Qumran itself, along a route the Copper Scroll refers to as "the way from Jericho to Secacah." Secacah, a site mentioned in the Bible, is named in four successive Copper Scroll site descriptions, and Allegro identifies it with Qumran, a view held by a number of scholars.[24]

In one of the Copper Scroll references to Secacah a site is described as "in a fissure . . . in the 'Solomon' reservoir." At Qumran there is some evidence of earthquake damage; one of the cisterns on the eastern side of the site is actually split down its length. According to Allegro's description, "one side dropped some two feet lower than the other," thus creating a fissure that "would have served well as a deposit for treasure."[25] The cavity was big enough to crawl into, which Allegro did, but found only a few potsherds. He concluded, nonetheless, that it was "such an obvious hiding place" that Roman soldiers would easily have found it when they destroyed the site in 68 A.D. and thereafter occupied it. "Doubtless they would have spent their spare time searching the ruins for any trophies or valuables their enemies might have left, and the gaping earthquake fissure would not have gone unnoticed."[26]

Allegro failed to find any of the treasure referred to in the Copper Scroll, nor did he identify a single site with any conviction, let alone certainty. He continued to speculate, however, that this or that location might be one of the sites mentioned in the scroll or that he had found what might be "the pit" or "the upper ditch" and concluded that "only a full excavation . . . could tell [if the identification was correct],"[27] since his metal-detecting equipment penetrated only eighteen inches,[28] and the treasure was sometimes buried as deep as ten feet below the surface.

Allegro readily conceded that in his identifications he had "strayed into the field of conjecture,"[29] but he was unquestionably correct as to the general vicinity of the burial places. Determining the exact spot, however, from the vague descriptions in the scroll is almost impossible.

He believed that many of the sites were in and around the Temple Mount in Jerusalem. In this, too, he is almost surely correct. Occasionally he excavated, but, again, without success. For example, he looked for "the tomb of Zadok" near the well-known trio of monumental Hellenistic tombs in Jerusalem's Kidron Valley that includes the Tomb of Absolom, but found nothing significant.

He also explored the Temple Mount, the Haram al-Sharif, as it is known in Moslem tradition. According to Allegro, approximately two dozen sites were located here, but "only persons having an intimate knowledge of the Temple courts and their chambers, their private names and functions, would be able to recognize them and rob them of their sacred treasure."[30]

He thought he could learn more by examining the underground chambers and cavities in the Temple Mount, which has never been done in modern times. The Moslem authorities were surprisingly cooperative, according to Allegro. "We found the authorities most willing to assist, from the governor of the city to the custodian of the sanctuary." But "suddenly . . . the good will we had been shown gave way to mumbled evasions and shamefaced looks."[31] The military commander of Jerusalem had decided, Allegro was told, that the timing was inopportune. Allegro assumed his problem was his enemies at the École Biblique, particularly de Vaux and Milik. As evidence, he cited a later article in the École's scholarly journal "rejoicing at the miscarriage of our plans." Thus "this priceless opportunity" had to be left "unexploited." Allegro concluded: "Until new blood and enterprise [are] injected into Palestinian archaeology, many priceless opportunities will continue to be lost."[32]

Although Allegro failed to identify a single site with certainty, many of his suggestions are generally reasonable. Allegro himself has said, "It would, of course, be absurd to dismiss the whole scroll as fiction,"[33] and Al Wolters, a recent translator of the Copper Scroll, believes that "a scholarly consensus seems to be emerging that the Copper Scroll is an authentic record of ancient treasure."[34] Whether any of the treasure still exists is another question. Allegro thought that "there is some possibility that, in the desert locations at least, it is still there."[35] Others hold that it is unlikely.

Whose treasure was it? Who buried it, and who hoped one day to retrieve it?

Here the scholarly speculation is no more reliable than a layperson's. Perhaps the treasure belonged to the Temple or to the Essene treasury. Or perhaps it's a second-century A.D. treasury related to the Second Jewish Revolt against Rome, the so-called Bar Kokhba revolt. From the nooks and crannies of ancient history books and from fertile scholarly imaginations come still other possibilities.

The most popular guess, with which I agree, is that the treasure belonged to the Temple in Jerusalem:

- The size of the treasure makes the Jerusalem Temple the prime candidate. It can be argued that the Essene community could also have had such a hoard, since its members placed all their property in a communal treasury, but this seems less likely.

- The number of sites in or near Jerusalem mentioned in the scroll also seems to me to favor the Temple treasury, though it has been argued that at least some of these Jerusalem sites are in areas where the Essenes lived.

- At a number of sites, cultic vessels and vestments are buried, including libation vessels (Site 13) and the priestly garment called the *ephod* (Site 4). This too seems to me to suggest the Jerusalem Temple.

- In the same vein, one site description refers to materials that are *herem,* that is, as Vermes tells us in his translation, items consecrated to the Temple.

- Another bit of evidence involves a disputed reading of a passage concerning Site 32. Some scholars see a reference here to Beth (house or family) of Hakkoz.[36] Others read Beth ha-Qos[37] or Beth Achsar.[38] Allegro translates the words as "Summer House."[39] If the correct reading is indeed Beth Hakkoz (as in the most authoritative reading[40]), the reference may be to the family that served as Temple treasurer. That the House of Hakkoz was a priestly family is clear; in Ezra 2:61 and Nehemiah 7:63, the sons of Hakkoz are referred to as members of a priestly family that returned from the Babylonian exile but were unable to prove their priestly lineage and so were assigned priestly duties that did not require genealogical purity. Nehemiah 3:4 refers to one Meremoth, son of Uriah, son of Hakkoz, who helped to repair the wall of Jerusalem. In Ezra 8:33, Meremoth, son of Uriah, was entrusted with the silver, gold, and Temple vessels that were brought back from the Babylonian exile. Supposedly the grandfather of this Meremoth was Hakkoz (Nehemiah 3:4). If this is so, it would hardly be surprising if some of the Temple treasure was buried near the residence of Beth Hakkoz. In the words of Kyle McCarter, "The Hakkoz family were the treasurers of the Temple!"[41]

The major difficulty with the Jerusalem Temple theory is that the Temple authorities would be unlikely to hide the key to their treasures in a cave in an area inhabited by their hated enemies the Qumranites, much less in the cave where the Qumranites stored their scrolls. Nevertheless, here is my own guess:

The First Jewish Revolt against Rome began in 66 A.D. and lasted four years, ending in 70 A.D. with the burning of Jerusalem and the destruction of the Temple. The Temple authorities took the precaution of hiding parts of the treasure in several places, some in Jerusalem and some in the ancient refugee route through the Kidron Valley toward the Dead Sea and the Wilderness of Judah. In 68 A.D. the advancing Roman legions destroyed Qumran, dispersing its Essene occupants (assuming Qumran was an Essene community in the first place). There is evidence that the Jewish militants who continued to occupy Masada after 68 A.D. also occupied Qumran at the same time. As the end approached (after the destruction of Qumran but before the destruction of Jerusalem itself), the Temple authorities decided to hide the copper plaque listing the secret hiding places of some of their treasury, which was written to be of little use to the uninitiated. As they rolled up the plaque, it broke in two. They then took the two halves to a cave near Qumran, occupied now by militants to whom they did not have the same doctrinal objections as to the former occupants. Perhaps realizing that the cave already held a hidden store, they cut a shelf in the rock wall at the rear of the cave and laid the two rolls of copper there, quite apart from the other scrolls in the cave. There it was found by archaeologists nearly two thousand years later.

But there are problems with this guess. The handwriting on the Copper Scroll is poor and full of errors, even taking into account the difficulty of pounding out the letters on metal.[42] For this reason, among others, Frank Cross doubts that the Copper Scroll describes real treasure.[43] And why would the people who hid the Copper Scroll choose a cave that others were already using as a hiding place?

Other anomalies add still further to the mysteries of the Copper Scroll. The Hebrew itself is peculiar. In the words of one expert, "[It has] no parallel in any of the hundreds of other scrolls from the eleven [Qumran] caves. . . . It is not identical to any Hebrew that we know." It might be a village dialect. The spelling too is unusual; "no orthographic system quite matches the one used in the Copper Scroll."[44]

The language, script, and spelling somewhat resemble Mishnaic Hebrew, the Hebrew of the Mishnah, the first great Rabbinic code, usually dated about 200 A.D. On this basis Milik originally dated the Copper Scroll to about 100 A.D., perhaps hoping to divorce it from the rest of the scrolls, since Qumran was destroyed in 68 A.D., and thus discourage treasure hunters like Allegro and his claims as to the scroll's nature. If the scroll dated only to 100 A.D., it was hardly likely that the impoverished Jews of the time would have had a treasury of this magnitude.

Less tendentiously, Frank Cross dates the scroll to between 25 and 75 A.D., and today most scholars would agree.[45] "Reviewing the evidence as a whole . . . a date before A.D. 68 imposes itself on the writer."[46]

Deepening the mystery still more are some strange letters in Greek appearing after a number of the descriptions of treasure. After Sites 1, 4, 6, 10, 14, and 17 there are sometimes two, sometimes three Greek letters. There also may be other signs that are not letters (especially after Site 17). The Greek letters do not form words or known abbreviations. One scholar has suggested that they may represent the quantities of treasure buried at the site.[47] Another recent suggestion is that they are abbreviations of names of priestly families responsible for the treasure at that particular site.[48] But why do the letters appear after these six sites and only these six?

On the other hand, these mysterious Greek letters may connect the Copper Scroll with other Qumran manuscripts, some of which also include cryptic Greek letters which puzzle scholars.[49]

One aspect of the Copper Scroll unrecognized by Milik, de Vaux, and Allegro was noticed by the talmudic scholar Manfred Lehmann, who found that the scroll contains considerable technical religious terminology from the Talmud. For example, the term *kli dema'*, which appears in the scroll several times, refers to "vessels of *terumah*," a portion of Temple sacrifices given to the priests, which Milik translates as "aromatic vases," and Allegro calls "tithe vessels."[50] Another term, *ma'aser sheni*, refers to the "second tithe"; still another, *herem*, refers to a "consecrated offering." The presence of these technical terms strengthens the connection of the scroll to the Temple.

Lehmann argues that the Copper Scroll reflects the Temple tax that continued to be self-imposed *after* the Temple's destruction. University of Chicago scholar Norman Golb, on the other hand, connects the Copper Scroll with the other Qumran scrolls to support his view that the scrolls as a whole represent not an Essene library or even a sectarian library but the mainstream Jewish library of the Temple. And so the debate goes on.

In 1993, the government of Jordan decided to allow conservation of the Copper Scroll, which, as one scholar said, had been gradually "disappearing."[51] The strips were taken to Paris, where a French team not only conserved the twenty-three semicircular segments but created an exact replica that could be flattened and joined, making photographing, reading, and studying the text far easier. The scroll is now back in Amman, and a new edition of the text is being prepared by Father Émile Puech of the École Biblique. Puech's work is also facilitated by digitalized high-resolution X-rays that can be manipulated on a computer screen. Whether all this will solve some of the mysteries of the scroll remains to be seen.

And what of Allegro? Shunned by the scholarly community, he ultimately left academia to pursue a career as a writer. During his scroll years, he was described as "cavalier, impudent, cheerfully iconoclastic," but in time the hostility of the scholarly community left him "weary and disillusioned."[52] In 1970, he committed scholarly suicide by publishing a book entitled *The Sacred Mushroom and the Cross,* in which he argued that Jesus never existed but was merely an image produced by early Christians under the influence of hallucinogenic mushrooms, that Christianity began as an orgiastic mushroom cult. In a letter to the London *Times,* fourteen prominent British scholars, including his old Oxford mentor, Godfrey Driver, repudiated the book and his publisher apologized for publishing it. Allegro remained in academic and literary exile until his death at sixty-five in 1988.

Frank Cross has described Allegro as "one of the few amoral people I have known. . . . the paranoid ravings about Vatican control [that] he gave to the tabloids, [he] knew very well [were] untrue." I once asked Cross if he could explain Allegro's motive. "[Allegro] told me," Cross replied, that it was "money. He did not bother with excuses. When he returned to the scrollery after a good deal of this slander had been printed, I confronted him. I said, 'John, were you correctly quoted in these interviews and newspaper stories?' He admitted that he had been quoted more or less accurately. I then expressed my scorn. I had no further dealings with Allegro. . . . He was a friendly and engaging person, but he was bent."[53] Nevertheless, without him, the Copper Scroll might still be regarded as fiction.

CHAPTER 12

LOOKING TOWARD THE FUTURE

The Dead Sea Scrolls have rightly been called the greatest archaeological discovery of the twentieth century, the only archaeological discovery that almost everyone has heard of. Yet, paradoxically, few people can tell why they are so important—or, more specifically, what they tell us that makes them so important.

This is because few descriptions have placed them in context. As we have seen, their significance becomes clear only when understood as part of a larger scholarly canvas—which has been the burden of this book.

For many, the most exciting aspects of the scrolls relate to what they tell us about Jesus and the early Christian community. Yet they tell us nothing about these matters directly. Jesus is not in the scrolls. Scholars have struggled for years to understand this critical moment in human history, and the scrolls are by no means the only materials they have used to understand how Christianity developed. But they are an important part of the puzzle—indeed, as we understand more of the scrolls, an increasingly important part.

Today a consensus exists among scholars that to understand Jesus, we must understand the Jewish world in which he lived. This is where the scrolls are important, for they are among our best windows on that world. This creates a problem for many New Testament scholars, schooled and expert in the Greek of the New Testament but not the Hebrew and Aramaic of the scrolls. Senior New Testament scholars must now learn new languages and absorb a whole new body of evidence. This may explain why many recent books on Jesus and early Christianity hardly mention the scrolls.

While the scrolls tell us nothing directly about Jesus or early Christianity, they tell us a great deal about the language Jesus spoke, about such concepts as "Messiah" and "Son of God," about the way Jesus and early Christians understood and interpreted the Hebrew Bible, about modes of thought of Jesus' contemporaries, and about the other Jewish movements that were swirling around in the ideological and theological maelstrom of Judea at the time. If the scrolls emphasize anything with regard to Christianity, it is that Jesus and his message were very much related to—were part of and grew out of—what was happening in the contemporaneous Jewish world.

Thus the scrolls tell us about Christianity by telling us a great deal about that world. The latest book of the Hebrew Bible, Daniel, dates to about 150 B.C. The earliest Rabbinic text is the Mishnah, redacted in about 200 A.D. The period between is a comparative black hole. The scrolls are a whole library of manuscripts from that dark period.

Yet the library apparently belonged to a marginal Jewish group that had separated itself from mainstream, or what scholars are now calling "common," Judaism. The Qumran group used a different calendar and despised the Jews who controlled the Jerusalem Temple. What can we learn from this group that will enlighten us about the history of Judaism at the turn of the era? We have seen that some of the scrolls are not sectarian; they apparently belonged to mainstream Judaism. Some of the scrolls describe the group's adversaries, if only polemically. And the scrolls in general reflect the ideas and modes of thought that engaged Jews, both mainstream and marginal, at the time. Thus, for example, we have seen that Jewish society, whether mainstream or fringe, was intensely concerned with purity and impurity. We still don't know why this was so. But it is clear that it *was* so. It is perhaps easier to understand why Jews at the time were concerned with the end of days and what scholars call apocalypticism, given the social conditions of the period. All of this is illuminated by the scrolls. But, again, it is part of a larger body of evidence that bears on these questions.

As we have seen, the scrolls also help us understand the Hebrew Bible and its development, how a variety of texts and versions were once widely accepted, how these texts emerged as different families of manuscripts (Masoretic, Septuagintal, and Samaritan), how the Rabbinic *textus receptus* was standardized and ultimately canonized, and how, side by side, other Bible-like books developed that were ultimately excluded from the canon.

These are some of the significant areas illuminated by the scrolls. But there are many more. Indeed, it would be more accurate to start from the other end: There is not a single question about the period from the third century B.C. to the second century A.D. that can be explored without asking whether the scrolls shed some light on the matter.

These new materials are not easily absorbed. They are fragmentary, elliptical, and written in arcane, symbolic, and metaphorical language. Indeed the scrolls have given rise to a whole new discipline, variously called Qumranology or simply Qumran studies. Just reading all the secondary literature would be an impossible task. A bibliography of Dead Sea Scroll studies published between 1970 and 1995 lists approximately six thousand items.[1]

Even the greatest scroll authorities have been unable to reach a consensus on such central questions in connection with the scrolls as who wrote them and what their relationship was to the ruins adjacent to the caves where they were found. The mysteries remain.

Now that all scholars have access to them, Dead Sea Scroll research has burgeoned. About this everyone agrees. As a result of the notoriety the scrolls have received, Qumran studies have attracted an abundance of bright young scholars. Whether they will eventually solve the many puzzles the scrolls present, however, remains a moot question. We may never know, for example, whether or not the sectarian scrolls are Essene documents.

Some of the questions, however, may one day be answered by still-undiscovered scrolls or by scrolls that have been discovered but are still in private hands. Nearly all scholars agree that more scrolls exist, either in the hands of antiquities dealers and private collectors or in caves near Qumran.

Recently there have been rumors in London, Washington, and Jerusalem that scrolls were being offered for sale on the antiquities market. For example, I was told that a complete scroll has already been purchased by a collector, who will one day make it public.

But not since 1967, when the famous Temple Scroll was recovered, has a scroll come to light. On the third day of the Six-Day War, with Israel newly in control of all Jerusalem and Bethlehem, Yigael Yadin sent a colonel in the Israeli army to confront Kando concerning a scroll that Yadin suspected Kando was hiding. Kando removed some tiles from the floor of his Bethlehem home and pulled out a Bata shoe box in which he had placed the Temple Scroll, which was immediately confiscated by the Israeli authorities. Ultimately, Kando was paid $105,000 for the scroll, though he had previously turned down an offer for $130,000.

From that day to this, not a single new scroll fragment that we know of has appeared on the antiquities market. (Of course, we don't know about clandestine sales.) According to one rumor, after the Temple Scroll incident, Kando smuggled all his remaining scroll materials to Damascus.

In 1994, John Strugnell told me that Lankester Harding, the last British Director of Antiquities in Jordan, claimed on his deathbed that shortly after the 1967 Six-Day War he had seen three intact Qumran scrolls in Aleppo, Syria. Strugnell said that he too had seen some scrolls that have never surfaced.

"I wouldn't be surprised if there were five other manuscripts . . . somewhere to be found in the near future," Strugnell continued. "I wouldn't be overwhelmed if there were seven or

eight. If none ever came to light, I would wonder who on earth had been having these hallucinations, or why they are being held back."

One reason more scrolls have not surfaced, we are told, is that the people who have them—collectors, investors, and dealers—fear they will be confiscated, as Kando's Temple Scroll was, or that they themselves will be held up to opprobrium instead of honored. Professional archaeologists often disdain collectors and dealers. The price of this high-mindedness may be that there have been no new scrolls since 1967.

Others—I among them—believe we must encourage people who have scroll materials to come forward. We want to learn what their treasures can tell us about our past. Eventually, these collections will pass to public museums. In many cases, public donors can be found who will finance their purchase on behalf of a museum, as happened with the great hoards of Dead Sea Scrolls. If the authorities hadn't dealt with the illegal excavators and their middlemen, the thousands of fragments from Cave 4, for example, would now be in hundreds of private hands all over the world. That today they are almost all in the Rockefeller Museum in Jerusalem—where fragments from the same scroll can be identified and reassembled and where scholars can assess the library as a whole—is a tribute to the common sense of the scholars who originally acquired the scrolls from Kando.

Other scrolls are almost certainly still in the caves. The entrances to these caves, however, have long been blocked and obscured by rockfalls caused by earthquakes. With the use of sonar equipment these caves may someday be located. Or another earthquake may open them. In the words of John Strugnell, "Every twenty-five years or so, the Jordan Valley is torn apart by earthquakes. That's when I expect old collapsed caves to be open. That's when I expect certain manuscripts to come to light."

Even in caves that have already been explored, scroll materials may lie buried under rockfalls that could not be moved either by the bedouin or by professional archaeologists with limited equipment. Nearly forty years ago, Pesach Bar-Adon, leading an Israeli team that was exploring caves in a nearby wadi, reported that the floors of tens of caves were covered with rockfalls that could not be moved. In one of these caves he found scroll fragments in Hebrew and Greek. "Perhaps the missing part of the complete scroll is yet pinned under these rocks," he said.[2] If so, it's still there.

In another case, a young kibbutznik managed to remove enough of the boulders in such a rockfall so that he could get a glimpse of the floor beneath. In the glare of his flashlight he saw, pinned beneath the rocks, a skeleton clothed in a white robe with a rope belt.[3] What else lies beneath this pile of rocks remains a mystery.

With modern equipment and the will to do so, it should be possible to explore what lies beneath some of the most promising rock piles. Frank Cross believes that someday that will happen: "I think I can say there are still scrolls, mostly in collapsed caves. One day these will come to light. It will be very exciting."[4]

Meanwhile, scholars continue to add to our understanding of the startling new literature that has already come to light. Their studies are often narrow and technical. But gradually, step by step, there will be enough for a more convincing synthesis than can be presented today. In the meantime, much work remains to be done.

NOTES

INTRODUCTION

1. André Dupont-Sommer, *The Dead Sea Scrolls: A Preliminary Survey* (Oxford: Basil Blackwell, 1952), p. 99.

2. Edmund Wilson, *The Scrolls from the Dead Sea* (New York: Oxford University Press, 1955).

3. Ibid., p. 102.

4. Ibid., p. 104.

5. Geza Vermes, *The Complete Dead Sea Scrolls in English* (New York: Allen Lane/Penguin Press, 1997), p. 7.

6. Josephus, *Jewish Antiquities,* Ralph Marcus, trans., Loeb Classical Library (London: Heinemann/Cambridge, Mass.: Harvard University Press, 1969), 12.5.1.

7. Shaye J. D. Cohen, in H. Shanks, ed., *Ancient Israel* (Washington, D.C.: Biblical Archaeology Society, 1988), p. 215.

1. EXPLORING THE LEGEND

1. The foundation was created in 1991.

2. On the other hand, it is claimed that edh-Dhib was not illiterate and had studied in the elementary school of the Lutheran Church at Bethlehem. William H. Brownlee, "Edh-Dheeb's Story of His Scroll Discovery," *Revue de Qumran* 3:12 (October 1962), p. 489.

3. See John C. Trever, *The Dead Sea Scrolls: A Personal Account* (Grand Rapids, Mich.: Eerdmans, 1965), p. 219, n. 17. Trever discounts,

on what basis is unclear, the accuracy of the claim (by another edh-Dhib?) that he left his initial find hanging in a bag for years.

4. Ibid., p. 98.

5. Ibid., p. 218, n. 6.

6. William H. Brownlee, "Some New Facts Concerning the Discovery of the Scrolls of 1Q," *Revue de Qumran* 4 (1963), p. 418. Lankester Harding also confused the matter by using the name edh-Dheeb for two persons. Harding gave a different account to the London *Times* from the one he published in *Discoveries in the Judean Desert I.*

7. William H. Brownlee, "Muhammad Ed-Deeb's Own Story of His Scroll Discovery," *Journal of Near Eastern Studies* 16 (1957), p. 236. See also Brownlee, "Some New Facts," p. 488.

8. John C. Trever, "When Was Qumran Cave 1 Discovered?" *Revue de Qumran* 3:9 (February 1961), p. 135. Two astute observers have recently noted that "the precise details concerning the discovery and removal of manuscript fragments from Cave 1 will never be known." George J. Brooke and James M. Robinson, "A Further Fragment of 1QSb: The Schøyen Collection MS 1909," *Journal of Jewish Studies* 46:120 (1995), p. 124. As early as 1955, Millar Burrows of Yale, who was director of the American School of Oriental Research in Jerusalem in 1947 and was a major player in the early years of scroll research, came to the same conclusion. Millar Burrows, *The Dead Sea Scrolls* (New York: Gramercy Publishing Company, 1955), p. 4.

9. See, for example, Brownlee, "Edh-Dheeb's Story," pp. 484–85.

10. According to William Brownlee, Faidi al-'Alami is "the only dealer in antiquities at Bethlehem which figures in any of the [early] accounts." Ibid., p. 490.

11. "[Najib S.] Khoury thinks the same man [known as Faidi Salahi] was known as Faidi al-'Alami in Bethlehem." Brownlee, "Some New Facts," p. 418.

12. Frank Moore Cross, *The Ancient Library of Qumran and Modern Biblical Studies,* rev. ed. (Grand Rapids, Mich.: Baker Book House, 1961, reprinted 1980), pp. 6–7, n. 2.

13. Ibid., p. 7.

14. Edward M. Cook, *Solving the Mysteries of the Dead Sea Scrolls* (Grand Rapids, Mich.: Zondervan, 1994), p. 13.

15. See Yigael Yadin, *The Message of the Scrolls* (New York: Simon and Schuster, 1957). Yadin draws upon the account in his father's diary.

16. There is some confusion about the exact date. Sukenik's diary says November 29. It could have been November 28.

17. Yadin, *Message of the Scrolls,* pp. 13–14.

18. Harry Thomas Frank, in Hershel Shanks, ed., *Understanding the Dead Sea Scrolls* (New York: Random House, 1992), p. 10.

19. The Nash Papyrus was dated from the second century B.C. to the second century A.D. before the evidence of the Dead Sea Scrolls became available. See Geza Vermes, *The Dead Sea Scrolls—Qumran in Perspective*, rev. ed. (Philadelphia: Fortress Press, 1981), pp. 35–36. Albright, even without the scrolls, dated it to the mid-second century B.C. See P. Kyle McCarter, Jr., *Ancient Inscriptions: Voices from the Biblical World* (Washington, D.C.: Biblical Archaeology Society, 1996), p. 157. With the refinements afforded by the scrolls, Albright's date has been confirmed. See Moshe Greenberg, s.v. "Nash Papyrus" in the *Encyclopedia Judaica* (c. 150 B.C.E.); Emanuel Tov, *Textual Criticism of the Hebrew Bible* (Minneapolis: Fortress Press, 1992), p. 118 (first or second century B.C.E.); and Ada Yardeni, *The Book of Hebrew Script* (Jerusalem: Carta, 1997), p. 45 (about the middle of the second century B.C.E.). According to Yardeni, the Nash Papyrus represents an early stage in the evolution of the Jewish cursive script (p. 172). A recently found marriage papyrus contract with a similar script suggests a date of 176 B.C.

20. Solomon Zeitlin, "The Zadokite Fragments: Facsimile of the Manuscripts in the Cairo Genizah Collection in the Possession of the University Library, Cambridge, England," *Jewish Quarterly Review,* Monograph Series 1 (Philadelphia: Dropsie College, 1952).

21. Quotations are from Harry M. Orlinsky, "The Bible Scholar Who Became an Undercover Agent," *Biblical Archaeology Review* 18:14 (July/August 1992), p. 26.

22. Yadin, *Message of the Scrolls,* p. 38.

2. ARCHAEOLOGISTS VS. BEDOUIN

1. Credit for finding the original cave is disputed. "The placing of the original text find into an archaeological context was due . . . to a bored Belgian army officer serving with the U.N. Observer force." Geza Vermes, "The Dead Sea Scrolls Forty Years On," a pamphlet published by the Oxford Centre for Postgraduate Hebrew Studies, 1987, p. 1. The Belgian army officer, Philippe Lippens, apparently instigated the search by the Arab Legion. See Millar Burrows, *Burrows on the Dead Sea Scrolls* (Grand Rapids, Mich.: Baker Book House, 1978), pp. 32–33.

2. Frank Moore Cross, Jr., *The Ancient Library of Qumran and Modern Biblical Studies,* rev. ed. (Grand Rapids, Mich.: Baker Book House, 1980), p. 12.

3. Ibid., pp. 12–13.

4. Robert Donceel in *The Oxford Encyclopedia of Archaeology in the Near East,* s.v. "Qumran."

5. I often rely on de Vaux's dating for lack of anything better, but as will be discussed, I do so without much confidence.

6. This is de Vaux's interpretation. Not everyone agrees. Israeli archaeologist Yizhar Hirschfeld believes that the 31 B.C. earthquake caused little if any damage at Qumran and that the apparent earthquake damage at the site occurred long after 68 A.D., at which time the site was destroyed by the Romans.

7. Yizhar Hirschfeld disputes de Vaux's conclusion regarding a Roman military occupation.

8. Cross, *The Ancient Library of Qumran,* p. 8.

9. Hershel Shanks, ed., *Frank Moore Cross: Conversations with a Bible Scholar* (Washington, D.C.: Biblical Archaeology Society, 1994), p. 115.

3. THE TEAM AT WORK

1. Hershel Shanks, ed., *Frank Moore Cross: Conversations with a Bible Scholar* (Washington, D.C.: Biblical Archaeology Society, 1994), p. 129.

2. Joseph Fitzmyer uses $5.60. Joseph Fitzmyer, *Responses to 101 Questions on the Dead Sea Scrolls* (New York: Paulist Press, 1992), p. 9. He gives no explanation for how he came up with this figure, precisely twice $2.80. Others (e.g., Frank Moore Cross, in Shanks, *Frank Moore Cross*) use $2.80, the rate confirmed by exchange-rate sources.

3. Shanks, *Frank Moore Cross,* pp. 119–20.

4. See letter of Frank Moore Cross in *Biblical Archaeology Review* 16:1 (January/February 1990), p. 18. Also Shanks, *Frank Moore Cross,* p. 124.

5. Edward M. Cook, *Solving the Mysteries of the Dead Sea Scrolls* (Grand Rapids, Mich.: Zondervan, 1994), p. 39.

6. John Strugnell, interview by Hershel Shanks, Cambridge, Mass., January 12, 1994.

7. Shanks, *Frank Moore Cross,* p. 141.

8. Ibid.

9. Ibid., p. 121.

10. "The Philistines and the Dothans—An Archaeological Romance: An Interview with Moshe and Trude Dothan" (Part 1), *Biblical Archaeology Review* 19:4 (July/August 1993), p. 26.

11. Strugnell, interview.

12. Shanks, *Frank Moore Cross,* p. 144.

13. Strugnell, interview.

14. Frank Moore Cross, Jr., *The Ancient Library of Qumran and Modern Biblical Studies,* rev. ed. (Grand Rapids, Mich.: Baker Book House, 1961, reprinted 1980), pp. 35, 37.

15. Ibid., p. 123.

16. Shanks, *Frank Moore Cross,* p. 128.

17. Strugnell, interview.

18. Starcky "was one lazy person." Strugnell, interview. A glance at Joseph Fitzmyer's *The Dead Sea Scrolls: Major Publications and Tools for Study,* rev. ed. (Atlanta: Scholars Press, 1990), will substantiate Strugnell's assessment; it will also return the accusation to Strugnell.

19. Strugnell, interview.

20. J. T. Milik, *The Books of Enoch: Aramaic Fragments of Qumran Cave 4* (Oxford: Clarendon Press, 1976).

21. See Hershel Shanks, "Debate on Enoch Stifled for 30 Years While One Scholar Studied Dead Sea Scrolls Fragments," *Bible Review* 3:2 (Summer 1987), p. 34.

22. Avraham Biran, interview by Hershel Shanks, July 27, 1996.

23. Strugnell, interview.

24. Yigael Yadin, *The Temple Scroll: The Hidden Law of the Dead Sea Scroll Sect* (London: Weidenfeld and Nicolson, 1985), p. 45.

4. FREEING THE SCROLLS

1. T. H. Gaster, *The Dead Sea Scriptures,* 2nd ed. (New York: Doubleday Anchor Press, 1976), p. xv.

2. Geza Vermes, *The Dead Sea Scrolls: Qumran in Perspective* (London: William Collins, Sons & Co., 1977), pp. 23–24.

3. Avi Katzman, "Chief Dead Sea Scroll Editor Denounces Judaism, Israel; Claims to Have Seen Four More Scrolls Found by Bedouin," *Biblical Archaeology Review* 17:1 (January/February 1991), pp. 64–72.

4. See the supplement to *The Qumran Chronicle* (December 1990).

5. "Poland Strikes Another Blow for Intellectual Freedom—MMT Once Again Available," *Biblical Archaeology Review* 18:6 (November/December 1992), p. 56.

5. UNDERMINING CHRISTIAN FAITH—OF A CERTAIN KIND

1. See Marcus J. Borg, "Profiles in Scholarly Courage: Early Days of New Testament Criticism," *Bible Review* 10:5 (October 1994), p. 40.

2. Ibid.

3. Citations to the literature may be found in Paul Rhodes Eddy, "Jesus as Diogenes? Reflections on the Cynic Jesus Thesis," *Journal of Biblical Literature* 115 (1996), p. 449.

4. N. T. Wright, *Anchor Bible Dictionary,* s.v. "Jesus, Quest for the Historical."

5. Cox's reference was to Daniel J. Harrington, "The Jewishness of Jesus," *Bible Review* 3:1 (Spring 1987).

6. Harvey Cox, "Jesus and Generation," in Marcus Borg, ed., *Jesus at 2000* (Boulder, Colo.: Westview Press, 1997), p. 101.

7. Harrington, "The Jewishness of Jesus."

8. Benedict T. Viviano, "Beatitudes Found Among Dead Sea Scrolls," *Biblical Archaeology Review* 18:6 (November/December 1992), p. 53. Viviano translates into English Émile Puech's original French translation of 4Q525 as published in E. Puech, "4Q525 et les péricopes des Béatitudes en Ben Sira et Matthieu," *Revue Biblique* 138 (1991), p. 80.

9. Helmut Koester, "The Gospel of Thomas (II,2)," in James H. Robinson, ed., *The Nag Hammadi Library in English,* 3rd ed. (San Francisco: Harper & Row Publishers, 1988), p. 132.

10. Geza Vermes, *The Complete Dead Sea Scrolls in English* (New York: Allen Lane/Penguin Press, 1997), pp. 391–92.

11. Daniel J. Harrington, S.J., called this to my attention.

12. Florentino García Martínez, *The Dead Sea Scrolls Translated,* Wilfred G. E. Watson., trans., 2nd ed. (Leiden: Brill, 1996), p. 127.

13. Vermes, *Complete Dead Sea Scrolls,* p. 159.

14. Michael Wise, Martin G. Abegg, Jr., and Edward M. Cook, *The Dead Sea Scrolls: A New Translation* (San Francisco: HarperSanFrancisco, 1996), p. 147.

15. The word is *yolid.* See the footnote in Vermes, *Complete Dead Sea Scrolls,* p. 159. Despite the computer enhancement on which Vermes relies, some scholars read *ytglh.* See Émile Puech, "La croyance des Esséniens en la vie future: Immortalité, résurrection, vie éternelle?" *Revue de Qumran* 16:62 (December 1993), p. 299.

16. Although in the last translation the *th* in "fathered" is in brackets, indicating a reconstruction, a computer enhancement at Oxford University indicates that it is there. Whether this will satisfy all doubters is unknown. See "A Textual Note" in James Charlesworth, ed., *The Dead Sea Scrolls: Hebrew, Aramaic, and Greek Texts with English Translations* 1 (Louisville, Ky.: Westminster John Knox Press, 1995), p. 109.

17. I thank P. Kyle McCarter for this observation.

18. Vermes, *Complete Dead Sea Scrolls,* p. 494.

19. John J. Collins, "A Pre-Christian 'Son of God' Among the Dead Sea Scrolls," *Bible Review* 9:3 (June 1993), p. 34, as supplemented by Vermes, *Complete Dead Sea Scrolls,* p. 577. Collins considers the various interpretations that have been given to "Son of God" in this text and concludes "with confidence" that it represents a messianic figure. Geza Vermes disagrees. See Vermes, *Complete Dead Sea Scrolls,* p. 576.

20. James Hoffmeier, "Son of God," *Bible Review* 13:3 (June 1997), p. 44.

21. See H. Neil Richardson, "The Old Testament Background of Jesus as Begotten of God," *Bible Review* 2:3 (Fall 1986), p. 22.

22. The New Jerusalem Bible adopts this version.

23. Hershel Shanks, ed., *Frank Moore Cross: Conversations with a Bible Scholar* (Washington, D.C.: Biblical Archaeology Society, 1994), pp. 156–57.

24. Joseph A. Fitzmyer, *Responses to 101 Questions on the Dead Sea Scrolls* (New York: Paulist Press, 1992), pp. 169–70.

25. See Joel 3:1 in the Hebrew Bible and 2:28 in most English versions.

26. The wine as blood is not mentioned in Luke.

27. Vermes, *Complete Dead Sea Scrolls*, p. 99.

28. Ibid., p. 111.

29. Ibid., p. 116.

30. Yigael Yadin, "The Temple Scroll: The Longest and Most Recently Discovered Dead Sea Scroll," *Biblical Archaeology Review* 10:5 (September/October 1984), p. 32.

31. Josephus, *The Jewish War*, H. St. J. Thackeray, trans., Loeb Classical Library (London: Heinemann/Cambridge, Mass.: Harvard University Press, 1976), 2:120.

32. See Otto Betz, "Was John the Baptist an Essene?" *Bible Review* 6:6 (December 1990), p. 18; Fitzmyer, *Responses to 101 Questions*, p. 107.

6. AN ESSENE LIBRARY?

1. See O. R. Sellers, "Radiocarbon Dating of Cloth from the 'Ain Feshka Cave," *Bulletin of the American Schools of Oriental Research* 123 (1951), p. 24.

2. In G. Ernest Wright, ed., *The Bible and the Ancient Near East: Essays in Honor of William Foxwell Albright* (New York: Doubleday, 1961).

3. See Hershel Shanks, "Carbon-14 Tests Substantiate Scroll Dates," *Biblical Archaeology Review* 17:6 (November/December 1991), p. 72; and Hershel Shanks, "New Carbon-14 Results Leave Room for Debate," *Biblical Archaeology Review* 21:4 (July/August 1995), p. 61.

4. Although Josephus does not name the fourth philosophy, many scholars identify it with the Zealots. See Josephus, *Jewish Antiquities*, L. H. Feldman, trans., Loeb Classical Library (London: Heinemann/Cambridge, Mass.: Harvard University Press, 1969), 18.6.

5. Josephus, *Life,* H. St. J. Thackeray, trans., Loeb Classical Library (London: Heinemann/Cambridge, Mass.: Harvard University Press, 1976), 4.5.

6. Josephus, *The Jewish War,* H. St. J. Thackeray, trans., Loeb Classical Library (London: Heinemann/Cambridge, Mass.: Harvard University Press, 1976), 2.4.

7. Bargil Pixner, "Jerusalem's Essene Gateway: Where the Community Lived in Jesus' Time," *Biblical Archaeology Review* 23:3 (May/June 1997), p. 22.

8. Josephus, *The Jewish War,* 2.4.

9. Josephus, *Jewish Antiquities,* 18.5.

10. Josephus, *The Jewish War,* 2.7.

11. Ibid.

12. Ibid., 2.6.

13. Ibid., 2.3.

14. Ibid.

15. Ibid.

16. Ibid., 2.3–4.

17. Ibid., 2.6.

18. Ibid., 2.7.

19. Ibid., 2.2.

20. Ibid.

21. Ibid., 2.13.

22. Ibid.

23. In 4Q270, 7i, 12–13 and also in a fragmentary state in 4Q267, 9vi, 4–5; quoted in Philip R. Davies, "Who Can Join the 'Damascus Covenant'?" *Journal of Jewish Studies* 46 (1995), p. 141.

24. Josephus, *The Jewish War,* 2.7.

25. Ibid., 2.9.

26. Ibid.

27. Hershel Shanks, "Outlook Grim for Final Report on Qumran Excavation," *Biblical Archaeology Review* 22:6 (November/December 1996), p. 44.

28. Josephus, *The Jewish War,* 2.10.

29. Ibid., 2.6.

30. Ibid., 2.6, 7.

31. Ibid., 2.7.

32. Ibid., 2.10.

33. Ibid., 2.11.

34. Josephus, *Jewish Antiquities,* Ralph Marcus, trans., Loeb Classical Library (London: Heinemann/Cambridge, Mass.: Harvard University Press, 1976), 13.9.

35. Ibid.

36. Josephus, *The Jewish War*, 2.14.

37. *Every Good Man Is Free*, 12.85–86, in *Philo*, F. H. Colson, trans., Loeb Classical Editions 9 (London: William Heinemann Ltd./ Cambridge, Mass.: Harvard University Press, 1961).

38. *Hypothetica*, 11.12, in *Philo*, F. H. Colson, trans., Loeb Classical Editions 9 (London: William Heinemann Ltd./Cambridge, Mass.: Harvard University Press, 1961).

39. Ibid., 11.1.

40. *Every Good Man Is Free*, 12.76.

41. *Hypothetica*, 11.14.

42. Ibid., 11.3.

43. *Every Good Man Is Free*, 12:84.

44. Ibid., 12:79.

45. We don't even know what the Hebrew word for "Essene" is. We have no Hebrew text with that word in it. All of its appearances are in Greek texts.

46. James H. Charlesworth, ed., *The Dead Sea Scrolls: Hebrew, Aramaic and Greek Texts with English Translations* 1 (Tübingen: J. C. B. Mohr/ Louisville: Westminster John Knox Press, 1994).

47. Geza Vermes, *The Complete Dead Sea Scrolls in English* (New York: Allen Lane/Penguin Press, 1997).

48. James C. VanderKam, *The Dead Sea Scrolls Today* (Grand Rapids, Mich.: William B. Eerdmans, 1994), p. 57.

49. Vermes, *Complete Dead Sea Scrolls*, p. 98.

50. Ibid., pp. 97–98.

51. Ibid., p. 108.

52. Ibid., p. 107.

53. Ibid.

54. Ibid.

55. Ibid., p. 105.

56. Ibid., p. 106.

57. Ibid., p. 105.

58. Ibid.

59. Ibid., pp. 107–8.

60. Ibid.

61. Ibid.

62. Josephus, *The Jewish War*, 2.9.

63. As noted by H. St. J. Thackeray, "Reinarch refers to a similar prohibition, applying to prayer-time, in Jerusalem Talmud (*Berachot*, iii, 5)" (Josephus, *The Jewish War*, p. 379, n.b.).

64. Vermes, *Complete Dead Sea Scrolls*, pp. 101–2.

65. Ibid., pp. 99–100.

66. Ibid., p. 99.

67. Ibid., p. 102.

68. Ibid., p. 103.

69. Ibid., p. 105.

70. Ibid., pp. 109–110.

71. Ibid., pp. 112–13.

72. Ibid., p. 115.

73. Raphael Levy, "First 'Dead Sea Scroll' Found in Egypt Fifty Years Before Qumran Discoveries," *Biblical Archaeology Review* 8:5 (September/October 1992), p. 38; and in Hershel Shanks, ed., *Understanding the Dead Sea Scrolls* (New York: Random House, 1992), pp. 63–78.

74. Solomon Schechter, *Documents of Jewish Sectaries: Fragments of a Zadokite Work* (Cambridge: Cambridge University Press, 1910), Introduction, pp. xv, xvi.

75. Louis Ginzburg, *An Unknown Jewish Sect* (New York: Jewish Theological Seminary of America, 1976).

76. R. H. Charles, ed., *The Apocrypha and Pseudepigrapha of the Old Testament in English* (Oxford: Clarendon Press, 1913), p. 790.

77. Joseph M. Baumgarten, "Sacrifice and Worship Among the Jewish Sectarians of the Dead Sea (Qumran) Scrolls," *Harvard Theological Review* 46 (1953), p. 141.

78. The Damascus Document, column 8, line 21. Translation from Vermes, *Complete Dead Sea Scrolls.*

79. Joseph M. Baumgarten and Daniel R. Schwartz in Charlesworth, ed., *Dead Sea Scrolls,* p. 4.

80. The Damascus Document, column 1, lines 2–4, 14–15; column 3, lines 10–11; column 4, lines 3–4; column 6, lines 5, 19; col. 19 (CD Ms B), lines 9–11. Translation from Vermes, *Complete Dead Sea Scrolls.*

81. Column 10, lines 7–9. Translation from Vermes, *Complete Dead Sea Scrolls.*

82. Column 12, lines 1–2. See also 11QTemple 45.11–12. Translation from Vermes, *Complete Dead Sea Scrolls.*

83. Charlesworth, ed., *Dead Sea Scrolls,* p. 61, 7. See also VanderKam, *Dead Sea Scrolls Today,* p. 57.

7. THE ARCHAEOLOGY OF QUMRAN

1. Roland de Vaux, *Archaeology and the Dead Sea Scrolls,* The Schweich Lectures of the British Academy, 1959 (Oxford: Oxford University Press, 1972, reprinted 1977), p. 30.

2. Ibid., pp. 11, 27.

3. Jean-Baptiste Humbert and Alain Chambon, *Fouilles de Khirbet Qumrân et de Ain Feshkha* (Fribourg: Éditions Universitaires Fribourg Suisse and Vandenhoeck/Göttingen: Ruprecht, 1994).

4. Yizhar Hirschfeld, "Khirbet Qumran—Hasmonean Desert Fortress and Herodian Estate Manor in the Kingdom of Judaea," forthcoming.

5. Jodi Magness, book review, *Dead Sea Discoveries* 3 (1996), p. 343.

6. See Hershel Shanks, "Death Knell for Israel Archaeology?" *Biblical Archaeology Review* 22:5 (September/October 1996), p. 48; and Hershel Shanks, "What Bones Tell Us," *Biblical Archaeology Review* 22:5 (September/October 1996), p. 52.

7. Robert Donceel, *The Oxford Encyclopedia of Archaeology in the Near East,* s.v. "Qumran."

8. De Vaux published an article about a small hatchet, which he regarded as a ritual object. Roland de Vaux, "Une hachette essénienne?" *Vetus Testamentum* 9 (1959), p. 399.

9. See Sidnie White Crawford, book review, *Bulletin of the American Schools of Oriental Research* 304 (1996), p. 102.

10. Ibid., p. 103.

11. Norman Golb, *Who Wrote the Dead Sea Scrolls?* (New York: Scribner, 1995).

12. Alan D. Crown and Lena Cansdale, "Qumran—Was It an Essene Settlement?" *Biblical Archaeology Review* 20:5 (September/October 1994), p. 24.

13. Philip R. Davies, "How Not to Do Archaeology: The Story of Qumran," *Biblical Archaeologist* 51 (1988), p. 205.

14. Ibid.

15. Kenneth W. Clark, "The Posture of the Ancient Scribe," *Biblical Archaeologist* 26 (1963), p. 64.

16. Ibid.

17. Ibid., pp. 71–72.

18. Ronny Reich, "A Note on the Function of Room 30 (the 'Scriptorium') at Khirbet Qumran," *Journal of Jewish Studies* 46 (1995), p. 157.

19. Ibid., p. 159.

20. Bruce M. Metzger, "The Furniture in the Scriptorium at Qumran," *Revue de Qumrân* 1 (1958), p. 509.

21. Clark, "Posture of the Ancient Scribe," p. 70.

22. Katherine G. Pedley, "The Library at Qumran," *Revue de Qumrân* 2 (1959), p. 21.

23. See Stephen Goranson, "Qumran, a Hub of Scribal Activity," *Biblical Archaeology Review* 20:5 (September/October 1994), p. 37. The inkwell Goranson discusses in this article apparently came from John Al-

legro, a member of the original editing team. See George J. Brooke and James M. Robinson, "A Further Fragment of 1QSb: The Schøyen Collection MS 1909," *Journal of Jewish Studies* 46 (1995), p. 121.

24. Roland de Vaux, "Fouilles de Khirbet Qumrân," *Revue Biblique* 63 (1956), p. 551.

25. Donceel, *Oxford Encyclopedia,* s.v. "Qumran."

26. These scholars include Jodi Magness (see her remarks in an interview in "The Enigma of Qumran," *Biblical Archaeology Review* 24:1 [January/February 1998], p. 24) and Ya'akov Meshorer. Magness bases her argument on the pottery, Meshorer, on the coins. Meshorer notes that when using coins for dating purposes, it is not the date they were struck but the date they were used that counts.

27. See "The Enigma of Qumran."

28. Magen Broshi, *The New Encyclopedia of Archaeological Excavations in the Holy Land,* s.v. "Qumran." Based on the coin evidence, Ya'akov Meshorer agrees with Broshi. From the numismatic viewpoint there is no gap in occupation.

29. Josephus, *The Jewish War,* H. St. J. Thackeray, trans., Loeb Classical Library IV (London: Heinemann/Cambridge, Mass.: Harvard University Press, 1976), 8:2.

30. Ibid., 9:1.

31. De Vaux, *Archaeology and the Dead Sea Scrolls,* p. 41.

32. Ibid., p. 38. No coins from the fourth or fifth year of the revolt were recovered in de Vaux's excavation.

33. Ibid., p. 84.

34. This cannot be seen on some of the Qumran plans that have been redrawn and published later; see, for example, the plan of Qumran by Robert Donceel in the entry on "Qumran" in the *The Oxford Encyclopedia of Archaeology in the Near East,* where walls in the Qumran "courtyard" have been omitted and conformed.

35. De Vaux, *New Encyclopedia of Archaeological Excavations.* Interestingly, in his *Archaeology and the Dead Sea Scrolls,* p. 62, de Vaux omits the word "religious" from this sentence.

36. Cf. Jean-Baptiste Humbert, "L'Espace Sacré à Qumrân: Propositions pour l'archéologie," *Revue Biblique* 101–2 (1994), p. 161.

37. Bryant Wood, "To Dip or Sprinkle? The Qumran Cisterns in Perspective," *Bulletin of the American Schools of Oriental Research* 256 (1984), p. 45.

38. Hirschfeld, "Khirbet Qumran," citing G. Garbrecht and Y. Peleg, "The Water Supply of the Desert Fortresses in the Jordan Valley," *Biblical Archaeologist* 57 (1994), p. 161.

39. Garbrecht and Peleg, "Water Supply," p. 161.

40. Donceel, *Oxford Encyclopedia*, s.v. "Qumran."

41. The number of people who lived at Qumran is a matter of considerable scholarly dispute, but the estimate of two hundred tends toward the high side. See "The Enigma of Qumran."

42. See Crown and Cansdale, "Qumran," p. 26.

43. Ibid.

44. See Ernest-Marie Laperrousaz, " 'Infra Hos Engadda,' notes à propos d'un article recent," *Revue Biblique* 69 (1962), p. 24; Jean-Paul Audet, "Qumrân et la notice de Pline sur Esséniens," *Revue Biblique* 68 (1961), p. 347.

45. But see Edward Cook, "A Ritual Purification Center," *Biblical Archaeology Review* 22:9 (November/December 1996), n. 1.

46. In one of Crown and Cansdale's examples, they claim that "in [Pliny's] description of the Palmyra region, he used the term 'below' to indicate that the cities of Beroea and Chalcis, in the Bekaa valley, were at a lower altitude than the Palmyra plateau" (Crown and Cansdale, "Qumran," p. 28). Bowersock disagrees, claiming that these cities are not altitudinally below the area with which they are compared (Bowersock, letter to Hershel Shanks, April 20, 1997).

47. Bowersock, letter to Hershel Shanks, April 20, 1997.

48. For example, Strabo refers to the Nabateans as "above" the Syrians in a passage where the Black Sea is the referent body of water, meaning that the Nabateans are farther from the Black Sea (in this case south).

49. De Vaux, *Archaeology and the Dead Sea Scrolls*, p. 135.

50. Ibid.

51. Ibid., pp. 235f.

52. Ibid., p. 137.

53. See also the remains described in Crown and Cansdale, "Qumran."

54. A few coins from the first century A.D. have been found at this site.

55. Robert Donceel and Pauline Donceel-Voûte observe that the number of coins found at Qumran is "exceptionally high" (Donceel and Donceel-Voûte, in Michael O. Wise, Norman Golb, John J. Collins, and Dennis G. Pardee, *Methods of Investigation of the Dead Sea Scrolls and the Khirbet Qumran Site*, Annals of the New York Academy of Sciences 722 [New York: The New York Academy of Sciences, 1994], p. 6), which de Vaux acknowledges contradicts the idea of Qumran as the site of an austere religious community (De Vaux, *Archaeology and the Dead Sea Scrolls*, pp. 129–30). According to Ya'akov Meshorer, the number of coins is not extraordinarily high (personal communication).

56. *Every Good Man Is Free,* 12.81, in *Philo,* F. H. Colson, trans., Loeb Classical Editions 9 (London: William Heinemann Ltd./Cambridge, Mass.: Harvard University Press, 1961).

57. Ronny Reich recently suggested that the dining hall might have functioned as a synagogue ("A Note on the Function of Room 30," p. 157, n. 3), but there is little to support this suggestion, in view of the contrast between this room and rooms at other sites that have been identified as pre-destruction synagogues.

58. Emanuel Tov, "Hebrew Biblical Manuscripts from the Judaean Desert: Their Contribution to Textual Criticism," *Journal of Jewish Studies* 39 (1988), p. 8.

59. *Every Good Man Is Free,* 12:78.

8. AN UNCERTAIN CONCLUSION

1. Frank M. Cross, "The Early History of the Qumran Community," in David Noel Freedman and Jonas C. Greenfield, eds., *New Directions in Biblical Archaeology* (Garden City, N.Y.: Doubleday, 1971), p. 77.

2. James C. VanderKam, "The People of the Dead Sea Scrolls: Essenes or Sadducees?" in Hershel Shanks, ed., *Understanding the Dead Sea Scrolls* (New York: Random House, 1992), p. 57.

3. Martin Goodman, "A Note on the Qumran Sectarians, the Essenes and Josephus," *Journal of Jewish Studies* 46 (1995), p. 161.

4. James H. Charlesworth, ed., *The Dead Sea Scrolls—Hebrew, Aramaic and Greek Texts with English Translations* 1 (Tübingen: J.C.B. Mohr/Louisville: Westminster John Knox Press, 1994).

5. VanderKam, "People of the Dead Sea Scrolls," p. 52.

6. Ibid., p. 53.

7. Goodman, "Note on the Qumran Sectarians," p. 165.

8. Cf. Edward M. Cook, "Qumran: A Ritual Purification Center," *Biblical Archaeology Review* 22:6 (November/December 1996), p. 39.

9. Frank M. Cross and Esther Eshel, "Ostraca from Qumran," *Israel Exploration Journal* 47 (1997), p. 17; see also Cross and Eschel, "The Missing Link," *Biblical Archaeology Review* 24:2 (March/April 1998).

10. As yet unpublished.

11. Martin Abegg on the Internet, citing Cook, "Qumran." Greg Doudna also significantly contributed to this Internet discussion.

12. "Pesach Bar-Adon and His Discoveries," *Biblical Archaeology Review* 19:4 (July/August 1993), pp. 36–37.

13. See Yigael Yadin, *Bar-Kokhba* (New York: Random House, 1971), especially Chapter 10, "The Letters Speak."

14. See Paul W. Lapp, "Bedouin Find Papyri Three Centuries Older Than Dead Sea Scrolls," *Biblical Archaeology Review* 4:1 (March 1978), p. 16; and Frank M. Cross, "The Historical Importance of the Samaria Papyri," *Biblical Archaeology Review* 4:1 (March 1978), p. 25.

15. Hershel Shanks, "So Far No Cigar," *Biblical Archaeology Review* 22:2 (March/April 1966), pp. 10–11.

16. Exhibit at Foundation for Ancient Research and Mormon Studies, Provo, Utah.

17. See Goodman, "Note on the Qumran Sectarians," p. 162.

18. Ibid., p. 165, n. 6.

19. Personal communication.

20. Norman Golb, "The Dead Sea Scrolls," *American Scholar* (Spring 1989), pp. 178–79; see also Norman Golb, *Who Wrote the Dead Sea Scrolls?* (New York: Scribner, 1995).

9. UNDERMINING THE JEWISH BIBLE

1. For example, the Philistines gouged out Samson's eyes (Judges 16:21). Later, the Babylonians did the same thing to the Judahite king Zedekiah (2 Kings 25:7; Jeremiah 39:7, 52:11).

2. Another, more complicated homeoteleuton is also possible. See James C. VanderKam, *The Dead Sea Scrolls Today* (Grand Rapids, Mich.: Eerdmans, 1994), pp. 131–32.

3. This occurs in over twenty cases.

4. Some scholars contend that there was no single original text; the search for the so-called "Hebraica veritas" is futile. In the words of Geza Vermes, "As far as the Bible is concerned, textual plurality precedes textual unity ("The Dead Sea Scrolls Forty Years On," The Fourteenth Sacks Lecture [Oxford: Oxford Centre for Postgraduate Hebrew Studies, 1987], pp. 10, 15). As Vermes notes, even the three master scrolls kept in the Temple, according to Rabbinic tradition contained variant readings (Yerushalmi, Ta'an 4:2 [68a]. See also Shemaryahu Talmon, "The Three Scrolls of the Law That Were Found in the Temple Court," *Textus* 2 [1962], p. 14).

5. See Harvey Minkoff, "The Aleppo Codex—Ancient Bible from the Ashes," *Bible Review* 7:4 (August 1991), p. 22.

6. The details are by no means clear. Recent rumors suggest that additional leaves may still be recovered.

7. The first edition came out in 1905.

8. In the sixteenth century, Protestant churches under Luther relegated these books to the Apocrypha.

9. Many of the most important differences are related to Samaritan theology: The Samaritans' holy mountain is Mount Gerizim (near Shechem, modern Nablus), whereas the Israelites' holy mountain is Jerusalem. Mount Gerizim became Israelite very early—during Joshua's conquest of the Promised Land, according to the biblical account; Jerusalem, on the other hand, did not become part of Israel until David's conquest of the city in about 1000 B.C. In MT, when, in the period prior to David's conquest (during the time of the Judges), the text refers to God's holy mountain (Jerusalem), it describes it as "the place that God *will choose*"; in these same passages in the Samaritan Pentateuch, the text says "the place that God *has chosen*," that is, Mount Gerizim. The earliest copy of the Samaritan Pentateuch dates to about the thirteenth or fourteenth century A.D. See Alan D. Crown, "The Abisha Scroll: 3000 Years Old?" *Bible Review* 7:5 (October 1991), pp. 13–21, 39.

10. 4QpaleoExod^m. See P. W. Skehan, E. Ulrich, and J. E. Sanderson, *Qumran Cave 4: IV. Paleo-Hebrew and Greek Biblical Manuscripts,* Discoveries in the Judean Desert IX (Oxford: Clarendon Press, 1992), pp. 53–130.

11. Except for the doctrinal change of "from the place that God will choose" to "the place that God has chosen" and except for the famous Samaritan addition of an eleventh commandment—to build an altar on the Samaritans' holy mountain, Mount Gerizim. This commandment is not in the Qumran manuscript.

12. Although the books of Samuel, Kings, Chronicles, and Ezra/ Nehemiah consist of two books each in modern Bibles, each is considered a single book in Jewish tradition. As to the possibility of a kind of Esther in Qumran, see Sidnie White Crawford, "Has Every Book of the Bible Been Found Among the Dead Sea Scrolls?" *Bible Review* 12:5 (October 1996), p. 28.

13. Emanuel Tov, "Hebrew Biblical Manuscripts," *Journal of Jewish Studies* 39 (1988), p. 7. See also Emanuel Tov, *Textual Criticism of the Hebrew Bible* (Minneapolis: Fortress Press, 1992), p. 117: "The reliability of the ancient translations, especially [LXX], is strengthened by the Qumran texts."

14. Kyle McCarter points out that Yahweh here may himself be a son of God. The text doesn't say that Yahweh did the dividing, but that the Most High (Elyon) did it. (Personal communication from Kyle Mc-Carter.)

15. See *The New Encyclopedia of Excavations in the Holy Land,* s.v. "Teman, Horvat."

16. Ibid. at "Qom, Khirbet El-."

17. *HarperCollins Bible Dictionary,* s.v. "Ten Commandments."

18. Emanuel Tov, "Biblical Texts as Reworked in Some Qumran Manuscripts with Special Attention to 4QRP and 4QParaGen-Exod,"

in Eugene Ulrich and James VanderKam, eds., *The Community of the Renewed Covenant* (University of Notre Dame Press, 1994), p. 134.

19. Emanuel Tov, *Textual Criticism,* p. 107. But Tov does find groups of texts that he calls "proto-Masoretic," "pre-Samaritan," and "proto-Septuagintal," or, more precisely, texts close to the presumed source of the Septuagint (pp. 107–8). Tov also identifies another group of biblical texts as "displaying a unique character" that he calls "Qumran [scribal] practice." The Qumran practice texts "may have used proto-Masoretic texts" as their source (p. 114).

20. Frank Moore Cross, "Some Notes on a Generation of Qumran Studies," in J. T. Barrera and L. V. Montaner, *The Madrid Qumran Congress Proceedings* (Leiden: E. J. Brill, 1992), p. 7.

21. Geza Vermes, too, disagrees with Cross: "Brilliant though [Cross's] theory may appear, explaining the threefold diversity of text-types by scribal activities in the three great centres of Jewish learning, it nevertheless fails to carry conviction" (Vermes, "Dead Sea Scrolls Forty Years On," p. 8).

22. Cross, "Some Notes," p. 7. In the same volume, see the replies to Cross's paper by Emanuel Tov ("Some Notes on a Generation of Qumran Studies: A Reply" [by Frank M. Cross]) and Eugene Ulrich ("Pluriformity in the Biblical Text, Text Groups, and Questions of Canon").

23. Tov, "Hebrew Biblical Manuscripts," p. 15.

24. Ibid.

25. Ibid., n. 38.

26. See James C. VanderKam, "Jubilees—How It Rewrote the Bible," *Bible Review* 8:6 (December 1992), p. 32.

27. Scrolls once thought to have come from Wadi Seiyal (and known as the Seiyal Collection) in fact came from Nahal Hever. See Emanuel Tov, *The Greek Minor Prophets Scroll from Nahal Hever (8HevXIIgr) (The Seiyal Collection I),* Discoveries in the Judean Desert 8 (Oxford: Clarendon Press, 1990).

28. With perhaps one exception.

29. Frank Cross believes this process was largely completed by 70 A.D. See his "The Text Behind the Text of the Hebrew Bible," in Hershel Shanks, ed., *Understanding the Dead Sea Scrolls* (New York: Random House, 1992).

30. See Eugene Ulrich, in Eugene Ulrich and James C. VanderKam, *The Community of the Renewed Covenant* (Notre Dame, Ind.: University of Notre Dame, 1994), p. 90, citing Emanuel Tov in *The Greek Minor Prophets Scroll from Nahal Hever.*

31. Emanuel Tov, "The Textual Base of the Corrections in the Biblical Texts Found at Qumran," in D. Dimant and U. Rappaport, eds., *The Dead Sea Scrolls—Forty Years of Research* (Leiden: E. J. Brill, 1992), p. 308.

Note the difference between the standardization of a text and its choice as authoritative.

32. Ibid., p. 311. Professor Shemaryahu Talmon of Hebrew University also believes the text was standardized after the Roman destruction: "Rabbinic Judaism established a *textus receptus* when the recitation of selected Bible texts became an integral component of the synagogue service, probably after 70 C.E." See Shemaryahu Talmon, "The Community of the Renewed Covenant: Between Judaism and Christianity" in Ulrich and VanderKam, *Community of the Renewed Covenant,* pp. 18–19.

Emanuel Tov takes a somewhat intermediate position: The Qumran period (mid-third century B.C.–68 A.D.) "was characterized by textual plurality." Nevertheless, "[I]t appears that in temple circles there existed a preference for one textual tradition, i.e., the texts of the Masoretic family." The biblical scrolls from Masada, whose latest date is 74 A.D., all "reflect" MT. But, "for every biblical book [at Qumran] one could find an almost unlimited number of texts, differing from each other, sometimes in major details." Emanuel Tov, *Textual Criticism,* p. 191. Tov maintains that the proto-Masoretic texts from Qumran are nearly identical to the second-century texts, reflecting standardization, but not canonization, at an earlier period.

33. Babylonian Talmud, Sukkah 20b.

34. See, for example, Luke 16:16, 29, 31; 24:27; Acts 26:22; 28:23.

35. See Frank M. Cross, "The Text Behind the Text of the Hebrew Bible," in Shanks, *Dead Sea Scrolls,* pp. 152–53.

36. Section C, lines 10–11, conveniently in Hershel Shanks, "For This You Waited 35 Years: MMT as Reconstructed by Elisha Qimron and John Strugnell," *Biblical Archaeology Review* 20:6 (November/December 1994), p. 56. I am indebted to Professor Steven Fraade of Yale University for these references. See his "Interpretive Authority in the Studying Community at Qumran," *Journal of Jewish Studies* 44 (1993), pp. 46–69.

37. Shanks, "For This You Waited 35 Years," p. 56 at Section B, lines 52–53.

38. See Eugene Ulrich, "The Bible in the Making: The Scriptures at Qumran," in Ulrich and VanderKam, *Community of the Renewed Covenant.*

10. ILLUMINATING JUDAISM

1. I believe Jacob Neusner was the first to use the term. He certainly popularized it.

2. Hershel Shanks, ed., *Frank Moore Cross: Conversations with a Bible Scholar* (Washington, D.C.: Biblical Archaeology Society, 1994), p. 155.

3. A careful reading of the Talmud, however, indicates that the sages were well aware of their opponents. As Lawrence Schiffman has pointed out, "The claim of a monolithic Sinai tradition was the Pharisaic view. They admitted that there other views. They just saw them as totally wrong" (personal communication).

4. Shanks, *Frank Moore Cross,* p. 109.

5. Joseph A. Fitzmyer, S.J., *Responses to 101 Questions on the Dead Sea Scrolls* (New York: Paulist Press, 1992), p. 37. Lawrence Schiffman in a personal communication disagrees with this interpretation, contending that Column 29 reflects "a pre-eschatological temple." This may be the view as well of Ya'akov Sussman, who has described the envisioned temple as "quasi-utopian" (in Elisha Qimron and John Strugnell, *Qumran Cave 4:* Discoveries in the Judean Desert 10 [Oxford: Clarendon Press, 1994], p. 183).

6. Sussman, in Qimron and Strugnell, *Qumran Cave 4,* p. 183.

7. Magen Broshi, "The Gigantic Dimensions of the Visionary Temple in the Temple Scroll," *Biblical Archaeology Review* 13:6 (November/December 1987), p. 37.

8. These Aramaic fragments have been found in Cave 1 (1Q32), Cave 2 (2Q24), Cave 4 (4Q554 and 555), Cave 5 (5Q15), and Cave 11 (11Q18). See Geza Vermes, *The Complete Dead Sea Scrolls in English* (New York: Allen Lane/Penguin Press, 1997), pp. 568–70.

9. Carol Newsom, *Songs of the Sabbath Sacrifice: A Critical Edition* (Atlanta, Ga.: Scholars Press, 1985), p. 59. Professor Newsom concludes that "the scroll of the Sabbath Shirot is a product of the Qumran community." In a personal communication, she has informed me that in the Discoveries in the Judean Desert edition of this text, she will back away from this conclusion somewhat. The Sabbath Shirot were certainly used by the Qumran community, but they may not have produced the scroll. It may have been used by other Jewish reformist movements, as well as the Qumran community.

10. Vermes, *Complete Dead Sea Scrolls,* p. 325. Carol Newsom (see previous note), translates *elohim* as "godlike"; she leaves *elim* untranslated. In a personal communication, she has advised me that when the text is republished in the official Discoveries in the Judean Desert series she will translate these terms as "gods." I leave the reader to ponder the implications for monotheism and polytheism within Second Temple Judaism.

11. John J. Collins, *HarperCollins Dictionary of the Bible,* rev. ed., s.v. "Apocalyptic Literature." Lawrence Schiffman, in a personal communi-

cation, notes that apocalypticism by no means completely died out in Judaism. Indeed, it enjoyed a revival in the third and fourth centuries, as well as later.

12. Shanks, *Frank Moore Cross,* p. 153.

13. Gershon Scholem, *The Messianic Idea in Judaism* (New York: Schocken Books, 1971), pp. 8–9.

14. Lawrence Schiffman, *Reclaiming the Dead Sea Scrolls* (Philadelphia: The Jewish Publication Society, 1994), p. xxv.

15. T. Shabbat 13b.

16. See, generally, Yitzhak Magen, "The Stone Vessel Industry During the Second Temple Period," in *Ancient Jerusalem Revealed* (Jerusalem: Israel Exploration Society, 1994).

17. The reconstruction and translations are those of Qimron and Strugnell. See Qimron and Strugnell, *Qumran Cave 4.*

18. The scrolls have many titles for this person in addition to the Wicked Priest: the Wrathful Lion, the False Oracle, the Cursed Man. See Shanks, *Frank Moore Cross,* p. 103; p. 177, n. 2.

19. "Others" may be referred to in the second person (you do that) or in the third person (they do that).

20. Ya'akov Sussman, "The History of the Halakha and the Dead Sea Scrolls" (Appendix I), in Qimron and Strugnell, *Qumran Cave 4,* p. 190.

21. Of course the priests would naturally get dirty in the course of reducing a cow to ashes. But this is not the impurity that the manufacturing process imparts. The rabbis were considering ritual impurity, not physical uncleanness.

22. Ecclesiastes Rabbah, 7:23, no. 4.

23. T. Yoma 1:2.

24. T. Yoma 239d.

25. The Sadducees were a major Jewish group who often vied with the Pharisees for power, including control of the Temple priesthood. The Sadducees tended to be more elitist than the Pharisees and traced their origins to the Zadokite priesthood installed by King Solomon.

26. In Qimron and Strugnell, *Qumran Cave 4,* p. 179.

27. I am indebted to James VanderKam for this observation. See his *The Dead Sea Scrolls Today* (Grand Rapids, Mich.: Eerdmans, 1994), p. 44.

28. The Bible itself has "nakedness" instead of "holy days."

29. The translation is from Vermes, *Complete Dead Sea Scrolls,* p. 484.

30. See Yigael Yadin, *The Temple Scroll* (Jerusalem: The Israel Exploration et al., 1983), Vol. 1, pp. 359–60.

11. TREASURE SEARCH—THE COPPER SCROLL

1. John Marco Allegro, *The Treasure of the Copper Scroll,* 2nd ed. (New York: Doubleday, 1964), p. 4. This edition differs from the first edition, published in 1960.

2. Ibid.

3. P. Kyle McCarter, "The Mysterious Copper Scroll—Clues to Hidden Temple Treasure?" *Bible Review* 8:4 (August 1992), p. 34; reprinted as "The Mystery of the Copper Scroll" in Hershel Shanks, ed., *Understanding the Dead Sea Scrolls* (New York: Random House, 1992), p. 233.

4. Ron Rosenbaum, "Riddle of the Scrolls," *Vanity Fair* 55:11 (November 1992), p. 287.

5. Allegro, *Copper Scroll,* 2nd ed., p. 35.

6. J. T. Milik, "Le rouleau de cuivre de Qumrân (3Q15): Traduction et commentaire topographique," *Revue Biblique* 66 (1959), p. 321.

7. J. T. Milik, "The Copper Document from Cave III of Qumran: Translation and Commentary," *Annual of the Department of Antiquities of Jordan* 4–5 (1960), p. 137.

8. John Allegro, *The Treasure of the Copper Scroll* (New York: Doubleday, 1960).

9. J. T. Milik, R. de Vaux, and H. W. Baker, "Le rouleau de cuivre provenant de la grotte 3Q (3Q15)," in M. Baillet, J. T. Milik, and R. de Vaux, *Les "Petites Grottes" de Qumrân,* Discoveries in the Judean Desert 3 (Oxford: Clarendon Press, 1962), pp. 201–301.

10. J. T. Milik, "The Copper Document from Cave III, Qumran," *Biblical Archaeologist* 19 (1956), p. 532.

11. *The Times* (London), June 1, 1956, p. 12.

12. Stephan Goranson, "Sectarianism, Geography, and the Copper Scroll," *Journal of Jewish Studies* 43 (1992), p. 284.

13. It may have broken in two when it was rolled up to hide in a safe place. According to Father Fitzmyer, it is "really not a scroll at all" (*The Dead Sea Scrolls: Major Publications and Tools for Study,* rev. ed. [Atlanta, Ga.: Scholars Press, 1990], p. 191).

14. McCarter, "Mystery of the Copper Scroll," p. 237. McCarter advises me that the metal is in fact bronze, not copper, as unpublished reports have revealed. He still subscribes to the other sentiments in this quotation.

15. Josephus, *Jewish Antiquities,* L. H. Feldman, trans., Loeb Classical Library (London: Heinemann/Cambridge, Mass.: Oxford University

Press, 1969), 14:4.5. Crassus later removed from the Temple an additional two thousand talents plus gold for eight thousand talents (Josephus, *Jewish Antiquities* 14:7.1).

16. James E. Harper, "26 Tons of Gold and 65 Tons of Silver," *Biblical Archaeology Review* 19:6 (November/December 1993), p. 44. See also Alan R. Millard, "Does the Bible Exaggerate King Solomon's Wealth?" *Biblical Archaeology Review* 15:5 (May/June 1989), p. 20.

17. These are Allegro's dates. See Allegro, *Copper Scroll,* 2nd. ed., p. 55. The exact dates are uncertain. The most precise dates I have seen are those given by Michael Wise in Michael Wise, Martin Abegg, Jr., and Edward Cook, *The Dead Sea Scrolls: A New Translation* (San Francisco: HarperSanFrancisco, 1996), p. 190. He states that Allegro "mounted two treasure-hunting expeditions: one in December 1959–January 1960, and another in March–April 1960." Father Fitzmyer says one was in December 1960 and the other in January 1961 (Fitzmyer, *Responses to 101 Questions,* p. 36). James VanderKam dates the Allegro expedition to 1962 (VanderKam, *The Dead Sea Scrolls Today* [Grand Rapids, Mich.: Eerdmans, 1994], p. 69).

18. Allegro, *Copper Scroll,* 2nd. ed., p. 21.

19. Ibid., p. 51. The most extensive account of Allegro's efforts to locate the sites mentioned in the Copper Scroll is in this revised edition, often overlooked by scroll researchers who confine themselves to the 1960 edition.

20. Ibid., p. 57

21. García Martínez, however, does translate "sepulcher monument." Florentino García Martínez, *The Dead Sea Scrolls Translated,* 2nd ed. (Leiden: E. J. Brill, 1996), p. 462.

22. Allegro, *Copper Scroll,* 2nd ed., pp. 57–58.

23. Ibid., p. 58.

24. See Zvi Greenhut, "The City of Salt," *Biblical Archaeology Review* 19:4 (July/August 1993), p. 36.

25. Allegro, *Copper Scroll,* 2nd ed., p. 65.

26. Ibid., pp. 65–66.

27. Ibid., pp. 75, 77.

28. Ibid., p. 67.

29. Ibid., p. 112.

30. Ibid., p. 117.

31. Ibid., pp. 130–31.

32. Ibid., pp. 131–32.

33. Ibid., p. 160.

34. Al Wolters, "History and the Copper Scroll," in *Methods of Inves-*

tigation of the Dead Sea Scrolls and the Khirbet Qumran Site (New York: New York Academy of Sciences, 1994), p. 291.

35. Allegro, *Copper Scroll,* 2nd ed., p. 160.

36. Michael Wise, in Wise, Abegg, and Cook, *Dead Sea Scrolls.*

37. Geza Vermes, *The Complete Dead Sea Scrolls in English* (New York: Allen Lane/Penguin Press, 1997).

38. García Martínez, *Dead Sea Scrolls,* p. 462.

39. Allegro, *Copper Scroll,* 2nd ed., p. 24.

40. McCarter, "Mystery of the Copper Scroll." McCarter is preparing a new edition of the scroll based on new photographs; it will include the translation of the critical phrase quoted in the foregoing citations.

41. Ibid.

42. Kyle McCarter thinks the scribe was illiterate, which may have been why he was chosen for the job (personal communication).

43. Frank Moore Cross, Jr., *The Ancient Library of Qumran and Modern Biblical Studies,* rev. ed. (Grand Rapids, Mich.: Baker Book House, 1980), p. 23. To the same effect: McCarter, "Mystery of the Copper Scroll," p. 235. On the other hand, Cross agrees that the scroll was probably meant to leave the erroneous impression that it described the Temple treasure. Cross, *Ancient Library,* p. 22.

44. McCarter, "Mystery of the Copper Scroll," pp. 235, 238.

45. Cross, *Ancient Library,* p. 24.

46. Ibid.

47. E. Ullendorff, "The Greek Letters of the Copper Scroll," *Vetus Testamentum* 11 (1961), p. 227.

48. See Bargil Pixner, "Unraveling the Copper Scroll Code: A Study on the Topography of 3Q15," *Revue de Qumrân* 11:3:43 (December 1983) p. 335, n. 32.

49. See Goranson, "Sectarianism, Geography, and the Copper Scroll," p. 284, n. 17.

50. See Manfred R. Lehmann, "Where the Temple Tax Was Buried," *Biblical Archaeology Review* 19:6 (November/December 1993) p. 38; Manfred R. Lehmann, "Identification of the Copper Scroll Based on Its Technical Terms," *Revue de Qumrân,* 6 (1964), p. 97.

51. McCarter, "Mystery of the Copper Scroll," p. 233.

52. Michael Baigent and Richard Leigh, *The Dead Sea Scroll Deception* (New York: Summit Books, 1991), pp. 59, 61.

53. Hershel Shanks, ed., *Frank Moore Cross: Conversations with a Bible Scholar* (Washington, D.C.: Biblical Archaeology Society, 1994), pp. 142–44.

12. LOOKING TOWARD THE FUTURE

1. Florentino García Martínez and Donald W. Parry, *A Bibliography of the Finds in the Desert of Judah 1970–95* (Leiden: E. J. Brill, 1996).

2. Pesach Bar-Adon, "Judean Desert-Caves Archaeology Survey in 1960," *Yediot* (Bulletin of the Israel Exploration Society) (1961), p. 36 (in Hebrew).

3. Baruch Safrai, "Recollections from 40 Years Ago—More Scrolls Lie Buried," *Biblical Archaeology Review* 19:1 (January/February 1993), p. 50.

4. Hershel Shanks, "We Haven't Seen the Last of the Scrolls," *Biblical Archaeology Review* 19:1 (January/February 1993), p. 57; see also Hershel Shanks, ed., *Frank Moore Cross: Conversations with a Bible Scholar* (Washington, D.C.: Biblical Archaeology Society, 1994), p. 141.

SELECT BIBLIOGRAPHY

OFFICIAL PUBLICATIONS

Discoveries in the Judaean Desert, Oxford: Oxford University Press, 1955– .

ENGLISH TRANSLATIONS

Martínez, Florentino García, trans. *The Dead Sea Scrolls Translated: Qumran Texts in English.* Leiden: E. J. Brill, 1994.

Vermes, Geza. *The Complete Dead Sea Scrolls in English.* New York: Allen Lane/The Penguin Press, 1997.

Wise, Michael, Martin G. Abegg, Jr., and Edward M. Cook. *The Dead Sea Scrolls: A New Translation.* San Francisco: HarperSanFrancisco, 1996.

TEXTS AND TRANSLATIONS

Charlesworth, James H., ed. *The Dead Sea Scrolls—Hebrew, Aramaic and Greek Texts with English Translations. Rule of the Community and Related Documents.* Vol. 1. Tübingen: J.C.B. Mohr; Louisville: Westminster John Knox Press, 1994.

Charlesworth, James H., ed. *The Dead Sea Scrolls—Hebrew, Aramaic and Greek Texts with English Translations. Damascus Document, War Scroll and Related Documents.* Vol. 2. Tübingen: J.C.B. Mohr; Louisville: Westminster John Knox Press, 1995.

GENERAL WORKS

Allegro, John Marco. *The Treasure of the Copper Scroll.* 2nd ed. New York: Doubleday, 1964.

Burrows, Millar. *More Light on the Dead Sea Scrolls: New Scrolls and New Interpretations with Translations of Important Recent Discoveries.* New York: Viking, 1958.

Burrows, Millar. *The Dead Sea Scrolls.* New York: Gramercy Publishing Company, 1955.

Campbell, Jonathan. *Deciphering the Dead Sea Scrolls.* London: Fontana Press, 1996.

Cook, Edward M. *Solving the Mysteries of the Dead Sea Scrolls.* Grand Rapids, Mich.: Zondervan, 1994.

Cross, Frank Moore, Jr. *The Ancient Library of Qumran and Modern Biblical Studies.* Rev. ed. Grand Rapids, Mich.: Baker Book House, 1958, 1961, reprinted 1980.

Davies, Philip R. *Qumran.* Cities of the Biblical World. Guilford, Surrey: Lutterworth; Grand Rapids, Mich.: Eerdmans, 1982.

Eisenman, Robert, and Michael Wise. *The Dead Sea Scrolls Uncovered.* New York: Penguin Books, 1992.

Fitzmyer, Joseph, *Responses to 101 Questions on the Dead Sea Scrolls.* New York: Paulist Press, 1992.

Golb, Norman. *Who Wrote the Dead Sea Scrolls? The Search for the Secret of Qumran.* New York: Scribner, 1995.

Martínez, Florentino García. *The People of the Dead Sea Scrolls— Their Writings, Beliefs and Practices.* Leiden: E. J. Brill, 1993.

Price, Randall. *Secrets of the Dead Sea Scrolls.* Eugene, Oreg.: Harvest House, 1996.

Ringgren, Helmer. *The Faith of Qumran—Theology of the Dead Sea Scrolls.* New York: Crossroad, 1995.

Schiffman, Lawrence. *Reclaiming the Dead Sea Scrolls.* Philadelphia: The Jewish Publication Society, 1994.

Shanks, Hershel, ed. *Understanding the Dead Sea Scrolls.* New York: Random House, 1992.

Silberman, Neil Asher. *The Hidden Scrolls—Christianity, Judaism, and the War for the Dead Sea Scrolls.* New York: G. P. Putnam's Sons, 1994.

Trever, John C. *The Dead Sea Scrolls: A Personal Account.* Grand Rapids, Mich.: Eerdmans, 1965.

VanderKam, James C. *The Dead Sea Scrolls Today.* Grand Rapids, Mich.: William B. Eerdmans, 1994.

Vermes, Geza. *The Dead Sea Scrolls—Qumran in Perspective.* Philadelphia: Fortress Press, 1981 (reprint).

Wilson, Edmund. *The Scrolls from the Dead Sea.* New York: Oxford University Press, 1955.

Yadin, Yigael. *Bar Kokhba: The Rediscovery of the Legendary Hero of the Second Jewish Revolt against Rome.* London: Weidenfeld and Nicolson, 1971.

Yadin, Yigael. *The Message of the Scrolls.* New York: Simon and Schuster, 1957.

PERIODICAL RESOURCES

These journals either are devoted to studies of the Dead Sea Scrolls and Qumran or publish a significant amount of material on the scrolls. For specific articles see notes.

Bible Review

Biblical Archaeologist

Biblical Archaeology Review

Bulletin of the American Schools of Oriental Research

Dead Sea Discoveries

Israel Exploration Journal

Journal of Jewish Studies

Journal of Near Eastern Studies

Revue Biblique

Revue de Qumrân

TRANSCRIPTIONS, REPRODUCTIONS, AND RECONSTRUCTIONS

Eisenman, Robert H., and James M. Robinson. *A Facsimile Edition of the Dead Sea Scrolls.* Vols. 1 & 2. Washington, D.C.: Biblical Archaeology Society, 1991.

Humbert, Jean-Baptiste, O.P., and Alain Chambon. *Fouilles de Khirbet Qumrân et de Aïn Feshkha.* Novum Testamentum et Orbis

Antiquus Series Archaeologica Vol. 1. Göttingen: Éditions Universitaires Fribourg Suisse/Vandenhoeck and Ruprecht, 1994.

Lim, Timothy H., and Philip S. Alexander, eds. *The Dead Sea Scrolls Electronic Reference Library.* Leiden: E. J. Brill, 1997. CD Rom.

Tov, Emanuel, and Stephen J. Pfann, eds. *The Dead Sea Scrolls on Microfiche.* Leiden: E. J. Brill, 1993. Microfiche.

Wacholder, Ben Zion, and Martin G. Abegg, eds. *A Preliminary Edition of the Unpublished Dead Sea Scrolls: The Hebrew and Aramaic Texts from Cave Four.* Vols. 1–4. Washington, D.C.: Biblical Archaeology Society, 1991–96.

STUDY TOOLS

Fitzmyer, Joseph A., *The Dead Sea Scrolls: Major Publications and Tools for Study.* Rev. ed. SBL Resources for Biblical Study 20. Atlanta, Ga: Scholars Press, 1990.

García Martínez, F., and A. S. Van Der Woude. *A Bibliography of the Finds in the Desert of Judah 1970–75.* Studies on the Texts of the Desert of Judah, Vol. 19. Leiden: E. J. Brill, 1996.

ACKNOWLEDGMENTS

No single scholar is expert in all the subjects covered in this book, least of all me. My indebtedness is vast, first, to those who have devoted their lives to studying the scrolls in their context and to those who have made a specialty of the archaeology of Qumran. Many have helped me indirectly through their writings. Almost as many have helped directly by talking to me about various subjects involving the scrolls. I think especially of Frank Cross. Some of our conversations about the scrolls eventually formed part of a book (Hershel Shanks, ed., *Frank Moore Cross: Conversations with a Bible Scholar* [Washington, D.C.: Biblical Archaeology Society, 1994]). Many others went unrecorded. I have always profited, as well, from talks with my friends Kyle McCarter and Jim Sanders, founder of the Ancient Biblical Manuscript Center.

A number of scholars—and friends—were kind enough to review an early draft of the manuscript: Geza Vermes of Oxford University, Larry Schiffman of New York University, Kyle McCarter of The Johns Hopkins University, Yizhar Hirschfeld of Hebrew University, and George Brooke of the University of Manchester. That they devoted the time and effort to doing this for me is the greatest compliment that I could ask for. They caught many errors and gave me much sage advice. I could not ask them to do their work a second time after the manuscript was in many ways revised, so I have special reason for the usual *mea culpa* accepting responsibility for the remaining errors.

I also received the invaluable support of that wonderful organization known as the Biblical Archaeology Society, especially of its executive director, Bridget Young, and my longtime editorial colleague, Suzanne Singer.

More directly helpful was the devoted, effective, and careful work of my research assistant, Allison Dickens, who worked with me on every aspect of the manuscript. In many ways this is her book. I am also grateful to our summer intern, Ben Soskis, who prepared the initial research notebooks for me.

With his usual acuity, my Random House editor, Jason Epstein, helped me substantially reshape a much bulkier manuscript into the reader-friendly book we hope it is. His capable assistant—and talented editor in her own right—Joy de Menil was an always-available shoulder whenever the editorial process got painful. Her suggestions are often incorporated here.

My agent, Robert Barnett, Esq., who handled the formalities with Random House, demonstrated once again that what is often regarded as a difficult, even adversarial, process can be both pleasant and effective.

To all, my profound gratitude.

HERSHEL SHANKS
Washington, D.C.
October 1997

INDEX

References to illustrations, maps, and plans
are in italics.

ABOUT THE AUTHOR

HERSHEL SHANKS is founder and editor of *Bible Review* and *Biblical Archaeology Review,* the most widely read and authoritative periodical on the subject. He is the editor of *Understanding the Dead Sea Scrolls,* a collection of essays, and the author of *The City of David: A Guide to Biblical Jerusalem, Judaism in Stone: The Archaeology of Ancient Synagogues,* and *Jerusalem: An Archaeological Biography.* An international authority on Jerusalem and the Dead Sea Scrolls, he has written about biblical archaeology for over twenty-five years.

ABOUT THE AUTHOR

HERSHEL SHANKS is founder and editor of *Bible Review* and *Biblical Archaeology Review,* the most widely read and authoritative periodical on the subject. He is the editor of *Understanding the Dead Sea Scrolls,* a collection of essays, and the author of *The City of David: A Guide to Biblical Jerusalem, Judaism in Stone: The Archaeology of Ancient Synagogues,* and *Jerusalem: An Archaeological Biography.* An international authority on Jerusalem and the Dead Sea Scrolls, he has written about biblical archaeology for over twenty-five years.

ABOUT THE TYPE

This book was set in Bembo, a typeface based on an old-style Roman face that was used for Cardinal Bembo's tract *De Aetna* in 1495. Bembo was cut by Francisco Griffo in the early sixteenth century. The Lanston Monotype Company of Philadelphia brought the well-proportioned letterforms of Bembo to the United States in the 1930s.